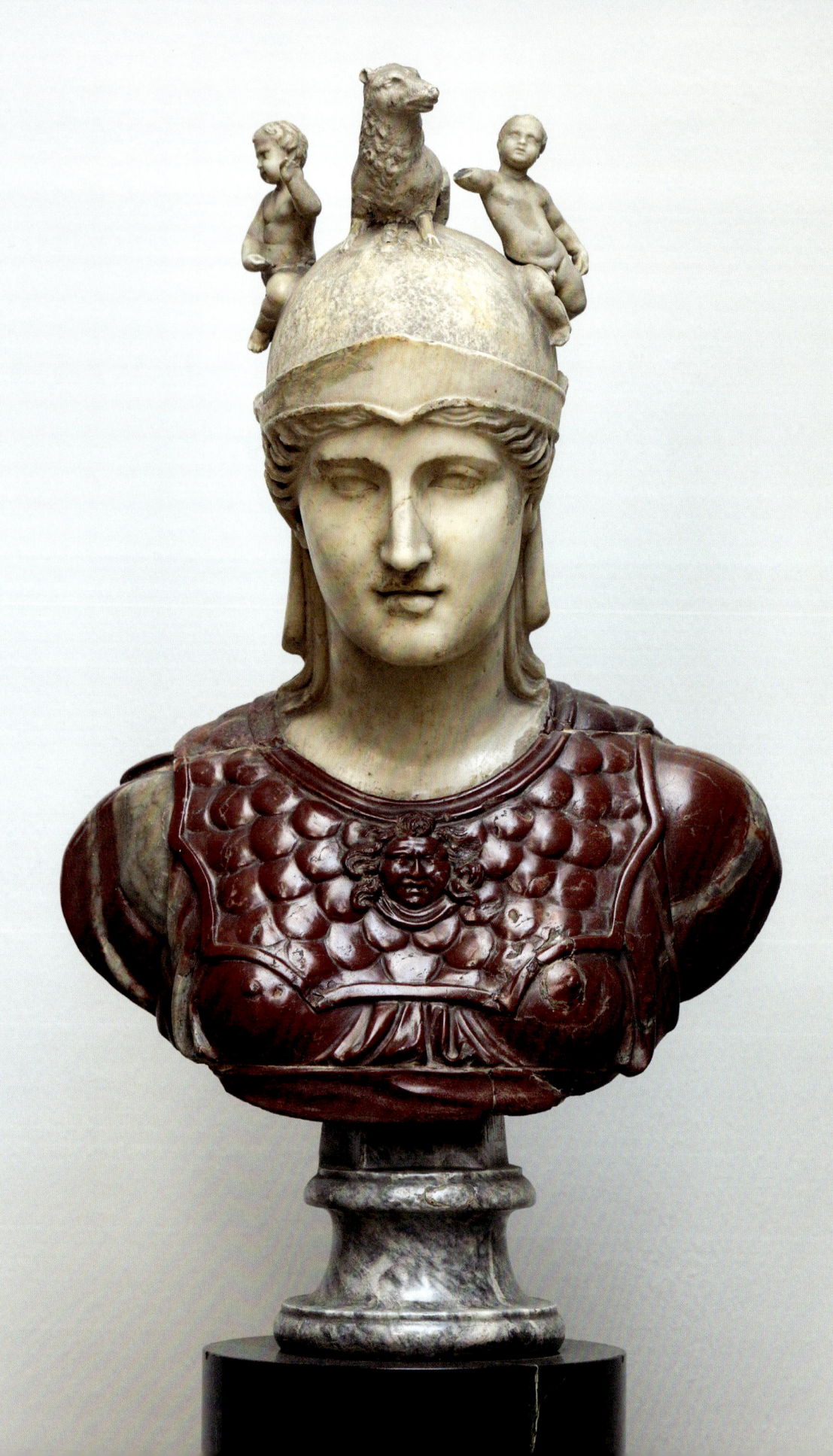

The Grand Tour

DESTINATION ITALY

ARIANE VAN SUCHTELEN

JANNEKE BUDDING

JON CULVERHOUSE

MATTHEW HIRST

LAURA NUVOLONI

MARIA DE PEVERELLI

VICTORIA POULTON

LUCY PURVIS

MAURITSHUIS THE HAGUE ◆ WAANDERS PUBLISHERS ZWOLLE

Powered by

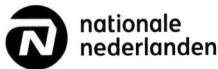

Top partners

VRIENDENLOTERIJ

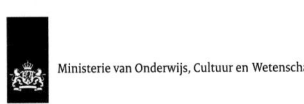

Ministerie van Onderwijs, Cultuur en Wetenschap

Exhibition partners

Friends of the Mauritshuis
The Johan Maurits Compagnie Foundation
M.A.O.C. Gravin van Bylandt Fund
Gilles Hondius Foundation

The exhibition has been supported by the Dutch government:
an indemnity grant has been provided by the Cultural Heritage Agency of the
Netherlands on behalf of the Minister of Education, Culture and Science.

CONTENTS

PREFACE

Young adults call it a gap year: the year between leaving school and continuing their education. If you're already working and feel the need for a change of scene, you take a sabbatical. Such a 'time out' seems to be typical of our times, but in fact it's an age-old phenomenon. The English upper classes, especially the young men, routinely left home for such reasons, only they called it a Grand Tour. As early as the seventeenth century, these young aristocrats crossed the English Channel and went on to explore Europe. We know quite a bit about what they did on these journeys thanks to the journals and letters that survive. But we know far less about the actual organisation of such a Grand Tour, how many servants went along, how many horses and carriages were necessary, where Grand Tourists slept and ate and how they planned their next destination. The reason – or pretext – for undertaking this long and costly journey is clear, however: to gain a better understanding of classical antiquity, and to acquire knowledge of other cultures and learn other languages.

Travelling also had another objective: to sow one's wild oats and then move beyond such youthful excesses to a more mature phase of young adulthood. The diaries kept on Grand Tours therefore recount as much about love affairs as about Roman antiquities. James Boswell, a Scottish lawyer and writer who embarked on a Grand Tour in 1764, was perfectly capable of combining the literature of antiquity and amorous adventures. Upon his arrival in Rome, he wrote: 'I remembered the rakish deeds of Horace and those other amorous Roman poets, and I thought that one might well allow one's self a little indulgence in a city where there are prostitutes licensed by the Cardinal Vicar.'

The fact that not all Grand Tourists took the educational aspect of their travels seriously is also confirmed by the French lawyer Charles de Brosses, a resident of Rome, who observed: 'There are some who will have left the city at the time without having seen anyone but other Englishmen and without even knowing where the Colosseum is.' The poet Samuel Rogers, who was in Italy in the 1820s, noted similar behaviour. He found it intolerable: 'Nothing can be more depressing to those who really value Rome than to meet Englishmen hunting in couples through the Vatican galleries, one looking for the number of the statue in the guide-book, the other not finding it; than to hear Americans describe the Forum as the dustiest heap of old ruins ever looked upon… or, of the Colosseum, that "it will be a handsome building when it is finished".' The intellectual Rogers was probably thinking 'Do not cast your pearls before swine' as he complained about the ignorance of his fellow tourists.

Nothing is more enjoyable for us than to read about the appreciation, or lack thereof, of cities and monuments that are now hotspots of mass tourism. Lady Mary Wortley Montagu wrote to her daughter in 1758: 'Of all towns in Italy, I am the least satisfied with Venice… Old and in general ill-built houses, ruined pictures and stinking ditches dignified with pompous denomination of canals; a fine bridge spoilt by two rows of houses upon it, and a large square decorated with the worst architecture I yet saw.'

The diaries of English travellers are full of their dissatisfaction with Rome and its inhabitants. Writing in 1820, Lady Morgan complained: 'You pass over miles of barren common, much like Hounslow Heath; and when at last you arrive at the gate of the Eternal City, the first impression is, I think, a feeling of disappointment… the habits of the people are in some measure restrained by the presence of the English. Still there is quite enough left to make me believe the Romans the nastiest people in Christendom – if I had not seen the Portuguese.' Rome and Venice were not the only cities that provoked displeasure; other European cities also fell short of expectations. Paris, for example, was described in travel journals as a dirty, stinking city.

Despite all this criticism, we have countless testimonials that praise the grandeur and riches of these Continental cities. After the French writer Stendhal visited Florence in 1817 and described his ecstasy at seeing the graves of Machiavelli, Michelangelo and Galileo Galilei in the stunning basilica of Santa Croce, many travellers longed for the same experience. More and more people undertook Grand Tours. There was also an increase in the number of female travellers, whether or not accompanied by their husbands. Today, too, tourists are moved, dazed, overcome by the antiquity and sheer beauty of such cities as Florence and Venice. And, like tourists nowadays, the Grand Tourists of the past wanted to take home something that reminded them of their journey. This gave rise to the souvenir (literally 'memory'), which became the third goal of the Grand Tour. In addition to gaining knowledge and maturity, Grand Tourists were bent on acquiring paintings, sculpture and antiquities. The carriages returning from Grand Tours were laden with souvenirs destined to decorate English country houses.

No place else in Europe can boast as many country estates with magnificent art collections as Great Britain, with its long tradition of wealthy, aristocratic families who commissioned the construction of splendid country houses surrounded by parks and gardens. Moreover, generations of travellers filled these stately homes with art collected largely on trips to the Continent. And because for centuries no war has been waged in England, these magnificent estates have often survived intact. The majority of England's country houses now belong to such organisations as the National Trust, but ten of the most beautiful properties are still in private hands and still inhabited by descendants of the original owners. These ten, collectively called Treasure Houses of England, welcome visitors for a large part of the year. The exhibition *The Grand Tour – Destination Italy* displays pieces on loan from three of these renowned Treasure Houses: Holkham Hall in Norfolk, Burghley House in Lincolnshire and Woburn Abbey in Bedfordshire.

The Mauritshuis is honoured to work, once again, with these exceptional English organisations. Previous collaborations resulted in the exhibitions *At Home in Holland: Vermeer and his Contemporaries from the British Royal Collection* (2016-2017) and *National Trust: Dutch Masters from British Country Houses* (2018-2019). This time we are presenting, instead of Dutch masters, foreign painters whose work is not commonly found in Dutch museums, including Pompeo Batoni, Canaletto, Joshua Reynolds, Angelica Kauffman, Carlo Dolci and Paolo Veronese, as well as works by artists who are no longer well known but were very successful in their day, such as Luigi Garzi, Pietro Fabris and Nathaniel Dance.

We are greatly indebted to our lenders, Lord and Lady Leicester of Holkham Hall, Miranda and Orlando Rock of Burghley House, and the Duke and Duchess of Bedford of Woburn Abbey, all of whom were willing to give us their costly artworks on temporary loan. Without their extraordinary generosity, this exhibition would not have been possible.

Our curator Ariane van Suchtelen was the initiator of this exhibition, on which she worked closely with Maria de Peverelli, Head of Collections at Holkham Hall. Together they selected the loans on display in the exhibition. The project group, under the supervision of Lieve Boiten, worked very hard to make *The Grand Tour – Destination Italy* a success. Thank you, Lieve – your first exhibition as project leader, well done! The design of the exhibition was in the capable hands of Caspar Conijn. Gert Jan Slagter designed the book, which was printed by Waanders Publishers. Dorine Duyster edited the texts and translated the English contributions into Dutch. Diane Webb translated the Dutch texts into English. The former curator-in-training at the Mauritshuis, Daphne Martens, and the present curator-in-training, Robin de Vries, assisted Ariane van Suchtelen, the editor of the catalogue.

This exhibition would not have been possible without the generous support of the NN Group, our Friends of the Mauritshuis Foundation, the VriendenLoterij, the Johan Maurits Compagnie Foundation, the M.A.O.C. Gravin van Bylandt Foundation and the Gilles Hondius Foundation. This exhibition is supported by an indemnity granted by the Cultural Heritage Agency of the Netherlands (RCE) on behalf of the Ministry of Education, Culture and Science (OCW).

Many thanks are due to Maria de Peverelli, Lucy Purvis, Katie Bolton and Laura Nuvoloni of Holkham Hall, Jon Culverhouse of Burghley House, and Matthew Hirst and Victoria Poulton of Woburn Abbey. We would also like to thank the following individuals: Tom Aalmoes, Janneke Budding, Arco Gnocchi, Nynke de Jong, Andrea Huntjens, Janneke Knüpfer and Vava Stojadinovic, Maria Smit, Marita Smit, Maud van Suylen, Joost van der Spek, Guy Sainthill and Roderik van der Weijden.

Martine Gosselink,
General Director Mauritshuis

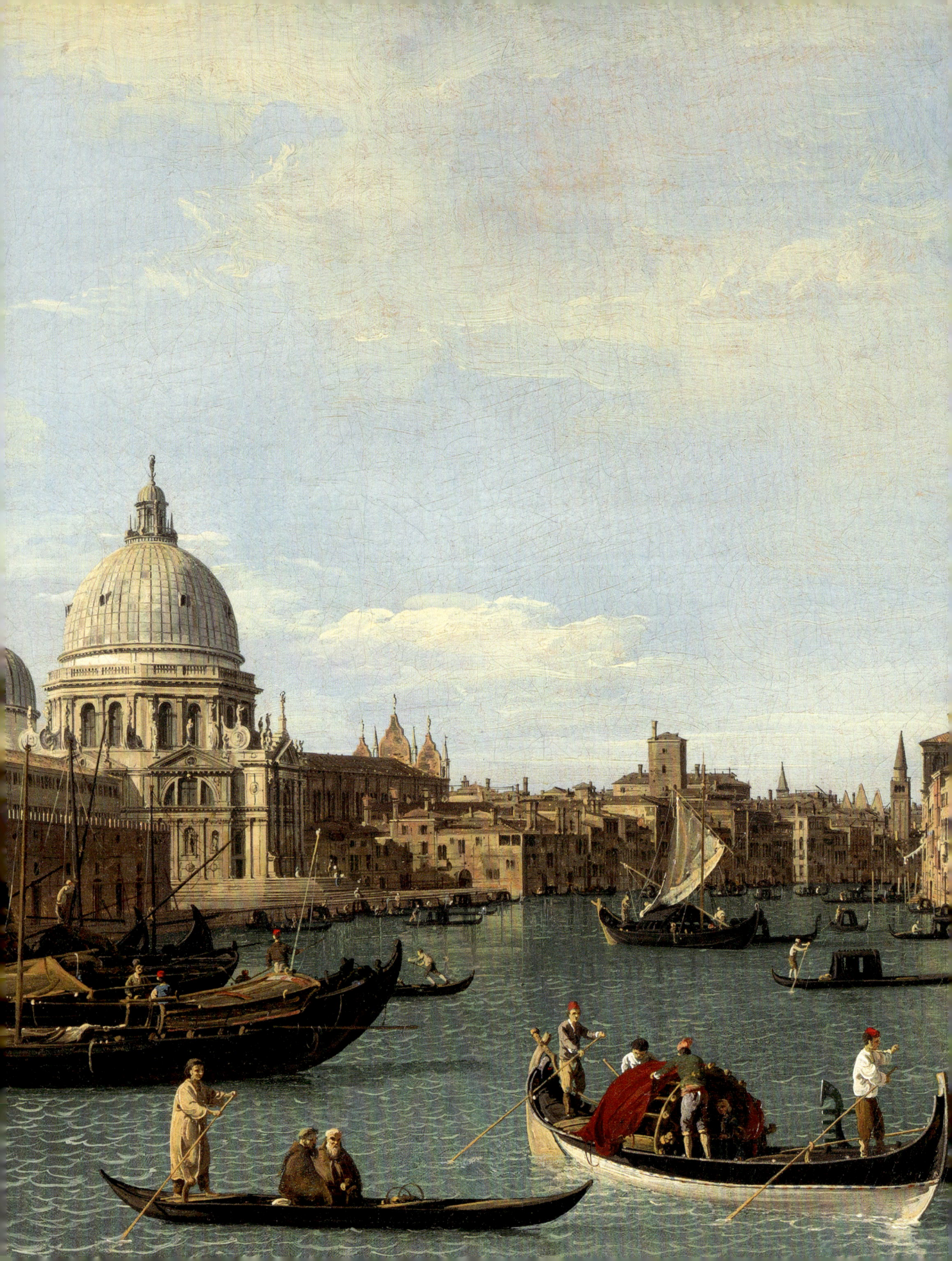

THE GRAND TOUR – DESTINATION ITALY
INTRODUCTION

Ariane van Suchtelen

School-leavers nowadays often take a gap year to go abroad and see other parts of the world, hoping to have a few adventures and to meet new people. Whether reluctantly or willingly, their parents let them go: after all, sooner or later their offspring have to grow up. Throughout history, young and old alike have had the desire to explore foreign countries, but in centuries past, this was beyond the means of most people. In the heyday of the Grand Tour, foreign travel was a costly, time-consuming and not infrequently risky undertaking (see pp. 17-21).

By the eighteenth century, the Grand Tour had become a familiar phenomenon, but even before this, young men had been sent abroad with private tutors and other attendants as a means of completing their education. The term Grand Tour was coined by Richard Lassels (1603-1668), an English travel-book writer and Catholic priest who travelled to Italy five times as a tutor. In 1670, Lassels' travel guide *The Voyage of Italy or a Compleat Journey through Italy* was published posthumously, in which he observed: 'No man understands Livy and Caesar...' (in other words, classical antiquity) 'like him, who hath made exactly the Grand Tour of France and the Giro of Italy'.

Rite of Passage

From the seventeenth to the mid-nineteenth century – when the construction of the railways changed European travel for good – the Grand Tour was a rite of passage for young men of the upper crust, especially the British, who travelled to the Continent with Italy as their ultimate destination. There they visited the famous monuments of Roman antiquity and became acquainted with the art and culture of the Renaissance. Grand Tourists visited not only Rome and Florence, but also Venice, for example, which was then just as popular among tourists as it is today. A natural phenomenon such as Vesuvius, the active volcano near Naples, was also a special attraction. The Grand Tour was considered an essential part of the cultural and social education of the elite, a period preceding adulthood that was meant for making useful contacts and acquiring good taste. It was nothing less than an intensive preparation course for a role in society. But the Grand Tour can also be defined more broadly. It was not only young unmarried men who undertook such travels. Somewhat older gentlemen also toured Europe, and in the course of the eighteenth century, more and more women followed suit, usually in the company of their husbands. Sometimes whole families went abroad, travelling with children, servants and horses parading in their wake. John Cecil, 5th Earl of Exeter, and his wife, Anne Cavendish, were pioneers in this respect. As early as the seventeenth century, they journeyed repeatedly through Europe, where they purchased a great many paintings and other objects intended for the decoration of Burghley House, their country estate. Who were the Cecils, and who were the other people who journeyed so far from home at a time when travel was not yet taken for granted? What did they look at, and what did they take home in the way of art and other souvenirs?

This exhibition focuses on a few exceptional travellers whose passion for collecting art, both old and new, provided the basis for the splendid collections at Holkham Hall, Burghley House and Woburn Abbey.

Notebooks and Other Documents

The archives of these three Treasure Houses of England, which are still inhabited by descendants of the original owners, contain a wealth of information on the foreign adventures experienced by these Grand Tourists of the past. Their holdings range from notebooks and account books, letters and inventory lists, to handwritten inscriptions on the backs of paintings and even a single piece of paper in a hardstone snuff box (fig. 1). On this paper Brownlow Cecil, 9th Earl of Exeter, noted that the three small rocks preserved in the box had been taken by English sailors from Pompey's Pillar in Alexandria, after drinking a bowl of punch at the top of this monument erected in honour of the Emperor Diocletian. The same note states that the precious box is made of lava from the island of Ischia near Naples.

The archives of Woburn Abbey contain a well-thumbed notebook that must have belonged to John Russell, 4th Duke of Bedford, the man who ordered an unprecedentedly large series of Venetian *vedute* from Canaletto (see cat. nos. 30-31). The notebook contains fragmentary notes made by Russell on his Grand Tour of 1728-1732. Perhaps this is the very book that Russell holds in his hand in the small portrait on ivory that he commissioned in Rome (fig. 2).

Steward Culpepper Tanner accompanied John Cecil, 5th Earl of Exeter, on various trips to the Continent. Tanner recorded every payment he made for Cecil and his entourage, including small amounts for the cold drinks sold at roadside stands near tourist attractions. Sometimes one of Tanner's notes can be linked to a particular souvenir, as is the case with the essence bottle 'carved in the form of a pine cone', which is so beautiful that it has been preserved to the present day at Burghley House (fig. 3). From Livorno, Tanner had crates of paintings shipped to England.

The most detailed records are to be found in the account book kept by the *valet de chambre* Edward Jarrett, who accompanied the young Thomas Coke on his Grand Tour of 1712-1718. Jarrett's bookkeeping is so meticulous that it makes readers feel like fellow travellers. We know, for example, that Coke and his company drank cocoa nearly every day, for Jarrett, too, recorded the smallest expenses. Even more importantly, Jarrett's account book provides insight into Thomas's determination to amass a collection of art, antiquities and valuable books with a view to installing these treasures in the stately home he intended to build after his return to England. His vision gave rise to the magnificence of Holkham Hall (pp. 24-31, 54-57).

Posing Along The Way – Portraits as Souvenirs

In the eighteenth century it became customary for Grand Tourists to have themselves portrayed abroad, as a souvenir of their Italian sojourn. In Rome one could go to the famous portraitist Pompeo Batoni (1708-1787), whose clientele were almost exclusively English. Batoni's portrait of Thomas William Coke of 1774 is an imposing example of just such a 'Grand Tour portrait' (fig. 4). Nineteen-year-old Thomas William Coke is portrayed full length, elegantly dressed in a red cloak trimmed with ermine, with a noble hunting hound at his feet. Behind him at right stands a Roman statue of Ariadne from the Vatican Collection that Batoni depicted in various portraits. The sitter could make an impression at home with such a monumental likeness. Another portraitist who was very popular with the English was Rosalba Carriera (1675-1757) in Venice. She painted portrait miniatures on ivory, but her fame was due mainly to her innovative pastel portraits on paper, which became her trademark. Carriera's small formats made it possible for travellers to pack up a portrait on ivory or paper and take it home in their luggage. In 1714, Thomas Coke commissioned Carriera to paint his portrait on ivory

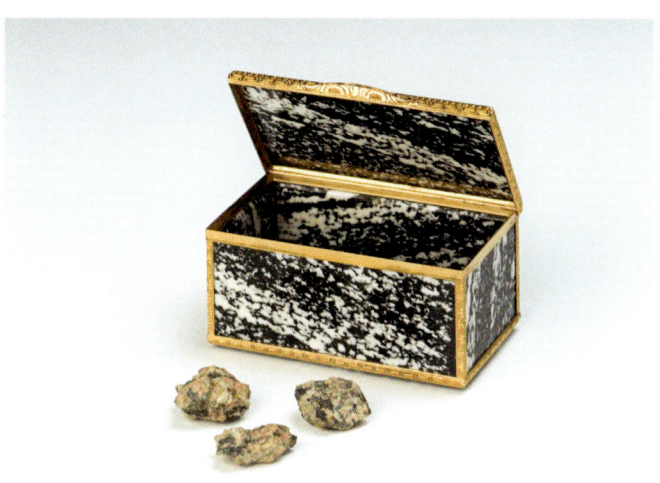

Fig. 1
Anonymous (Italy), *Snuff box with rocks*, before 1767. Hardstone (black and white polished lava), gold, width 7.5 cm. Burghley House (cat. no. 24)

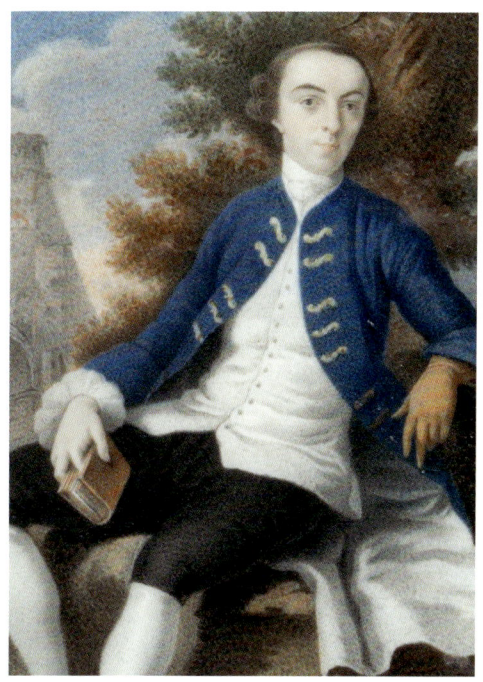

Fig. 2
Detail of Orsola Urbani (attributed to), *Portrait of a Man Traditionally Identified as Lord John Russell, later 4ᵗʰ Duke of Bedford (1710–1771)*, c.1730. Watercolour on ivory, 15.4 x 12 cm, Woburn Abbey (cat. no. 26)

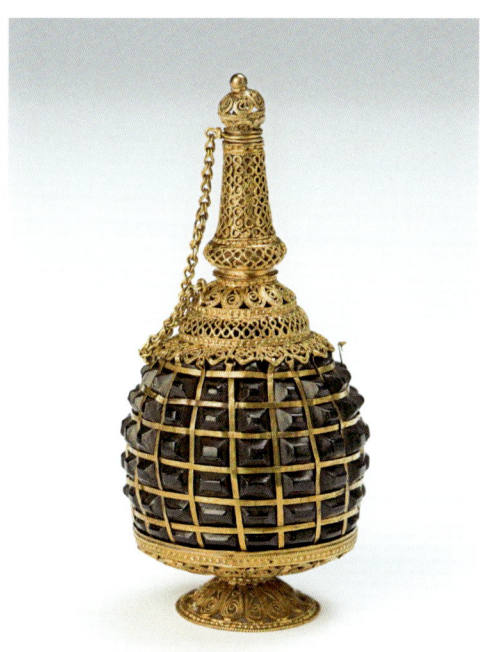

Fig. 3
Anonymous Indo-Portuguese artist, *Essence Bottle Carved in the Form of a Pine Cone*, 17ᵗʰ century. Organic material, garnished with gold wire, height 7.8 cm, Burghley House (cat. no. 25)

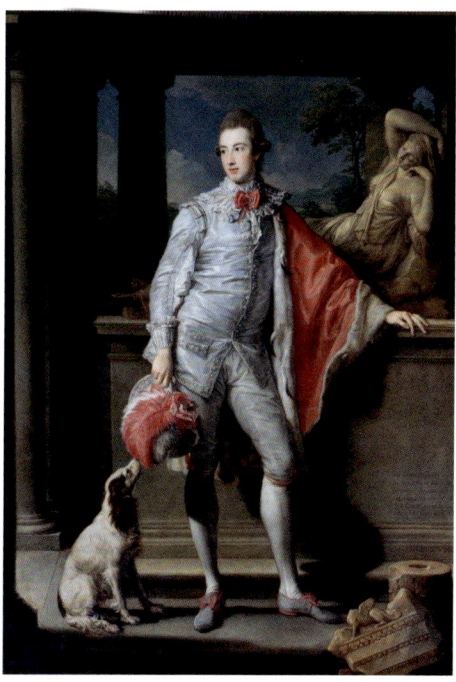

Fig. 4
Pompeo Batoni, *Portrait of Thomas William Coke (1754–1842)*, 1774. Canvas, 248.8 x 170.3 cm. Holkham Hall (cat. no. 3)

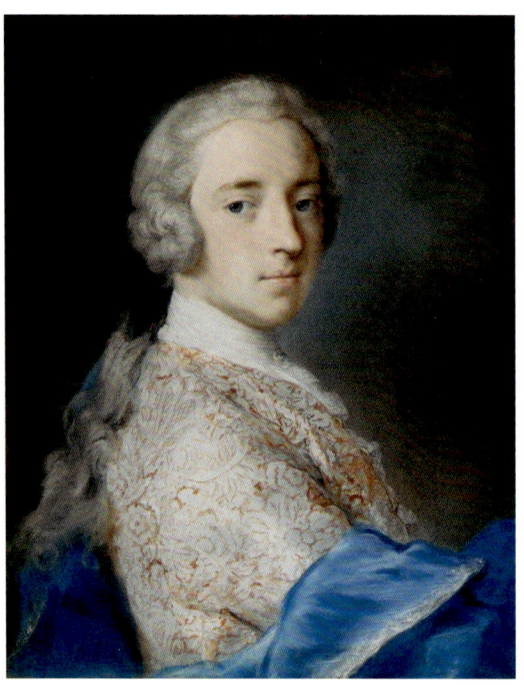

Fig. 5
Rosalba Carriera, *Portrait of Viscount Edward Coke*
(1719-1753), c.1739. Pastel on paper, 50.8 x 43.2 cm.
Holkham Hall (cat. no. 2)

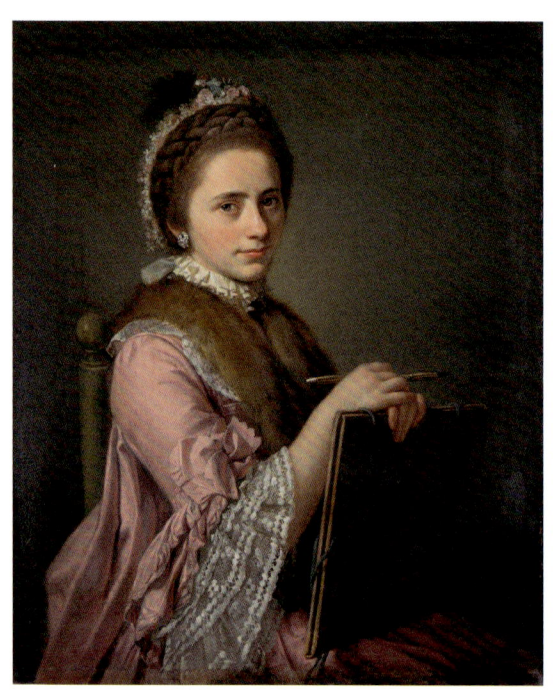

Fig. 6
Nathaniel Dance, *Portrait of Angelica Kauffman*
(1741-1807), 1764. Canvas, 83 x 69 cm. Burghley House
(cat. no. 11)

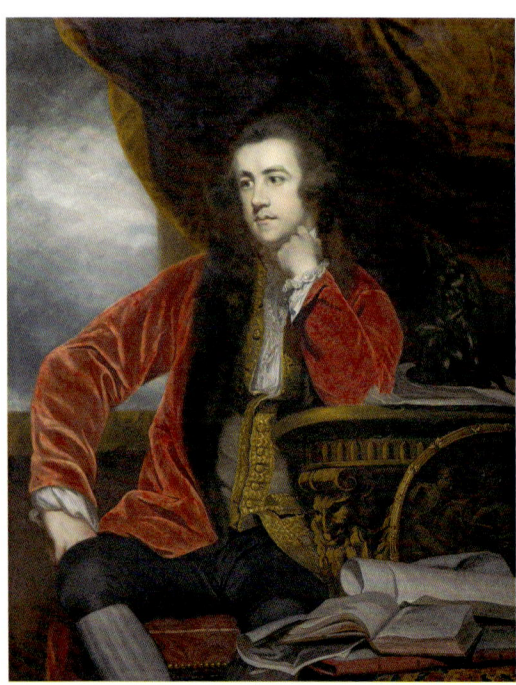

Fig. 7
Joshua Reynolds, *Portrait of Francis Russell, Marquess*
of Tavistock (1739-1767), 1765-1766. Canvas, 123 x 98 cm.
Woburn Abbey (cat. no. 27)

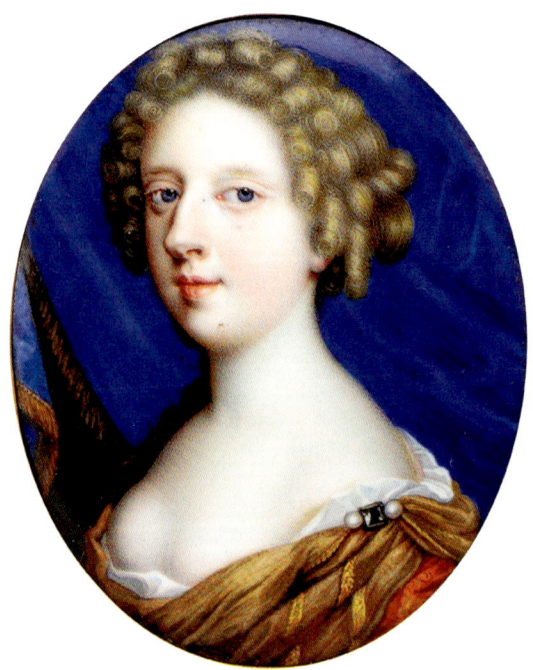

Fig. 8
Jean Petitot the Younger after Peter Lely, *Portrait of Anne*
Cavendish (1649-1703), c.1677. Miniature, height 38 cm.
Burghley House

(see cat. no. 1). Some twenty-five years later it was his son Edward's turn to pose for the artist in Venice. Edward chose the pastel technique, which had meanwhile become very fashionable (fig. 5). This engaging portrait of Edward Coke, who met an untimely death in his mid-thirties, is a highlight of Carriera's refined portraiture and immediately makes clear why her colourful pastels were so much in demand.

In Italy there were also a number of foreign artists who were eager to paint travellers' portraits. The most famous was undoubtedly the Swiss-Austrian Angelica Kauffman (1741-1807). A superstar in her own lifetime, she had flocks of admirers who were just as interested in their idol's love life as they were in her art. In 1764 in Naples, Kauffman painted the portrait of Brownlow Cecil, 9th Earl of Exeter, who travelled to Italy for the first time as a 38-year-old widower (see cat. no. 10). In the background of Cecil's portrait, Kauffman depicted the Bay of Naples with the smoking Vesuvius, the volcano that never failed to put on a spectacular, fiery display (see cat. no. 12). Shortly after Kauffman painted his likeness, Cecil bought a portrait of the artist herself, painted in Rome by the Englishman Nathaniel Dance (fig. 6). Cecil was so impressed by Kauffman that he eventually became one of the most important collectors of her work.

The *Portrait of Francis Russell, Marquess of Tavistock* by the English portraitist Joshua Reynolds (1723-1792) looks like a typical Grand Tour portrait, but in reality it was painted a few years after the sitter's return to England (fig. 7). Tavistock had a small bronze after Michelangelo, which he had purchased in Italy, depicted on the table next to him as a reference to his travels (see cat. no. 28). Bronze copies of antique and Renaissance statues were extremely popular as classy souvenirs. This portrait provided proof of the good taste Tavistock had acquired on his Grand Tour.

Several Protagonists and their Grand Tour Purchases

The narratives reconstructed in this exhibition are based on the histories of the most important Grand Tourists of Burghley House, Holkham Hall and Woburn Abbey: John Cecil, 5th Earl of Exeter, and his wife, Anne Cavendish, who purchased hundreds of contemporary Italian paintings for Burghley House, the country estate they renovated; Thomas Coke, who had Holkham Hall built after his Grand Tour; John Russell, 4th Duke of Bedford, to whom Woburn Abbey is indebted for the series of Venetian views by Canaletto; and Brownlow Cecil, 9th Earl of Exeter, who, following in the footsteps of his great-grandparents, journeyed twice to Italy, where he purchased art that further enriched the collection of Burghley House, his family home.

John Cecil (1648-1700) owed his great fortune to his marriage to Anne Cavendish (1649-1703), daughter of the immensely wealthy Earl of Devonshire (fig. 8). The couple first travelled to the Continent in 1679-1681, and before 1700, Lord Exeter undertook three more European tours, sometimes in the company of his wife.

Purchases were made on a grand scale in France and Italy for the embellishment and enrichment of Burghley House, which, thanks to Anne's money, was transformed from a somewhat outmoded sixteenth-century Tudor house into a magnificent and richly decorated palace (see pp. 60-69). A fortune was spent during those Continental travels on furnishings for Burghley House – pieces of furniture, tapestries, textiles, and no fewer than three hundred paintings by contemporary Italian masters, many of which are still preserved there. Never before had so much art been purchased for an English country house.

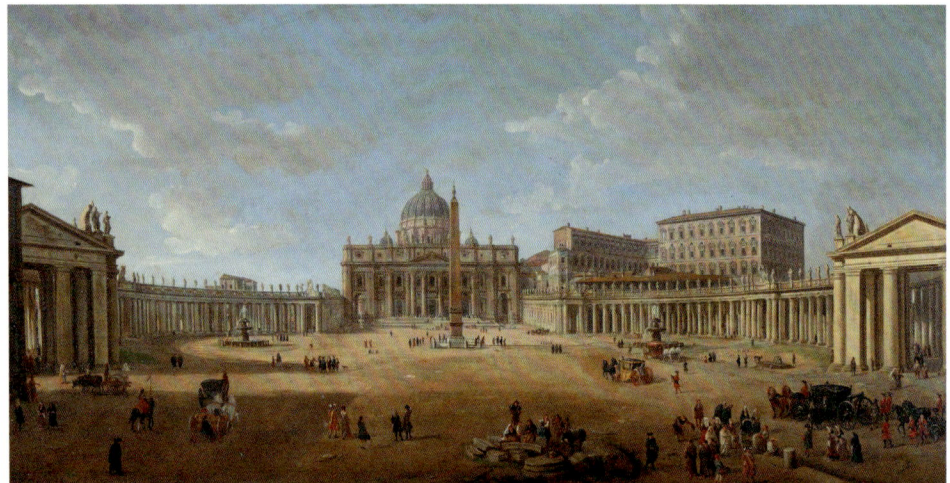

Fig. 9
Caspar Adriaansz van Wittel, known as
Vanvitelli, *View of Saint Peter's Square,
Rome*, 1716. Canvas, 54.6 x 114.3 cm.
Holkham Hall (cat. no. 5)

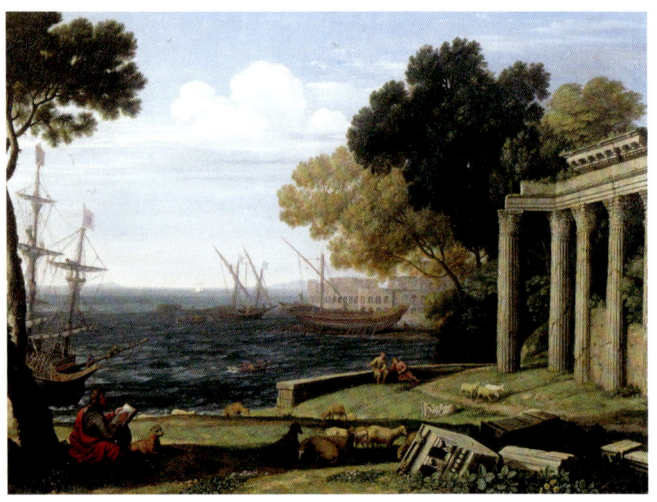

Fig. 10
Claude Gellée, named Lorrain, *View of a Seaport and Amphitheatre*,
1652(?). Canvas, 73.6 x 91.1 cm. Holkham Hall (cat. no. 4)

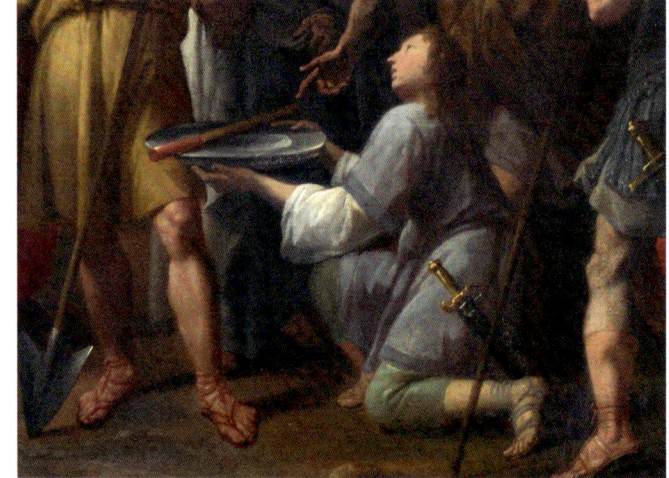

Fig. 11
Detail of Luigi Garzi, *Cincinnatus at the Plough*, 1716.
Canvas, 182.8 x 21.9 cm. Holkham Hall (cat. no. 6)

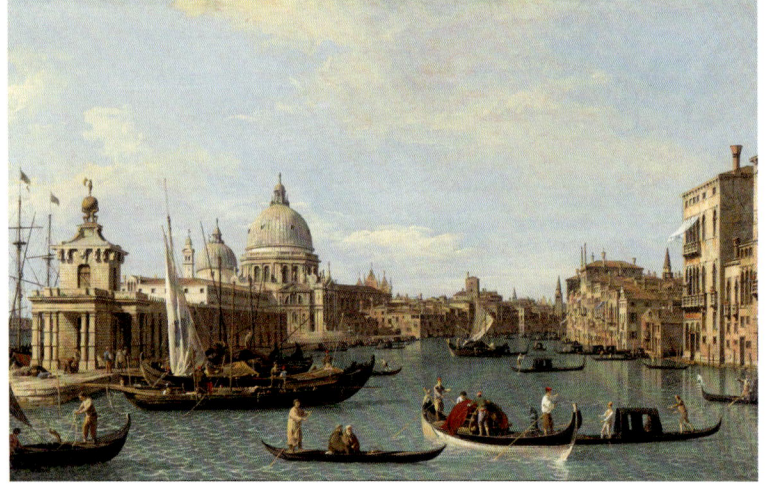

Fig. 12
Giovanni Antonio Canal, named Canaletto,
The Grand Canal in Venice, Looking West,
c.1732–1736. Canvas, 47 x 79 cm.
Woburn Abbey (cat. no. 30)

Thomas Coke, Earl of Leicester (1697-1759) was the very model of the classic Grand Tourist: a young man sent abroad to complete his education. He was still just fifteen when he set out in 1712 in the company of various attendants, among them his tutor, Dr Thomas Hobart, Fellow of Christ's College, Cambridge, and the previously mentioned Edward Jarrett. Thomas stayed away from home all of six years, much longer than the average Grand Tourist.

One of the people he met during his travels was the architect William Kent (1685-1748), who would later play a crucial role in the design and construction of Holkham Hall. Despite his tender age, Thomas Coke had a mission: the formation of an art collection to decorate his future family home. He bought paintings, drawings, statues, books and illuminated manuscripts for his library, and much, much more. From Caspar van Wittel (1653-1736) of Amersfoort, who had settled in Italy, he acquired views of the cities he had visited, a highlight being the resplendent view of St Peter's in Rome (fig. 9). It was Van Wittel who had introduced the cityscape, a genre that had emerged a century before in Dutch art, to Italy (where he was known as Vanvitelli). Thomas Coke was the most avid English collector of this Dutchman's work. Coke also collected the work of the French landscape painter Claude Lorrain (1600-1682), who was extremely popular in England and whose Arcadian depictions of the Italian countryside were in great demand. *View of a Seaport and Amphitheatre* portrays an artist sketching a Roman temple (fig. 10). Coke's wide-ranging interests included a partiality for contemporary Italian history painting. From Luigi Garzi (1638-1721) – then one of the most sought-after painters in Rome – he commissioned *Cincinnatus at the Plough*, in which he had himself portrayed kneeling at the feet of this Roman military leader (fig. 11).

John Russell (1710-1771) undertook a Grand Tour in the years before he became the 4th Duke of Bedford in 1732. In the spring of 1731 he was in Venice, the city whose enchanting beauty appealed to the imagination of many foreign visitors. For these travellers, the souvenir of choice was a painted cityscape, a postcard *avant la lettre*. Canaletto (1697-1768) succeeded as none other in meeting the demand for such mementos with his lively *vedute*. Through the British consul, Joseph Smith, whose palazzo on the Canal Grande served as a showroom for Canaletto's art, Russell placed his first orders. This led to the unparalleled series of twenty-four views of Venice by this peerless Venetian painter (fig. 12). These Canalettos were initially kept at Bedford House in London, but since around 1800 the ensemble has decorated the dining room of Woburn Abbey.

Brownlow Cecil, 9th Earl of Exeter (1725-1793), was the great-grandson of John Cecil, the 5th Earl. He was nearly forty when he first travelled to the Continent, and his interests were broader than those of his seventeenth-century predecessors. During his two trips to Italy, he not only bought the work of living artists, but also went in search of paintings by masters of the past. In Rome he managed to acquire a painting then ascribed to Leonardo da Vinci. This attribution proved too optimistic: the painting in question, *Madonna with the Cherries*, has since been recognized as a work by the sixteenth-century Flemish painter Joos van Cleve (c. 1485-1540) (fig. 13). On his second trip to Italy, the 9th Earl purchased a couple of costly paintings by Paolo Veronese (1628-1588), which had come from a church on the island of Murano in the lagoon of Venice. Typical of Grand Tour souvenirs are the micro-mosaics made by Cesare Aguatti (see cat. no. 17), which Cecil ordered in Rome through Thomas Jenkins, a British art and antique dealer who had a rather shady reputation. Another object he acquired

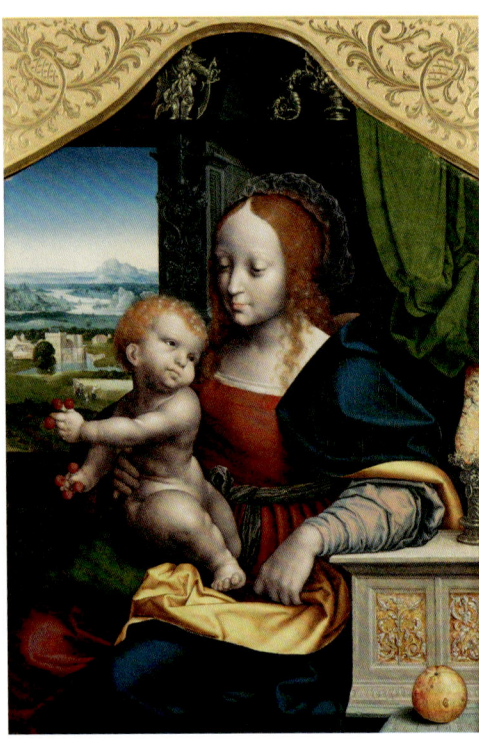

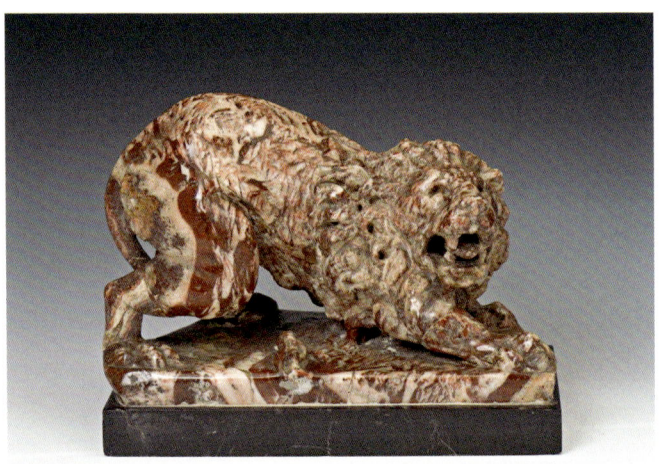

Fig. 13
Joos van Cleve, *Madonna with the Cherries*. Panel, 76 x 55.5 cm.
Burghley House

Fig. 14
Anonymous, *A Crouching Lion*, probably 18th century. Pink marble,
16.5 x 23 cm. Burghley House (cat. no. 22)

from Jenkins is the small marble statue of a crouching lion (fig. 14). An inventory of
the contents of Burghley House states that the statue was found in 1725 in the ancient
Roman port of Ostia. Jenkins had presumably let the buyer believe that it was an
antique Roman sculpture. But the fact that this lion does not stem from antiquity is
compensated for by its charm as a work of art.

Fascinating stories can be told about art collecting, stories in which colourful personages
play the leading role. Thanks to the three Treasure Houses participating in this exhibition
– Holkham Hall, Burghley House and Woburn Abbey – a wealth of information has
come to light about the Grand Tourists whose pursuit of art, in Italy in particular, led
to the formation of such marvellous collections.

THE GRAND TOUR
TRAVEL AND CULTURE IN THE EIGHTEENTH CENTURY

Janneke Budding

A trip abroad is nothing out of the ordinary nowadays,[1] but this was not the case in the eighteenth century. In those days, foreign travel was a privilege enjoyed by the elite, and it cost not only much effort and money, but also a great deal of time. A Grand Tour to France and Italy, an essential part of the education of young British men of a certain standing, took anywhere from six months to more than two years. The journey was not undertaken alone, but in the company of one or more servants. Add to that the cost of travel and lodgings, and it is clear that a Grand Tour was reserved for the nobility and the upper classes. To make sure that their dear son did not abandon himself to frivolous pursuits while travelling abroad, the parents usually hired a tutor. This person, often mockingly called a 'bear leader', was expected to keep his pupil on the straight and narrow path of art, science and culture (figs. 1 and 2).

The Grand Tour was not reserved exclusively for men. In the second half of the eighteenth century in particular, upper-class British women often journeyed to France and Italy in the company of their husbands. Examples include Mrs Hester Lynch Piozzi and Lady Anna Miller, both of whom published accounts of their travels.[2]

The classic Grand Tour required thorough preparation. The first arrangements to be made involved the route to be taken after crossing over to France and which means of transport to use. One's own carriage was a possibility, but an alternative was to buy a coach and team of horses on the other side of the Channel and sell them before returning home. Travelling by diligence was the least expensive mode of transport, and therefore had the least standing.

The fashionable city of Paris was the first stopping point on the Grand Tour. Because most British travellers spent a relatively long time there, it was practical to hire a French *valet de place* for the duration of their stay, even for those who had brought along servants. Such a manservant was acquainted with the city and its ways, and also knew which tailors and other tradesmen to go to in order to acquire a new wardrobe and accessories. In the words of the Scottish writer Tobias Smollett: 'When an Englishman comes to Paris, he cannot appear until he has undergone a total metamorphosis. At his first arrival he finds it necessary to send for the tailor, perruquier, hatter, shoemaker, and every other tradesman concerned in the equipment of the human body. He must then change his buckles, and the form of his ruffles.'[3] Grand Tourists who dressed with extreme flamboyance were mockingly called 'macaroni' (fig. 3).

From Paris the journey continued to Lyon, where Grand Tourists had to decide how to travel to Italy. They could take the diligence to Marseille, where there was a boat to Genoa – a sea crossing that was not without danger, owing to pirates – or cross the Alps via the 2100-metre Mont Cenis pass. This route meant being carried in a so-called sedan chair, equipped with two long poles, front and back, for the porters. (fig. 4). When no longer necessary, this portable chair was dismantled and carried by mules like the rest of the baggage. Sedan chairs were reasonably comfortable: the passenger's feet rested on a rope, the elbows on wooden armrests. The poles were provided with straps that went over the porters' shoulders, to distribute the weight. Many a Grand Tourist praised the swiftness and sureness of foot with which the 'chair men', wearing spiked shoes, negotiated the steep mountain paths.

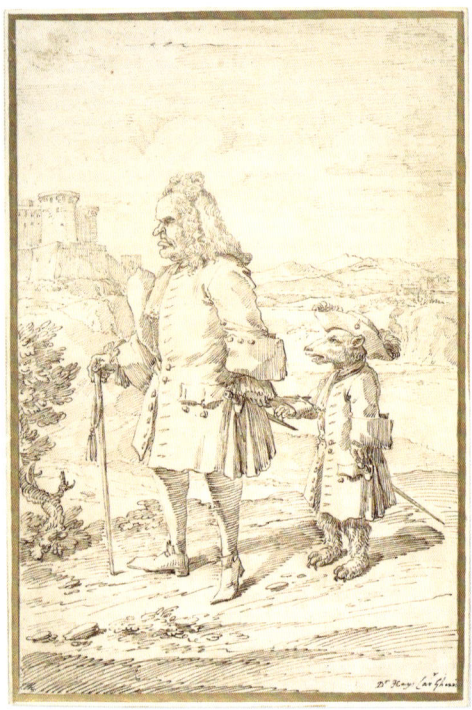

Fig. 1
Pier Leone Ghezzi, *Dr James Hay as 'bear leader'*,
c.1725. Pen and brown ink, 163 x 243 mm. British
Museum, London

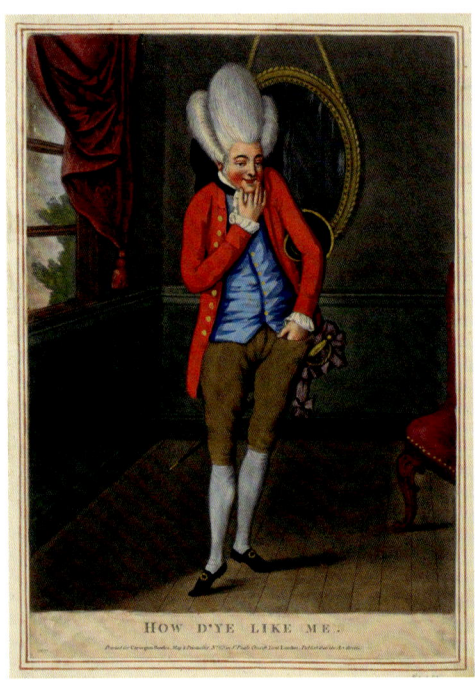

Fig. 2
Katherine Read, *British Gentlemen in Rome*, c.1750.
Canvas, 94.5 x 134.5 cm. Yale Center for British Art,
Paul Mellon Collection, New Haven

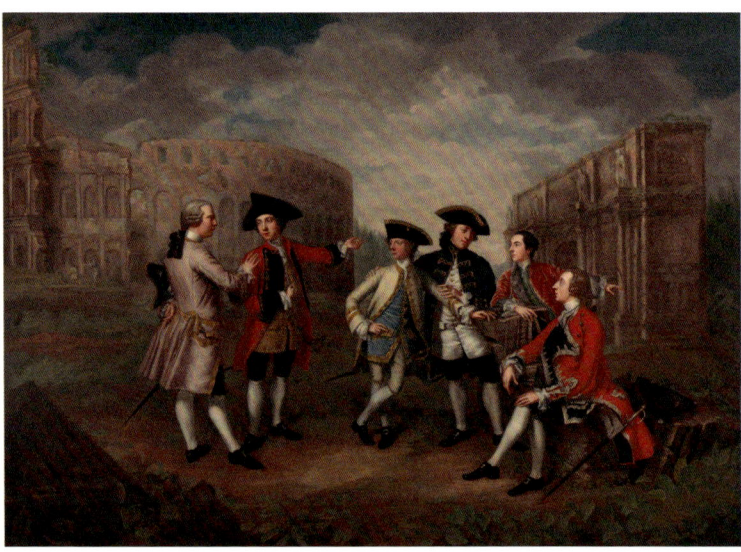

Fig. 3
Philip Dawe, *The Macaroni*, 1773. Mezzotint,
351 x 250 mm. British Museum, London

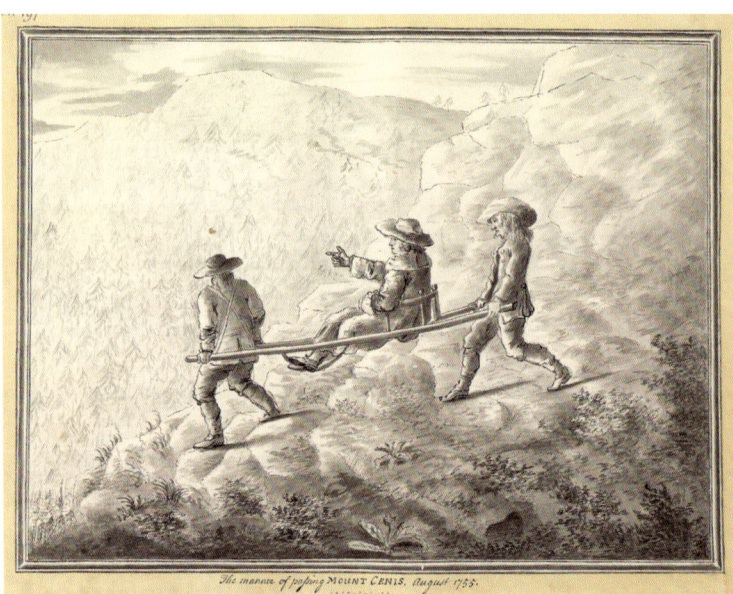

Fig. 4
George Keate, 'A Manner of Passing Mount Cenis', from an
album of 232 drawings of a journey through France, Switzerland
and Italy, 1754–1756. Pen and black ink, grey wash, 178 x 236 mm.
British Museum, London

Once they had arrived in Piemonte, Grand Tourists were delighted, even ecstatic, to find themselves in Italy, the cradle of the Renaissance. But their delight did not always extend to their accommodation en route. The inns and hotels in Italy's famous centres of culture were generally good, but outside the large cities they had a very bad reputation. Dr Sharp, a renowned British surgeon who toured Italy in 1765 and 1766, fulminated: 'At Turin, Milan, Venice, Rome, and, perhaps, two or three other towns, you meet with good accommodation but no words can express the wretchedness of the other inns. No other beds than one of straw, with a matrass [*sic*] of straw, and next to that a dirty sheet, sprinkled with water, and, consequently, damp.'[4]

Grand Tourists were attracted to Venice for a variety of reasons (see cat. nos. 30-31), not least its unique situation in a lagoon and its impressive art and architecture. Another enticement was its age-old reputation as the city of sin. In addition to the *ridotti* (gaming houses, at which it was obligatory to wear a mask), there were many prostitutes, who, according to the historian and author Thomas Nugent, were considered by some Grand Tourists to be the only reason to travel to Italy.[5] Thomas Coryat, who travelled around Italy at the beginning of the seventeenth century,[6] reported that Venice had all of 20,000 'courtisanes' in a population numbering 200,000.

Although Venice itself had much to offer, this was far from true of Venetian cuisine. Lady Miller complained about the 'wretched cooks' and was disgusted by the local custom of using animal blood in soups and ragouts.[7]

Most Grand Tourists proceeded from Venice via Bologna to Florence and Rome. Because the road passed through mountainous terrain, on this leg of the journey carriages were drawn by six horses, two more than in ordinary circumstances. In the Eternal City, the prime destination was St Peter's Basilica (see cat. no. 5). Lady Miller was impressed by the appearance St Peter's, which in her opinion was 'much more splendid' in reality than in the famous etchings by Giovanni Battista Piranesi that she had studied in England (fig. 5). Yet in spite of this favourable impression, she noted many points of criticism. The colonnade, for example, displayed 'a most striking fault in the architecture; the pillars, which are of stone, show heavy and crowded'. She also criticized the façade of St Peter's: 'There are so many ornaments, such twisting and turning.'[8]

Young *milordi inglesi*, for whom the traditional sights of the Grand Tour were of secondary importance, met in the coffee houses on the Piazza di Spagna, the 'English ghetto'. Grand Tourists who had seen enough of Rome were also inclined to travel a further thirty kilometres to higher-lying Tivoli, to inspect in comparative coolness the summer palaces and ample gardens of the Italian nobility and also Tivoli's villas and temples of antiquity.

It was customary for British Grand Tourists to have their portrait painted in Italy or at least to commission copies of famous paintings. During their travels, they acquired paintings and sculptures, both originals and copies, as well as cameos, fossils, archaeological finds, coins and maps. In 1764 the renowned British actor David Garrick wrote from Rome to a friend: 'You must know that I am antiquity hunting from Morning to Night & my poor wife drags her lame leg after me.'[9]

A number of Grand Tourists travelled on from Rome to Naples. The food and accommodation on this stage of the trip were notorious. Lady Miller was appalled by the 'rotten eggs, and some ragouts of liver and brains stewed in oil, out of the same reservoir with that used in the lamp.'[10] Dr Samuel Sharp wrote: '[A]ll the way to Naples we never once crept between the sheets, not daring to encounter the vermin and nastiness of those beds.'[11]

After visiting Pompeii, climbing Vesuvius (see cat. no. 12), and experiencing the pleasures of Naples, it was time for the return journey. Back home, the *milord*'s portrait, with a view of Rome or Florence in the background, was hung in pride of place.

Grand Tourists and the Servants Who Accompanied Them

Grand Tourists who aspired to return to Great Britain as connoisseurs were advised to see the sights of Rome in the company of a hired antiquarian: an expert in art and archaeology. To such a serious programme one might have to devote three hours a day for a full six weeks.

A reliable antiquarian was not easy to find. Many people, undeterred by their lack of specialist knowledge, offered their services. The excessively frugal Tobias Smollett refused to hire an antiquarian and instead found a servant who knew his way around Rome. The English writer and politician William Beckford (1760-1844), who travelled to Italy in 1782 with a retinue of more than twenty servants – including a tailor, a cook, a barber, an artist entrusted with making sketches, and his personal physician – would not even contemplate exploring Rome under the guidance of an alleged expert.

> '*I absolutely will have no antiquary to go prating from fragment to fragment, and tell me, that were I to stay five years at Rome, I should not see half it contained. The thought alone, of so much to look at, is quite distracting, and makes me resolve to view nothing at all in a scientific way; but straggle and wander about, just as the spirit chuses.*'[12]

A Grand Tourist had to cope with many unforeseen circumstances. To ease the discomfort of travelling, however, there were always servants, whether brought from home or hired locally. It was the job of the tutor to find such temporary personnel. The ideal servant answered as much as possible to the following description:

> '*A servant selected to accompany a gentleman on his travels should be conversant with the French language. Moreover, he should write a legible hand and bleed well in case his master should meet with an accident where no surgical aid is to be expected.*'[13]

In addition, the ideal servant was dependable, well-trained and had a great sense of responsibility. But not all travelling servants were endowed with these qualities. The poet-Lord Byron (1788-1824), who travelled around Italy in the company of an English servant from 1816 to 1819, complained:

> '*The perpetual lamentations after beef and beer, the stupid, bigoted contempt for everything foreign, an insurmountable incapacity for acquiring even a few words in any language, rendered him like all other English servants, an incumbrance.*'[14]

British personnel seem to have been remarkably eager to travel as servants abroad. The London newspaper *The Morning Post* published, in 1815 alone, around a thousand advertisements placed by 'travelling servants' seeking work, among them numerous women.

> '*Wants a situation, a young person as lady's-maid, or to attend upon an elderly lady. She fully understands her business, and has no objection to travel.*'[15]
> '*Respectable Young Woman, 23 years of age seeks a job as a lady's maid and would prefer going abroad.*'[16]

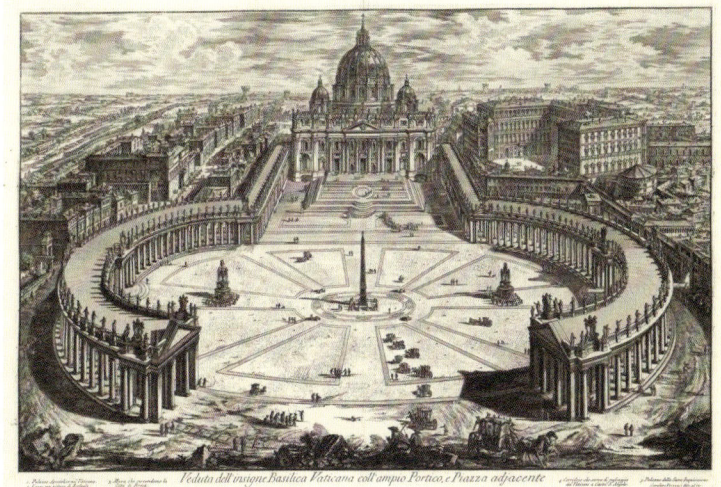

Fig. 5
Giovanni Battista Piranesi, *View of St Peter's Square with
St Peter's*, from the series *Vedute di Roma*, 1748-1778. Etching,
477 x 712 mm. Rijksmuseum, Amsterdam

The majority of those keen to travel were men, however. One of them presented himself
in *The Morning Post* as follows:

> As TRAVELLING SERVANT, an Englishman, who has been to Paris, travelled in
> Germany, all over Italy and Sicily, speaks Italian well, French and German enough
> for business; if with a Single Gentleman he will dress his dinner when necessary; lived
> four and a half years in his last situation.'[17]

In the eighteenth and nineteenth centuries, all foreign travellers, including Grand
Tourists and their personnel, were inevitably exposed to danger. The roads were often
bad, the horses might bolt, carriages could turn over. There was also a good chance of
disgusting food and squalid rooms, not to mention the risk of disease.

These discomforts were redoubled for the servants, who had to make do with
food and accommodation that was decidedly worse than their masters'. If only one
bed was available, the servant usually slept on the floor, using his coat as a blanket.
Travelling servants were the first to get up and the last to go to bed. They helped their
masters dress and nursed them in case of illness.

Unfortunately, few journals kept by travelling servants survive. An exception
is the account written by the Scotsman John MacDonald, who in 1790 published his
experiences abroad under the title *Memoirs of an Eighteenth-century Footman*. The
picture MacDonald sketches reveals that he actually enjoyed his foreign travels, which
made it possible for him to meet new people, see places of interest, and delight in the
unknown.

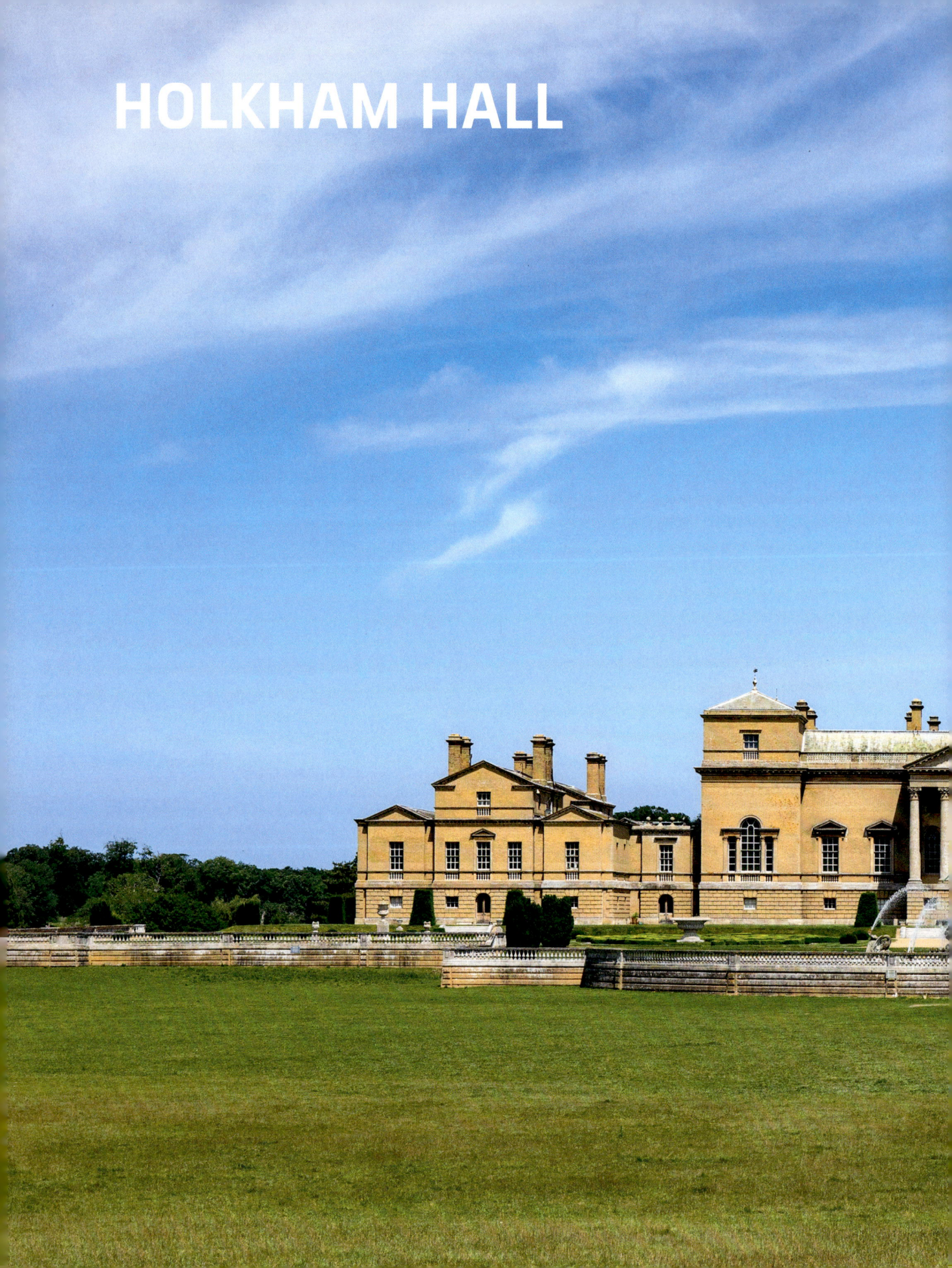

HOLKHAM HALL

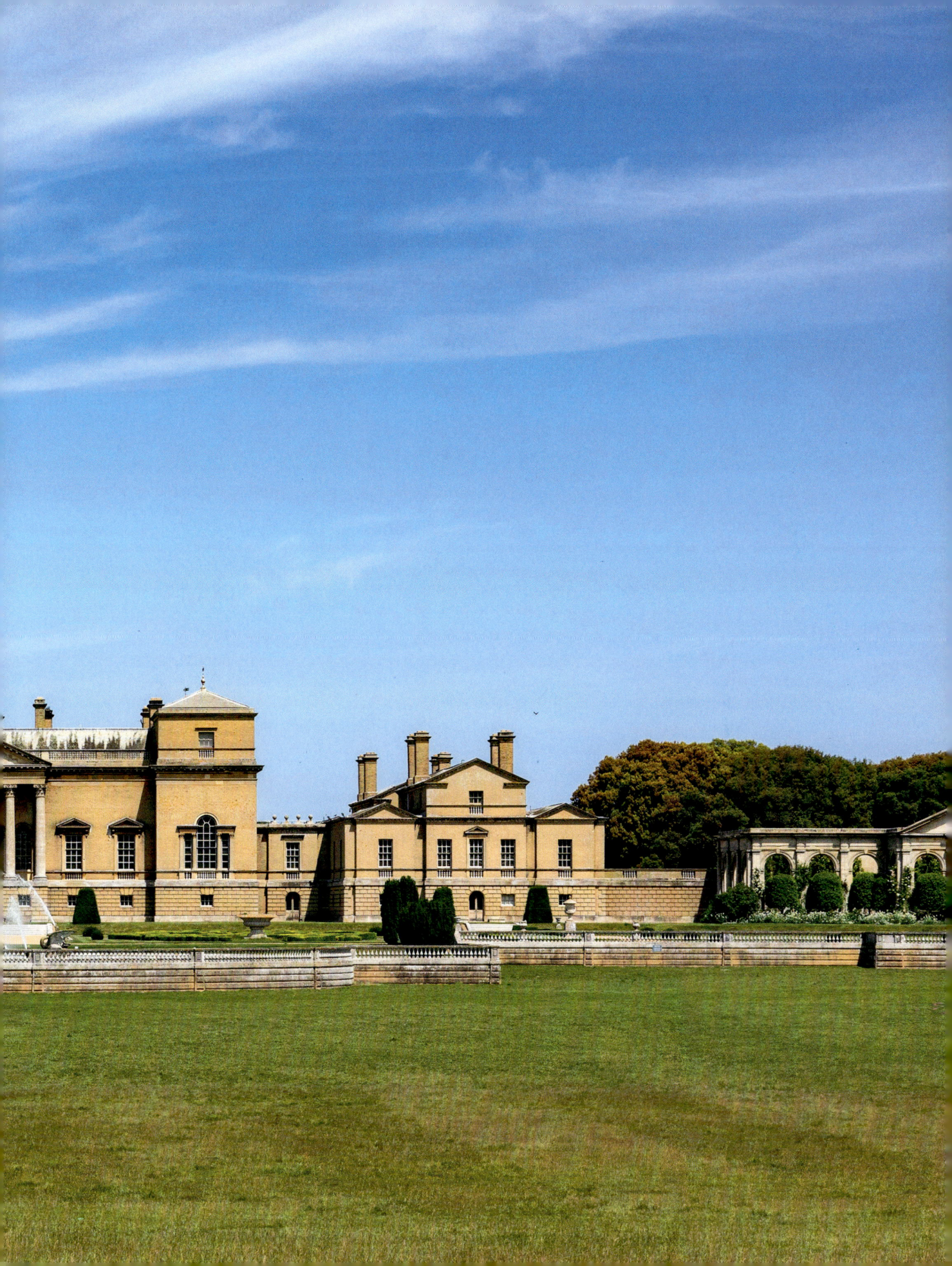

HOLKHAM HALL AND THE GRAND TOUR

Maria de Peverelli

Thomas Coke (1697-1759) was a man of vision and determination, and Holkham Hall was the embodiment of his dream (fig. 1). It all began in 1712, when, at just 15 years old, Thomas – an orphan of great wealth but without a title or seat – was sent on a Grand Tour by his guardians. The journey would last six years and change his life forever. He set out as an undisciplined youth – brilliant, headstrong, with a passion for cockfighting and gambling – and returned with a deep knowledge of art and architecture, a profound appreciation of classical culture, and a treasure trove of books, manuscripts, drawings, paintings, and sculptures. Most importantly, he came back with a vision: to build a house worthy of housing all he had acquired – Holkham Hall.

At the time, Britain was Europe's richest nation and the first constitutional monarchy. Its elite, educated in the classics, eagerly embraced the ideals and aesthetics of Ancient Rome, along with a widespread enthusiasm for classical art and architecture. By the early eighteenth century, the Grand Tour had become a rite of passage for the British upper classes, offering a chance to expand intellectual and worldly horizons. Travelers journeyed to Italy via France or the Low Countries, often stopping in Switzerland, Germany, and Austria, with Rome as the ultimate destination.

Rome, long celebrated as the heart of both the Roman Empire and the Christian Church, had drawn visitors for centuries. But in the eighteenth century, it emerged as the cultural epicentre for Grand Tourists. They admired ancient ruins and Baroque masterpieces, visited churches and aristocratic palaces, attended ceremonies and festivals, mingled with fellow countrymen, and eagerly acquired art. The works of Raphael (1483-1520), Annibale Carracci (1560-1609), and Guido Reni (1575-1642), in particular, were revered as the pinnacle of classical ideals. Often, travellers engaged local agents – frequently British artists or architects with close Italian ties – to assist in their purchases.

From these journeys, thousands of works of art were brought back to Britain to adorn palaces and country houses. It was nothing less than a cultural transfusion, enriching the very fabric of the nation's artistic and architectural heritage. Bringing home a portrait, a *veduta* (painting of a cityscape), and either an ancient sculpture or a cast of one, was in fact the ultimate prize for any Grand Tourist – a tangible testament to their cultural journey. Thomas did this on a grand scale, armed with the wealth, ambition, and vision to create a collection – and ultimately a home – worthy of his aspirations.

Thomas was accompanied on his journey by a governor, Dr Thomas Hobart (d.1727), the bibliophile Domenico Ferrari (1685-1744), two grooms, and the valet Edward Jarrett – whose account book would later become an invaluable source of insight into the entire journey (see pp. 54-57). After a prolonged stay in France, they arrived in Turin in November 1713. Aside from an excursion through Switzerland, Germany, and France in 1715, he spent the next three years immersed in Italy. Travelling from north to south, he was among the first Grand Tourists to venture as far as Sicily.[18] Jarrett's account book shows that as early as January 1714, during a month-long stay in Venice, Thomas had already begun acquiring books, an activity he continued throughout his journey (cat. nos. 8 and 9).

By February 1714, Thomas had reached Rome, where he remained for six months. Here, he began purchasing and commissioning paintings from leading artists and visiting numerous aristocratic collections. He also met William Kent (1685-1748), an English artist who became both a travelling companion and a trusted agent, later playing a vital role in the design of Holkham Hall.

A defining moment in Thomas's Roman experience – and a clear signal of his desire to be seen as a classical scholar – was his commission of a painting from Sebastiano Conca (1680-1764) depicting *The Vision of Aeneas in the Elysian Fields* (fig. 2). Inspired by frescoes Thomas had admired at Palazzo Pamphili, the painting likely portrays Thomas himself as the young lyre-player, representing the classical poet Virgil (70-21 BCE) or the mythical musician Orpheus.[19] Although lesser-known today, Conca was among Rome's most influential painters at the time, along with Giuseppe Bartolomeo Chiari (1654-1727), Andrea Procaccini (1671-1743), Francesco Trevisani (1656-1746), and Benedetto Luti (1666-1724) – all artists Thomas commissioned during this stay.[20] Luti, in particular, in whose studio Kent had worked, was also a great collector of drawings, probably influencing Thomas in his acquisitions. Payments for Conca's painting are recorded by Jarrett in 1716, during Thomas's second visit to Rome – a trip in which he also settled payments for works he had commissioned earlier from Chiari and Procaccini.[21] Thomas would go on to commission three more paintings in which he was depicted as a character of the story. Of the four, only two survive at Holkham: one by Luigi Garzi (1638-1721; see cat. no. 6), and the aforementioned work by Conca. Both of these paintings dealt with mythological or historical subjects, illustrating tales of magnanimity and clemency, virtues that Thomas evidently sought to associate with his own image.

The year 1716 was significant for another reason: it marked Thomas's first acquisition of a work by Caspar van Wittel (1653-1736): a *veduta* of the Colosseum. This purchase would inaugurate what would eventually become the largest collection of Van Wittel's works in Britain (cat. no. 5).

It was also during this second stay in Rome that Jarrett records another milestone in Thomas's collecting: the acquisition of his first sculpture, a colossal marble portrait head (fig. 3).[22] Collecting ancient sculptures and marbles was a privilege reserved for the wealthiest travellers, who, through specialised brokers, could secure important works for export (cat. no. 7). On his earlier visit to Rome, Thomas – armed with a copy of Paolo Alessandro Maffei's (1653-1716) *Raccolta di Statue Antiche e Moderne* of 1704, a compendium of classical, Renaissance, and Baroque sculptures – had sketched pieces in various private collections and commissioned drawings of notable antiquities. Other major acquisitions, including statues of Diana, Lucius Antonius, Jupiter and Apollo, were made in his subsequent journeys, with Kent acting as his agent.

Drawings, too, were among Thomas's passions. Jarrett records a payment for a book of drawings attributed to Raphael, with additional purchases made later in Naples – through Kent – and Florence.[23] Thomas's remarkable eye for quality is confirmed by his acquisition, also during this trip, of the group of drawings by Leonardo da Vinci (1452-1519) now known as the Codex Leicester – today famously owned by Bill Gates.

After touring Italy's northern cities, Thomas returned to Rome in January 1717, where he resumed acquiring sculptures and once again took up architectural lessons – an interest he had pursued since his earliest days in Italy. This laid the intellectual groundwork for the grand house he would eventually build. Shortly before departing Rome to begin his journey home, he commissioned a portrait from Trevisani, another leading painter of the time, who depicted him with all the attributes of the cultivated gentleman he aspired to embody (fig. 4).

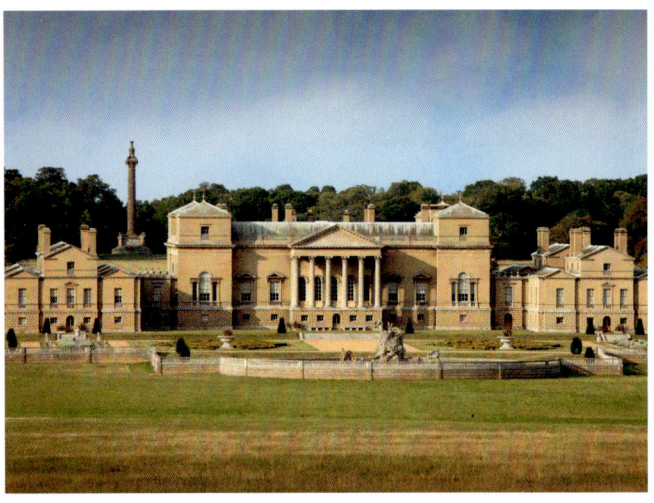

Fig. 1
View of Holkham Hall, Norfolk

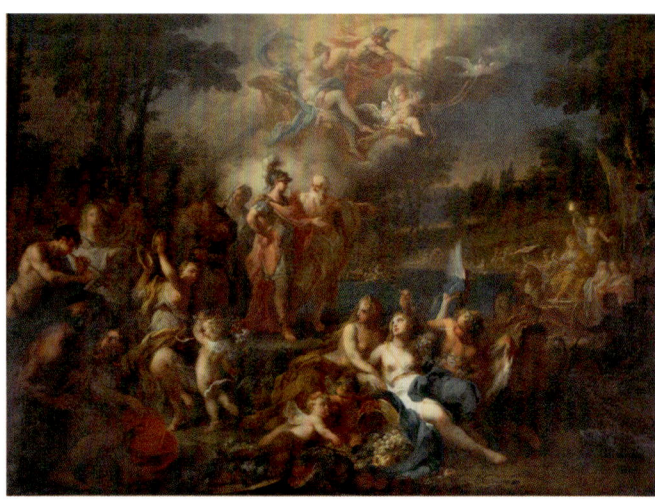

Fig. 2
Sebastiano Conca, *The Elysian Fields*, 1716-1718.
Canvas, 216 x 299.7 cm. Holkham Hall

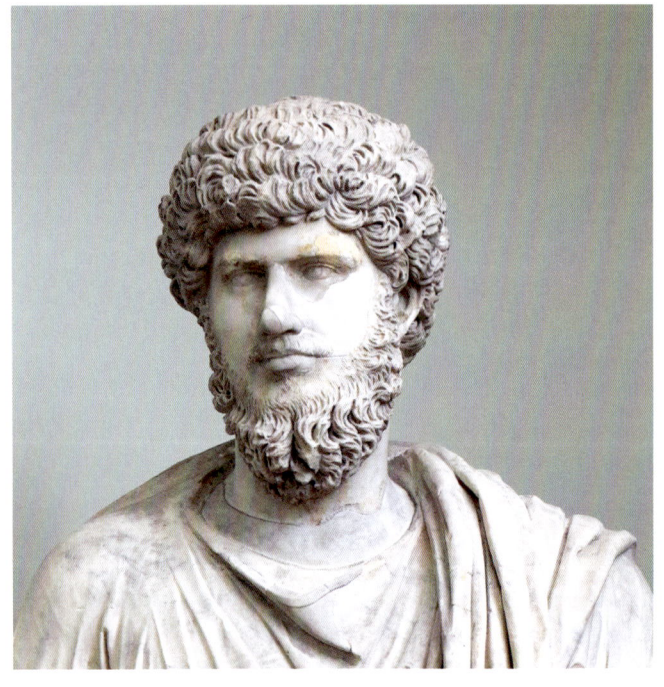

Fig. 3
Monumental Marble Portrait Head, 2nd century CE,
height 95 cm. Holkham Hall

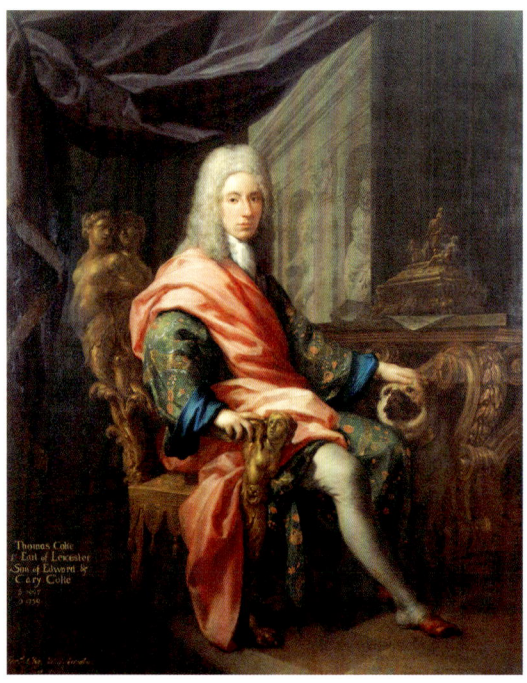

Fig. 4
Francesco Trevisani, *Portrait of Thomas Coke (1697-
1759)*, 1717. Canvas, 198 x 160 cm. Holkham Hall

In the summer of 1717, Coke embarked on the journey back to Britain, stopping in Vienna, Prague, Dresden, Berlin, Amsterdam, The Hague, and Paris, making significant acquisitions of manuscripts and paintings along the way. One of the most important purchases from this final leg was the monumental equestrian portrait of the Duke d'Arenberg by Anthony van Dyck (1599-1641), which today hangs in the Saloon at Holkham (fig. 5).

Once back in Britain, Thomas married Margaret Tufton (1700-1775) and set about planning his own temple of the arts. Financial losses from the South Sea Bubble delayed construction until 1734, and it would take 30 years to complete.[24] The project was the fruit of a remarkable collaboration between four men: Thomas himself – who not only conceived the project but actively contributed to its design; Kent – then working on parliamentary buildings in London and responsible for early drawings of the facades and interiors; Richard Boyle, 3rd Earl of Burlington (1694-1753) – the leading champion of Palladian architecture[25] in England, who had travelled in Europe with Kent; and Matthew Brettingham (1699-1769), a local architect and master builder, who helped bring their vision to life.[26]

Inspired by the Palladian villas and Roman temples he admired during his Grand Tour, Thomas envisioned a grand house: a central block with four corner towers and four pavilions. With its perfect proportions and harmonious composition, Holkham Hall would become celebrated as the finest example of Palladianism in England.[27]

The relatively austere exterior, built of soft, sand-coloured brick, gives little hint of the overwhelming splendour within. Visitors enter the Marble Hall – monumental in scale, clad not in marble but Staffordshire alabaster – with a coffered ceiling inspired by the Parthenon and a colonnade recalling Rome's Temple of Portunus (fig. 6). From this austere magnificence, visitors move into the sumptuous Saloon, draped in deep red velvet and lined with paintings with grand gilded frames, leading into a grand enfilade of state rooms.

While the building stands as the finest architectural example of Palladianism, the interiors represent an almost perfectly preserved Grand Tour collection – an extraordinary and meticulously documented time capsule. The product of Thomas's vision is documented in detail in the 1760 inventory (drafted after his death), Lady Margaret's detailed inventory of furnishings (down to protective fabric covers) and library volumes, Brettingham's 1761 publication *Plans, Elevations and Sections of Holkham*, and his son's revised editions – adding *A Descriptive Account of the Statues, Pictures and Drawings* in 1773 and 1776 – all kept in Holkham's archives and library.[28]

As construction advanced, Thomas launched a second phase of acquisitions in Italy and Britain, mostly through agents, to decorate the house. Between 1747 and 1754, Matthew Brettingham the Younger (1724-1803), son of Holkham's master builder, acted as Thomas's agent in Italy. While he primarily acquired sculptures – 13 statues and 21 busts – he also secured paintings by Claude Lorrain (1604/05-1682) and Van Wittel, mosaic tables from Villa Hadriana, a small fresco attributed to Carracci (*Polyphemus and Galatea*), and the famous copy of Michelangelo's (1475-1564) *Battaglia di Cascina* by Bastiano da Sangallo (1481-1551), today the most celebrated painting in the collection (fig. 7). Brettingham's account book, still preserved at Holkham's archives, records these invaluable acquisitions.

Thomas's preference for Italian art extended beyond his purchases abroad. Even in England, he favoured Italian artists: in 1744 – the year he was created the 1st Earl of Leicester – he commissioned Andrea Casali (1705-1784), a pupil of Conca and

Trevisani, to paint family portraits. In 1758, Casali visited Holkham to paint nine full-length portraits. Most were based on miniatures, except for Thomas and Lady Margaret, whose portraits were painted from life. Casali, who had arrived in London under Lord Carlisle's patronage in 1741, also operated as an art dealer, enabling Thomas to expand his collection further. Through Casali, Thomas acquired important works, such as a *Madonna and Child* (now attributed to Giulio Romano (1492/99-1546), but then thought to be by Raphael), and the cartoon for Raphael's *La Belle Jardinière* – sadly sold in 1991 and now at the National Gallery of Art in Washington, D.C.

Though dominated by artists born or working in Italy – such as Lorrain and Van Wittel – Thomas's tastes were not exclusively Italian. He also admired Flemish and Dutch painters, particularly those whose works he had encountered in England, like Peter Paul Rubens (1577-1640) and Van Dyck. In 1745, he acquired a monumental *Flight into Egypt* by Rubens, intended to complement an equestrian portrait by Van Dyck he had purchased in Paris. Among his more unconventional acquisitions were two paintings by Melchior d'Hondecoeter (1635/36-1695), purchased in 1746, in which bird motifs symbolised political and military conflict – specifically the campaigns of King William III of Orange (1650-1702; fig. 8).

Beyond paintings and sculptures, the state rooms were enriched with fine tapestries, luxurious wall coverings, and exquisite eighteenth-century furniture, much of it commissioned from leading London craftsmen like Paul Saunders (1722-1771) and Benjamin Goodison (c.1700-1767). Two rooms in particular owe their existence entirely to the Grand Tour: the Statue Gallery and the Landscape Room. The Statue Gallery, with on each end octagonal tribunes replicating the apses from Rome's Temple of Venus, was the first gallery in England dedicated exclusively to sculpture. To this day, it still houses the statues and busts exactly as Thomas intended. The Landscape Room (fig. 9), likely inspired by the *Sala dei Paesaggi* in Palazzo Colonna, features 22 landscapes by the greatest masters of the genre – Lorrain (of whom Holkham owns the largest collection in Britain; cat. no. 4), Andrea Locatelli (1695-1741), Gaspard Dughet (1615-1675; who created the *Sala dei Paesaggi*), Salvator Rosa (1615-1673), and Claude-Joseph Vernet (1714-1789). Interestingly, Thomas kept the *vedute* (cityscapes) by Van Wittel (cat. no. 5) and Canaletto (1697-1768) for his private apartments rather than the state rooms.

Although Holkham Hall embodied Thomas's dream, he died heirless in 1759, having drawn little joy from it late in life, famously lamenting: 'It is melancholy living to stand alone in one's own country... My nearest neighbour is the King of Denmark'.[29] After his death, it was his widow, Lady Margaret, who oversaw the final completion of the house and arranged part of the display of the paintings and the sculptures. Her role in the decoration and management of the house, but also of the grounds, has often been underestimated.[30]

Thomas Coke was not the only member of his family to embark on the Grand Tour. His son, Edward (1719-1753), followed in his footsteps, leaving Britain in 1738 and returning two years later. Like his father, Edward spent much of his time in Italy, where he sat for a portrait by Rosalba Carriera in Venice (1673/75-1757; cat. no. 2).

Nearly 30 years later, Thomas's great-grandnephew, Thomas William Coke (1754-1842), was similarly sent to Italy – a trip supported by his great-aunt and Thomas's widow, Lady Margaret, who was seeking a proper heir to the estate. His travels took him through Turin, Macerata, Rome (which he visited three times), Florence, Naples, Genoa, and Milan.[31] He was portrayed by Pompeo Batoni (1708-1787), the most celebrated portraitist of the Grand Tour era (cat. no. 3), and returned home with some cameos and a fine mosaic.

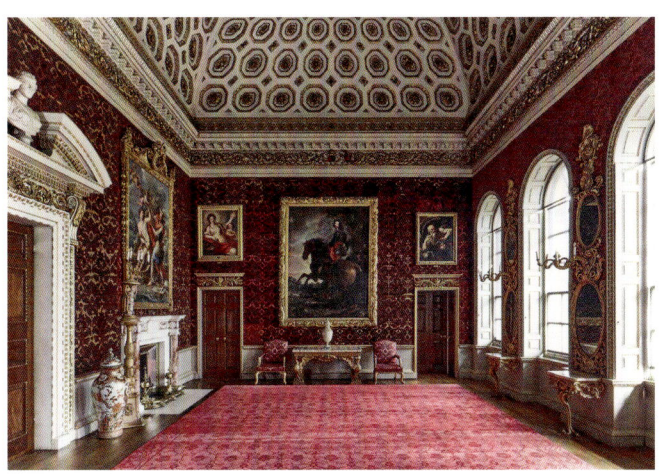

Fig. 5
View of the Saloon at Holkham, with Anthony van Dyck's
Equestrian Portrait of Duke d'Arenberg

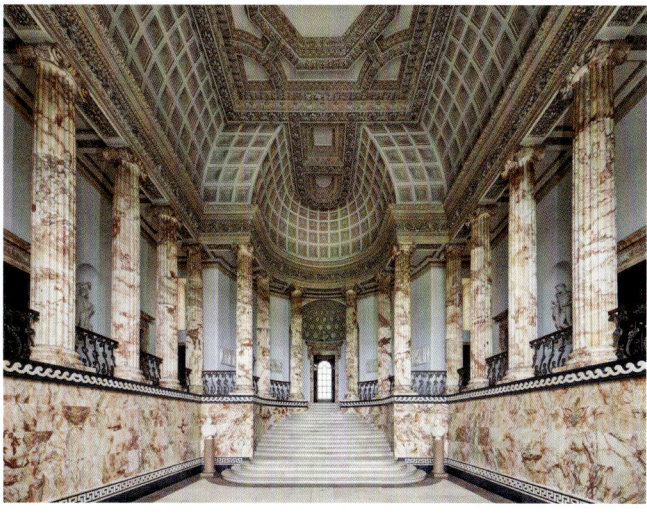

Fig. 6
View of the Marble Hall at Holkham

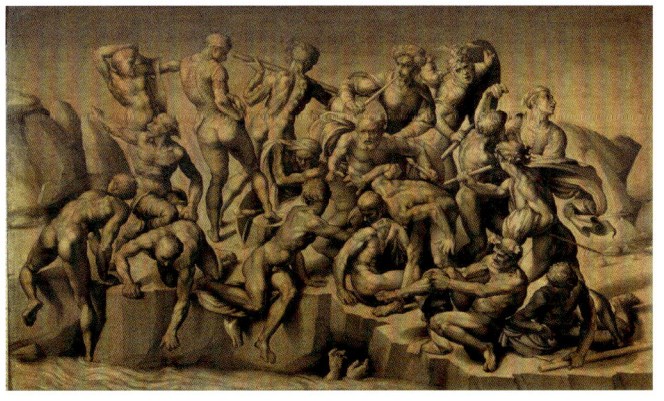

Fig. 7
Bastiano da Sangallo, *Copy of Michelangelo's Battaglia di Cascina*,
c.1542. Panel, 77 x 130 cm. Holkham Hall

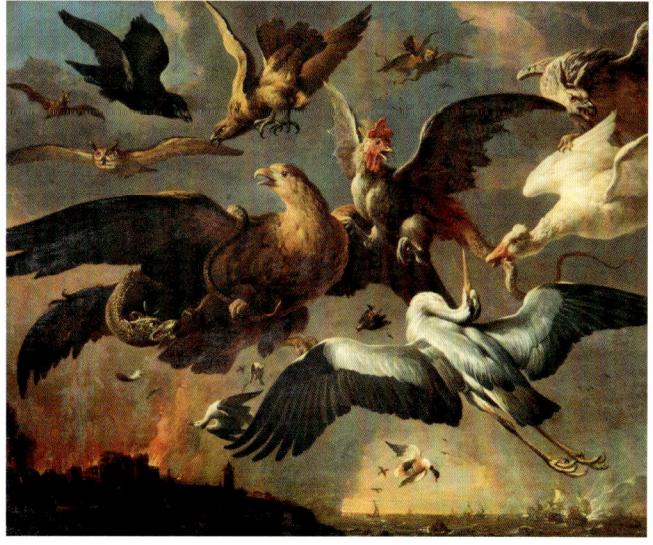

Fig. 8
Melchior d'Hondecoeter, *The Wars of William III (1650-1702)*, c.1680.
Canvas, 152.4 x 190.5 cm. Holkham Hall

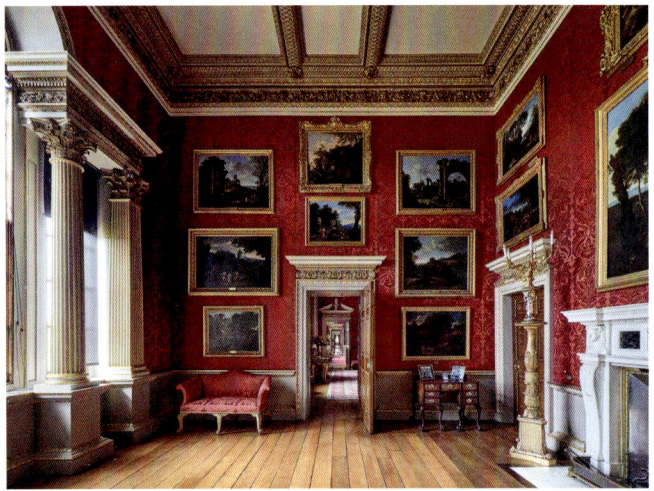

Fig. 9
View of the Landscape Room at Holkham

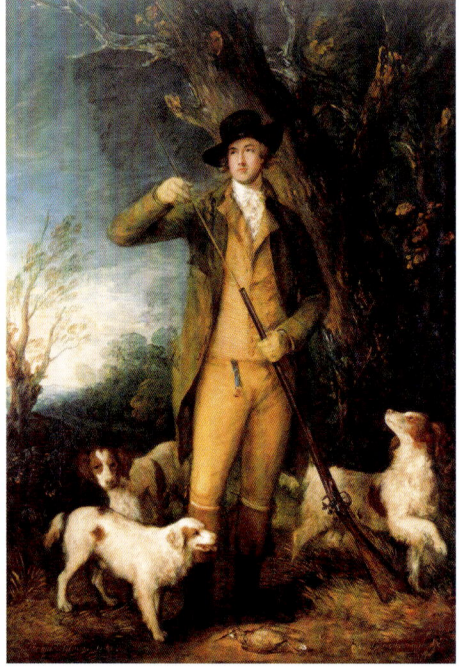

Fig. 10
Thomas Gainsborough, *Portrait of Thomas William Coke (1754-1842)*, 1778-1786.
Canvas, 242.5 x 170 cm. Holkham Hall

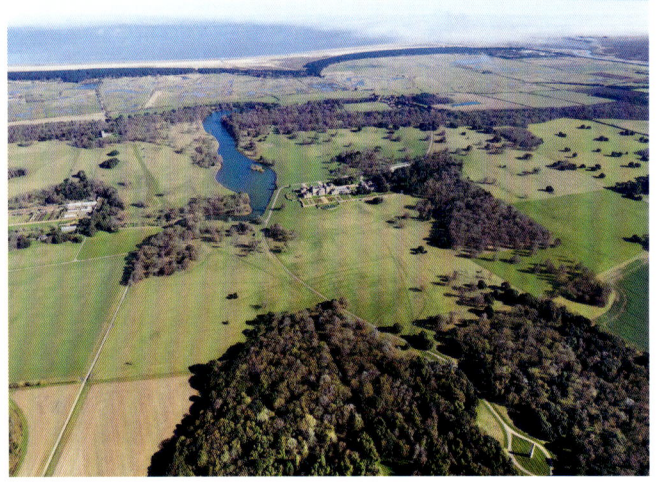

Fig. 11
Aerial view of the Holkham Estate

Once home, Thomas William expanded the collection of Italian paintings through the acquisition of a group of Renaissance works from the collection of his friend William Roscoe (1753-1831). Among these were a documented copy by Giorgio Vasari (1511-1574) of Raphael's *Pope Leo X with Cardinals* (now in the Uffizi), and a *Salvator Mundi* once attributed to Da Vinci. Both paintings still hang in the Chapel Gallery at Holkham.

When it came to commissioning contemporary works, however, Thomas William took a different path from his ancestor. Rather than favouring Italian artists working in England, he championed the Royal Academy and formed friendships with leading British painters, whose works still adorn Holkham's walls. Among them was Thomas Gainsborough (1727-1788), who painted a full-length portrait of Thomas William, now displayed alongside the Batoni (fig. 10). The two portraits present strikingly different images. Batoni captures Thomas William as a dashing young Grand Tourist, while Gainsborough depicts him as the country gentleman he had become. He is shown wearing the very suit he wore on 3 March 1778, when he presented a petition to the King, on behalf of Parliament, against the war in America. Thomas William later recalled: 'I was the individual who moved to put an end to that war... I was the only member out of twelve in this country who voted against the war, and I thank God for it... I carried out my address as an English country gentleman, in my leather breeches, boots and spurs'.[32]

Subsequent owners modernised Holkham Hall until preserving the estate became increasingly challenging. After World War II, financial collapse threatened its survival. It was Edward Coke, 7th Earl of Leicester (1936-2015) and father of the present Earl, who reversed the estate's fortunes, restoring farming profitability and ensuring Holkham's future. Though not a collector in the traditional sense, he was deeply committed to the Hall's art and library collections; one of his lasting contributions was the meticulous recreation of the original hanging in the Landscape Room and the Saloon, guided by historical inventories. For him, Holkham Hall was the heart of the estate, and everything done at Holkham was in service to its protection and preservation.

Today, Holkham Hall remains a private home, where the 8th Earl of Leicester lives with his wife and four children. His vision is to make Holkham the UK's most pioneering and sustainable rural estate, while continuing to share the house and its treasures with visitors (fig. 11).

1

ROSALBA CARRIERA

Portrait Miniature of Thomas Coke (1697-1759)
as a Young Man, **1714**
Gouache on ivory, 795 x 605 mm

_____

Holkham Hall

This miniature portrays Thomas Coke, the builder of Holkham Hall, aged 17. Like many of his peers, during his visit to Venice in 1714 in the second year of his Grand Tour, he sat to the much sought after portraitist Rosalba Carriera (1673-1757). The account book of Thomas's valet, Edward Jarret, is an invaluable record that makes Thomas's six-year journey one of the best-documented Grand Tours of the time (see pp.54-57). It notes a payment of 217 livres to Carriera on 17 August 1714.[33] However, it does not specify whether this sum was for the present miniature or a now-lost pastel portrait.

The portrait captures a young, smiling Thomas, dressed in the height of contemporary fashion: a voluminous white wig and a rosy-orange coat, left open to reveal an embroidered waistcoat. Given the tastes of the time, it is unsurprising that Thomas, like many of his contemporaries, chose Carriera to paint his likeness. At the peak of her career, a celebrated interpreter of grace and elegance, she was courted by Europe's aristocracy and adored by Venetian high society.

Carriera learnt to draw at an early age and initially chose miniature on ivory as her preferred technique. Ivory is a non-absorbent material and painting on it requires extraordinary skill and a lot of patience: one has to be able to paint with the tiniest, most delicate strokes of the brush.[34] Following a long-standing Venetian tradition, Carriera began by painting snuff boxes before transitioning to portraiture. She capitalised on the steady influx of wealthy foreign visitors, eager for a souvenir of their stay and willing to pay huge sums for her portrait miniatures.[35] Miniature portraits had the advantage of being quickly executed, sparing sitters the ordeal of long posing sessions. They were also easy to transport. The British,

in particular, were avid collectors of Carriera's work, inundating her with commissions. So much so that in 1721, she lamented that she had been 'attacked by the English'.[36]

Although Carriera may not have been the first artist to use ivory as a support for miniatures, she elevated the technique to new heights. It was a miniature, *Maiden with Dove*, that secured her admission to the painters' guild Accademia di San Luca in Rome in 1705 as a *'pittrice e miniatrice veneziana'* (Venetian painter and miniaturist). Her reputation grew rapidly, leading to her introduction into the Accademia Clementina in Bologna in 1720 and into the Académie Royale in Paris in 1721. Following the invitation of the French banker and art collector Pierre Crozat (1665-1740), Carriera spend about a year in Paris, where she painted portraits of the likes of king Louis XIV (1638-1715) and the painter Antoine Watteau (1684-1721).[37]

Carriera spent most of her life in Venice, where she achieved international fame for her pastels.[38] She also painted at least 80 miniatures until around 1730, when deteriorating eyesight forced her to stop miniature painting. She eventually went blind and died in 1757.

After leaving Venice, Thomas continued his travels through Florence, Rome, Naples, and other Italian cities, before returning to England in 1717. During his third and final visit to Rome, he commissioned Francesco Trevisani (1656-1746) to paint his portrait – not as the youthful, delicate figure rendered by Carriera, but as the refined and educated gentleman he had turned into, surrounded by examples of ancient sculpture and architecture that would inspire his vision for Holkham Hall.

MdP

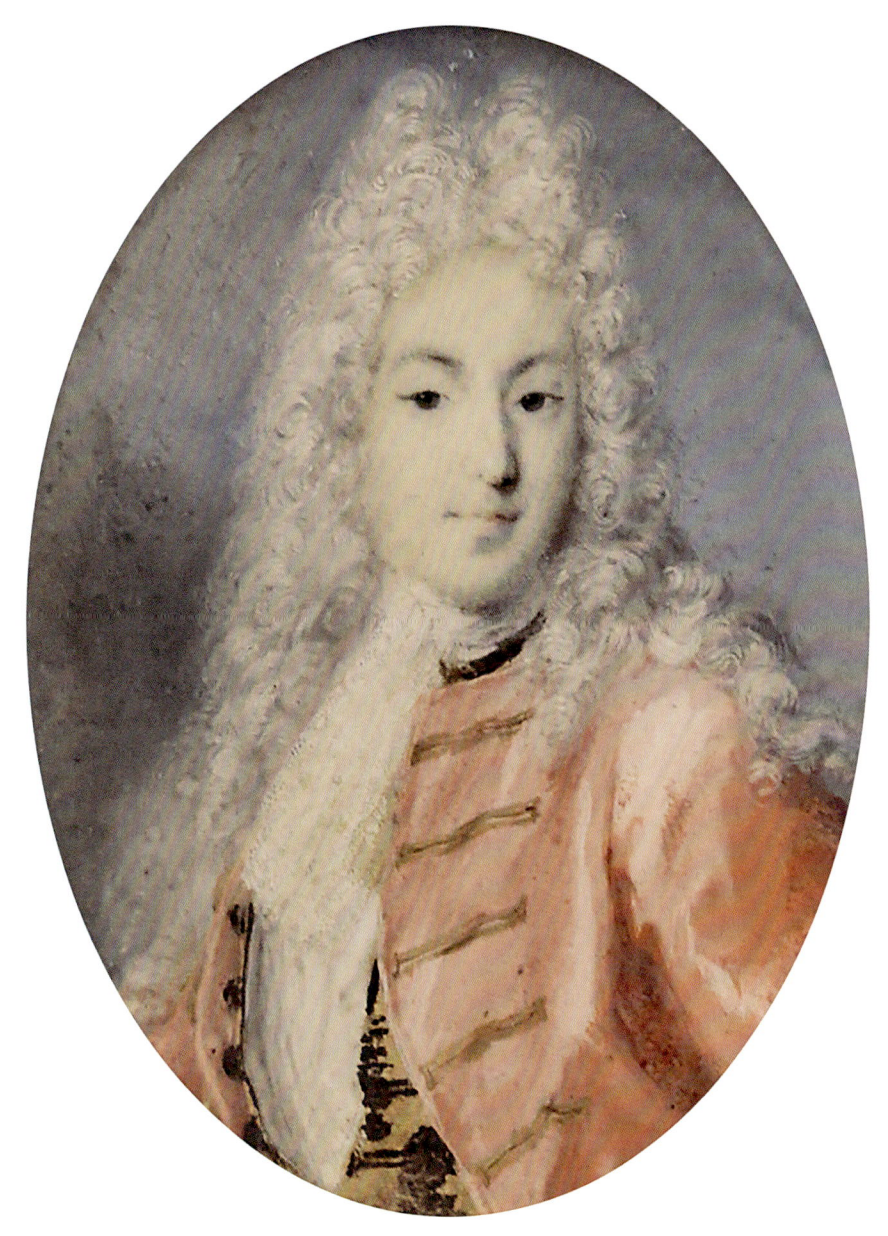

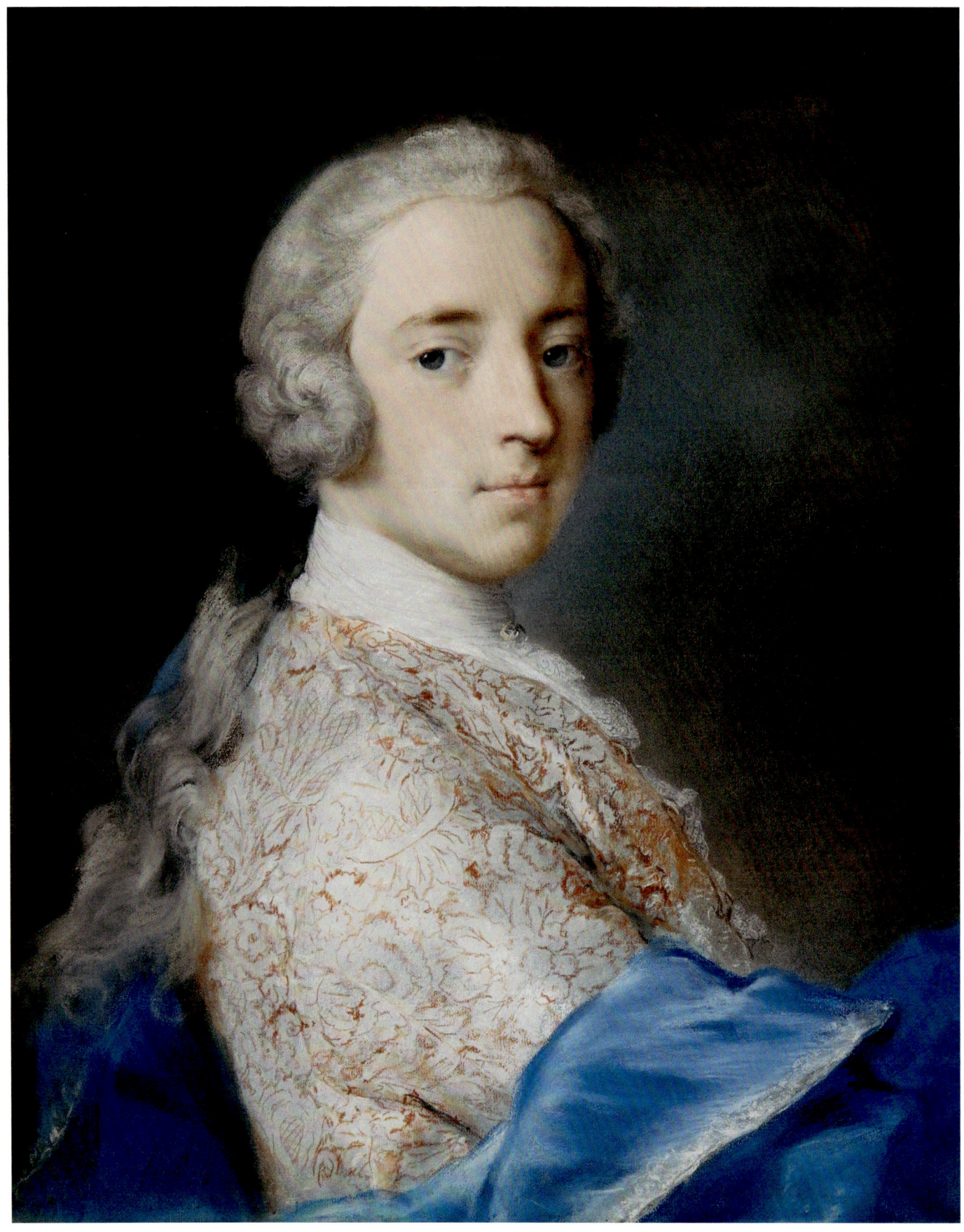

2

ROSALBA CARRIERA

Portrait of Viscount Edward Coke (1719-1753), c.1739
Pastel on paper, 508 x 432 mm

———————

Holkham Hall

This exquisite pastel, exceptional for its directness and immediacy, depicts Edward, the only surviving son of Thomas Coke, 1st Earl of Leicester (1697-1759). Like his father, he embarked on a Grand Tour and when in Venice in 1739 also sat for Rosalba Carriera (1675-1757).[39] Referred to as the Venetian queen of pastel, Carriera was instrumental in elevating this technique to a dignity equal to that of oil painting. Her first documented pastel dates from just before 1700 and portrays Anton Maria Zanetti (1689-1767), a Venetian artist and collector.

Pastel painting requires a high level of technical skill. This is mainly due to the inherent inability of pastel colours to mix. In addition, although the process is quick, the result is a surface of great delicacy, a consequence of the fact that the pastel particles never fully adhere to the paper. Rosalba's successful use of the medium was due to her exceptional technical skills but also to the increased availability of sets of crayons in a wide range of tones and colours on whose 'behaviour' one could count.

Carriera's knowledge of the English language and her ability in keeping the sittings brief, contributed to the popularity of her portraits among the 'flock of travelling boys' as the British writer and politician Horace Walpole (1717-1797) once called them: English, Welsh and Irish young men between the age of 18 and 26, children of the most exclusive elite that were passing through Venice as part of their education.[40] The artist is known for taking particular care in the way she packed and protected her pastels, sealing them in a black wooden frame with glass and usually adding a tiny holy card (a _santino_) – often depicting the three Magi – to the backing boards of the frame as talisman against evil during travel.[41]

In this portrait, the youthful Edward, with his captivating and casual countenance, exudes elegance as he meets the viewer's gaze with a subdued yet profound expression, devoid of a smile on his delicate lips. His attire – a long powdered wig tied back with a black ribbon, a vaporous white shirt, an intricately designed pink jacket, and a soft blue cape – reflects the hedonistic spirit of the time.

Just prior to his return to England in 1740, his father described Edward as 'sober as to wine' and possessing a 'meek temper'. He desired to marry him off to a lady of virtuous character who could shield him from the vices of the era.[42] Looking at the young man's features in Carriera's portrait, one wouldn't anticipate the grim turn Edward's life would take. Already in 1748, Walpole painted a starkly different picture: 'Lord Coke has demolished himself very fast... always drunk, lost immense sums at play, and seldom returns home to his wife till eight in the morning'.[43] His life ended on an even sadder note: he died childless in 1753, six years before his father, leaving Holkham Hall without an heir.

MdP

3

POMPEO BATONI

Portrait of Thomas William Coke (1754-1842), 1774
Canvas, 248.8 x 170.3 cm
Signed and dated on the lower left corner: P. Batoni
pinxit Romae an 1774, with a later inscription: *THIS
PORTRAIT PAINTED FOR/ THE COUNTESS OF ALBANY,
WIFE/ OF PRINCE CHARLIE WAS/ PRESENTED BY HER TO*

*MR/ T.W. COKE, AFTERWARDS/ VISCOUNT COKE AND
EARL/ OF LEICESTER.*
Lower left on the base of the column: *THOMAS WILL.
COKE.*

———————

Holkham Hall

This portrait of Thomas William Coke, known as Coke of
Norfolk, is considered one of the finest examples of Pompeo
Batoni's (1708-1787) late portraiture and shows the artist's
unabated zeal to impress his patrons.

Born in Lucca, Batoni spent his entire career in Rome
and was undoubtedly the most celebrated painter of all the
international visitors to Rome in the mid-eighteenth century.
He perfected an irresistible formula for his portraits, and this
painting is its perfect embodiment: technical virtuosity in the
handling of costume combined with freshness and immediacy
in the portrayal of the sitter. Furthermore, his prices were
lower than those of British society painters such as Joshua
Reynolds (1723-1792) or Allan Ramsey (1713-1784).[44]

It is indeed a splendid depiction of a wealthy young
Englishman on the Tour, posing for posterity among the
symbols and sculptures of Rome. Like his great-uncle Thomas
(see cat. no. 1) and his son Edward (see cat. no. 2), Thomas
William went on the Grand Tour and between 1771 and 1774
travelled to Italy, visiting Turin, Florence, Rome and Naples. In
1773, while in Rome, he attended a masquerade ball organised
by the Countess of Albany, wife of Charles Edward Stuart
(1720-1788) – the last Stuart claimant to the British throne.
Here, he most probably wore the white dress in which Batoni
portrayed him in this painting. The young Thomas, whom
contemporaries described as particularly handsome, is shown
wearing a white 'Van Dyck costume', inspired by the portraits
of the seventeenth century painter Anthony van Dyck (1599-
1641). He paired this with an ermine-trimmed scarlet cloak,

a splendidly intricate lace collar, Stuart 'rose' shoe buckles
and an ostrich feather-plumed hat in his hand. The imposing
classical statue beside him is the recumbent Ariadne, now
in the Vatican Museums. At the time it was one of the most
popular Roman sculptures among the cultural elite and has
been used by Batoni in several of his portraits.

The later inscription 'This portrait painted for the
countess of Albany […] was presented by her to Mr T.W. Coke
[…]' supports the rumour that the Countess of Albany was
infatuated with the young '*bel anglais*' and commissioned the
portrait as a gift to him. To add a further romantic aura to the
painting, it has also been suggested that her features can be
recognised in the sculpture of Ariadne.[45]

Thomas William was an important Whig politician and
great agriculturalist, who pioneered modern farming methods
and improved the breeds of cattle and sheep on his estates.
He was created Earl of Leicester (of the second creation)
in 1837, his great uncle's peerage having been extinct on
death. Though better known for his looks, his passion for
agriculture, and his support of the American Revolution,
Thomas William also made contributions to the collections at
Holkham, including a magnificent Roman mosaic and several
Renaissance paintings he acquired from the collection of this
friend William Roscoe (1753-1831), a famous banker, lawyer and
writer. All are still at Holkham.

MdP

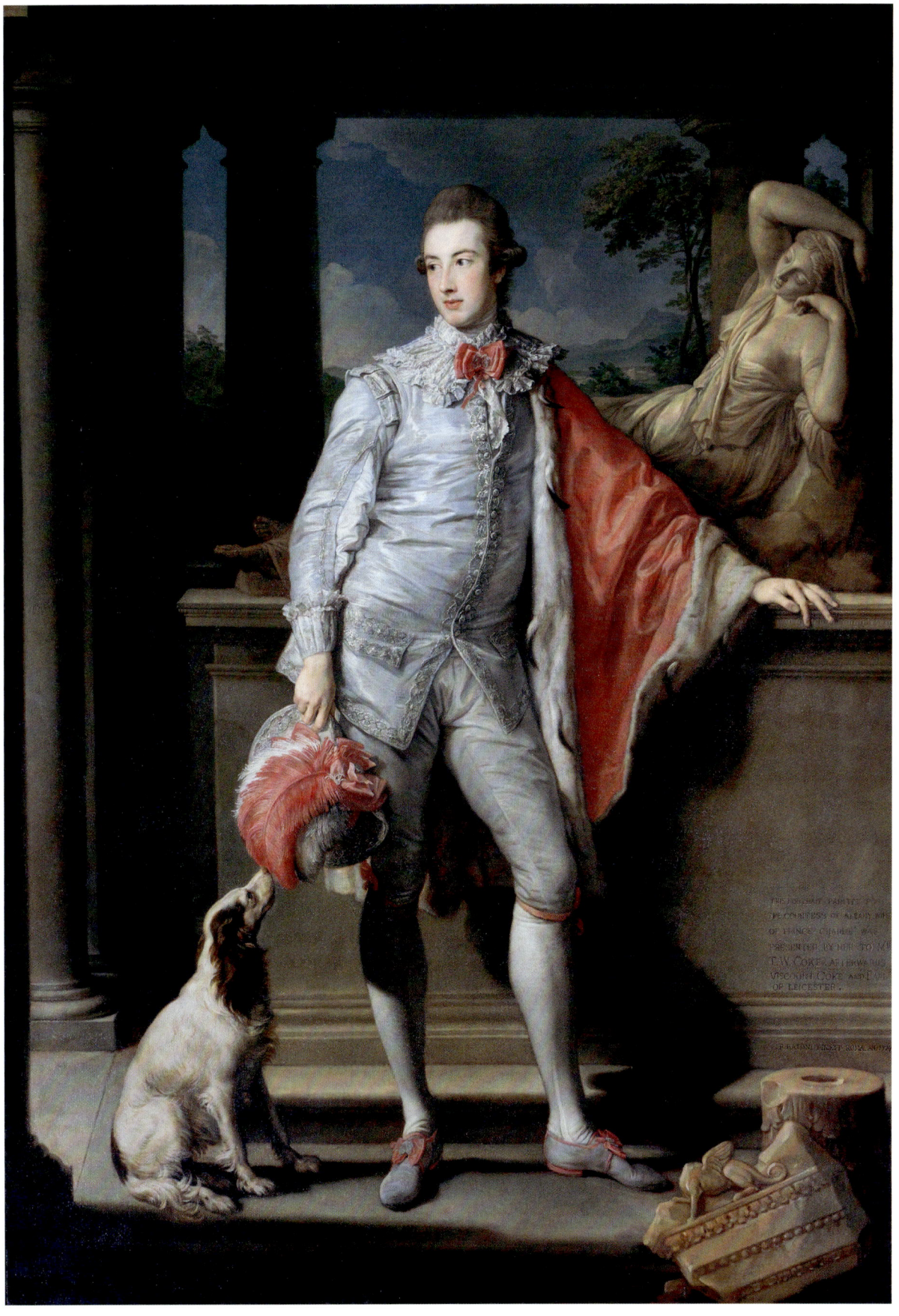

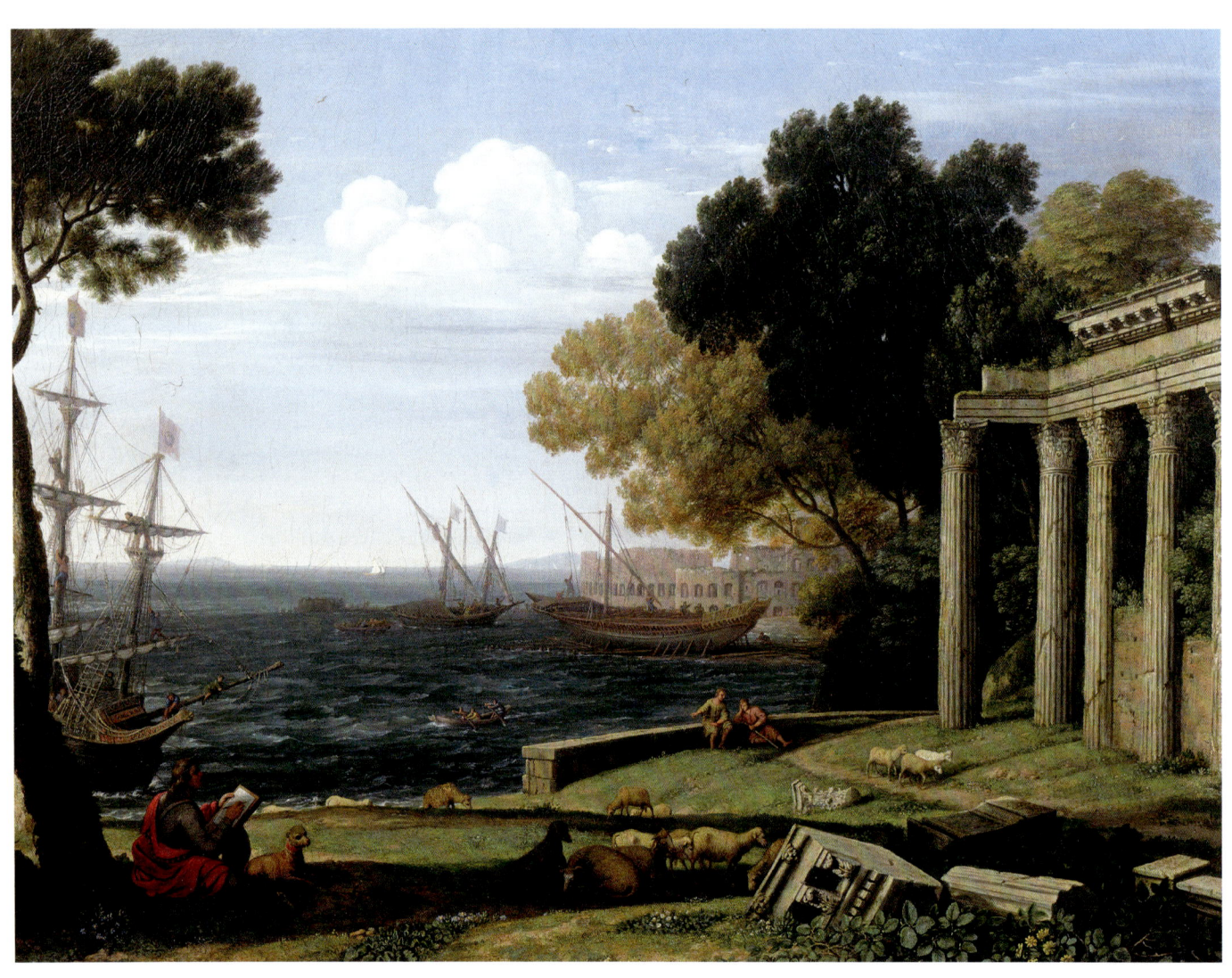

4

CLAUDE GELLÉE, CALLED LORRAIN

View of a Seaport and Amphitheatre, 1652(?)
Canvas, 73.6 x 91.1 cm
Signed and dated on the stone block on the lower right:
CLAVDI IVF ROMA 165[?][46]

Holkham Hall

In November 1756, Gavin Hamilton (1723-1798) and Matthew Brettingham (1699-1769), acting as agents for Thomas Coke (1697-1759), acquired two paintings by the hugely popular French painter Claude Lorrain (1600-1682) from Cardinal Alessandro Albani (1692-1779) in Rome: the one described here, and another work depicting Apollo guarding the flocks of Admetus.[47] Like many other Grand Tourists, Thomas was a great admirer of Lorrain's work, eventually amassing ten paintings by the artist, along with an equal number of drawings, all of which are still at Holkham Hall.

Lorrain, born in a village near Nancy, moved at a young age to Rome where he spent the rest of his life, with the exception of a protracted stay in Naples and a brief one in Nancy. His career and artistic practice are well documented thanks to two contemporary biographers, Joachim von Sandrart (1606-1688) and Filippo Baldinucci (1624-1697). In Rome, he first trained with the Italian landscape and architectural painter Agostino Tassi (1580-1644), and then shared a house and studio with the Dutch landscape painter Herman van Swanevelt (1603-1655). By the 1630s, his paintings, which had moved from the realistic and descriptive tradition of Dutch landscapes to idealised scenes, had become so popular that he began keeping what he called his *Liber Veritatis* (book of the truth): a record of his complete paintings – usually with a reference number, signature and the name of the patron – that he created to distinguish his paintings from those of forgers.

By 1650, he had become one of the most sought-after painters in Rome, admired not only by local high society, but also by Europe's royal and aristocratic families. Inspired by his walks in the Roman countryside, Lorrain created idealised landscapes bathing in a golden light, with classical ruins and mythological figures recalling Arcadia, a legendary place in ancient Greece celebrated by poets like Virgil (70-19 BCE).

Lorrain's influence on future generations of artists was widespread, but nowhere were his compositions more appreciated than in Britain, where great landscape painters like John Constable (1776-1837) and especially William Turner (1775-1851) drew inspiration from his work. His fame in Britain was such that, according to the artist Joshua Reynolds (1723-1792) 'there would be another Rafaelle before there would be another Claude. His landscapes have all that is exquisite and refined in art and nature'.

Most of the composition of the present painting is taken up by a seaport with an amphitheatre in the distance, traditionally identified as the one in Pula (Croatia), although it probably has the Colosseum as its model. In the left foreground, an artist is seen sketching classical ruins, surrounded by grazing sheep. The painting can be connected to one of the composition drawings in Lorrain's *Liber Veritatis*.[48] An inscription on the back of this drawing, however, indicates that the corresponding painting, dated 1634, was commissioned by Cardinal Rospigliosi – a work that has remained in the collection of his heirs to this day.[49] Compared to the latter painting of almost twenty years earlier, the landscape at Holkham Hall shows a number of variations in the left foreground, including a large ship, a tree trunk and a sketching artist.

Thomas Coke's passion for landscape painting extended beyond Lorrain. The so-called Landscape Room in Holkham Hall – probably inspired by the Sala dei Paesaggi in palazzo Colonna in Rome, which he saw during his Grand Tour – boasts 22 landscape paintings by masters such as Gaspard Dughet (the painter of the Sala dei Paesaggi), Domenichino, Paolo Anesi, Salvator Rosa, Andrea Locatelli, Frans van Bloemen, Claude-Joseph Vernet, and, of course, Claude Lorrain.

MdP

5

CASPAR ADRIAANSZ VAN WITTEL, KNOWN AS VANVITELLI

View of Saint Peter's Square, Rome, 1716
Canvas, 54.6 x 114.3 cm
Dated on the base of the column in the centre
foreground 1716

———————

Holkham Hall

Just as today we take photos with our mobile phones or buy postcards, eighteenth-century Grand Tourists bought or commissioned views of Rome as visual souvenirs. Thomas Coke (1697-1759) was no exception. He arrived in Rome for the first time in February 1714, but it was not until his second visit that he acquired his first work by Caspar van Wittel (1653-1736): a view of the Colosseum, that appears in his valet's account book on 17 July 1716. In the following year, the same account book records the purchase of another, unidentified, view of Rome by Van Wittel. In all, 17 works by the artist would reach Holkham, all still in situ: 5 large views (three of which of Rome), 3 smaller oils, 4 gouaches and 5 wash drawings. Thomas was one of the artist's greatest British patrons, the only one to buy directly from him.

Van Wittel was born in Amersfoort, where he studied under the still life and landscape painter Matthias Withoos (1627-1703). In 1675, at the age of 22, he is recorded as living in Rome, where he would spend the rest of his life, with the exception of brief visits to Venice and Northern Italy and a year in Naples. While other northern artists were more attracted to classical buildings and the light of the Roman *campagna* (countryside), Van Wittel showed a particular interest in topography, introducing the Dutch seventeenth-century cityscape tradition in Italy. He was the first artist to make Rome the main subject of his artistic production. His highly detailed views of the Eternal City were, as his contemporary biographer Lione Pascoli (1674-1744) tells us, highly sought

after by both the Roman aristocracy and the Grand Tourists.[50] Matthew Brettingham (1724-1803), son of one of Holkham Hall's architects and agent of Thomas in Italy, greatly praised the paintings by the artist in his 1773 edition of the plans of Holkham, noting in particular 'the fine glow of the Flemish colouring'.[51]

Understanding his patrons' desire for an accurate record of the great cities they had visited, Van Wittel often repeated his most popular views. Rome, with its unparalleled combination of antique, Renaissance and modern art and architecture was the unmissable stop for every Grand Tourist. Saint Peter's Square – with its modern colonnade completed by Gian Lorenzo Bernini (1598-1680) in 1667, Carlo Maderno's façade (1556-1629), and Michelangelo's (1475-1564) famous dome – represented the counterpart to the Colosseum, the most famous building of ancient Rome. It was one of Van Wittel's most popular compositions.

At least sixteen versions of this view are known to have been painted by Van Wittel between 1684 and 1721.[52] The Holkham version is the only dated one. These images for the first time, through a 'wide-angle', provide a sweeping view of the square. Van Wittel had prepared the composition in a drawing which is kept in the Biblioteca Nazionale in Rome, as part of a series of 52 views of Rome he made in situ.

MdP

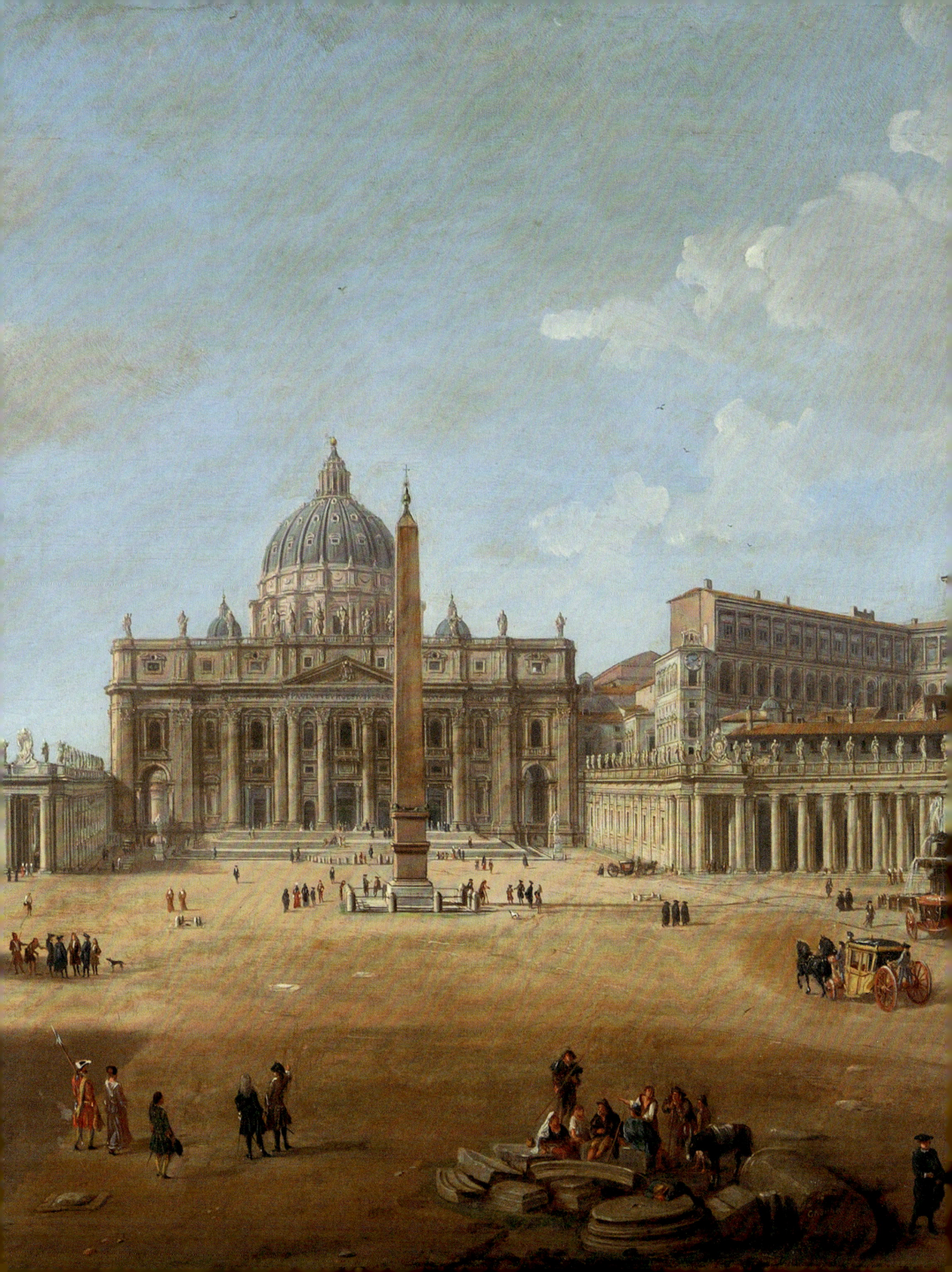

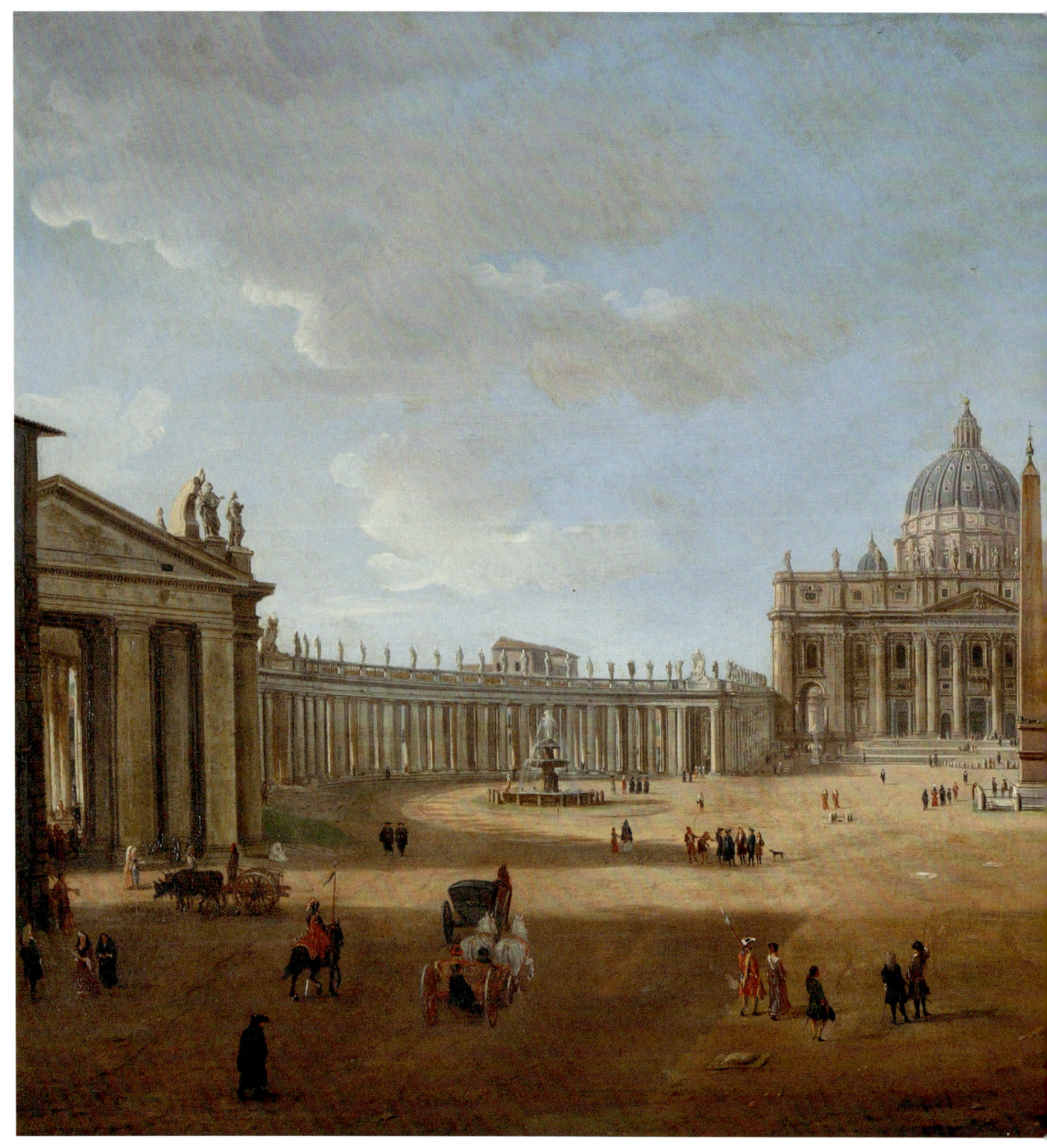

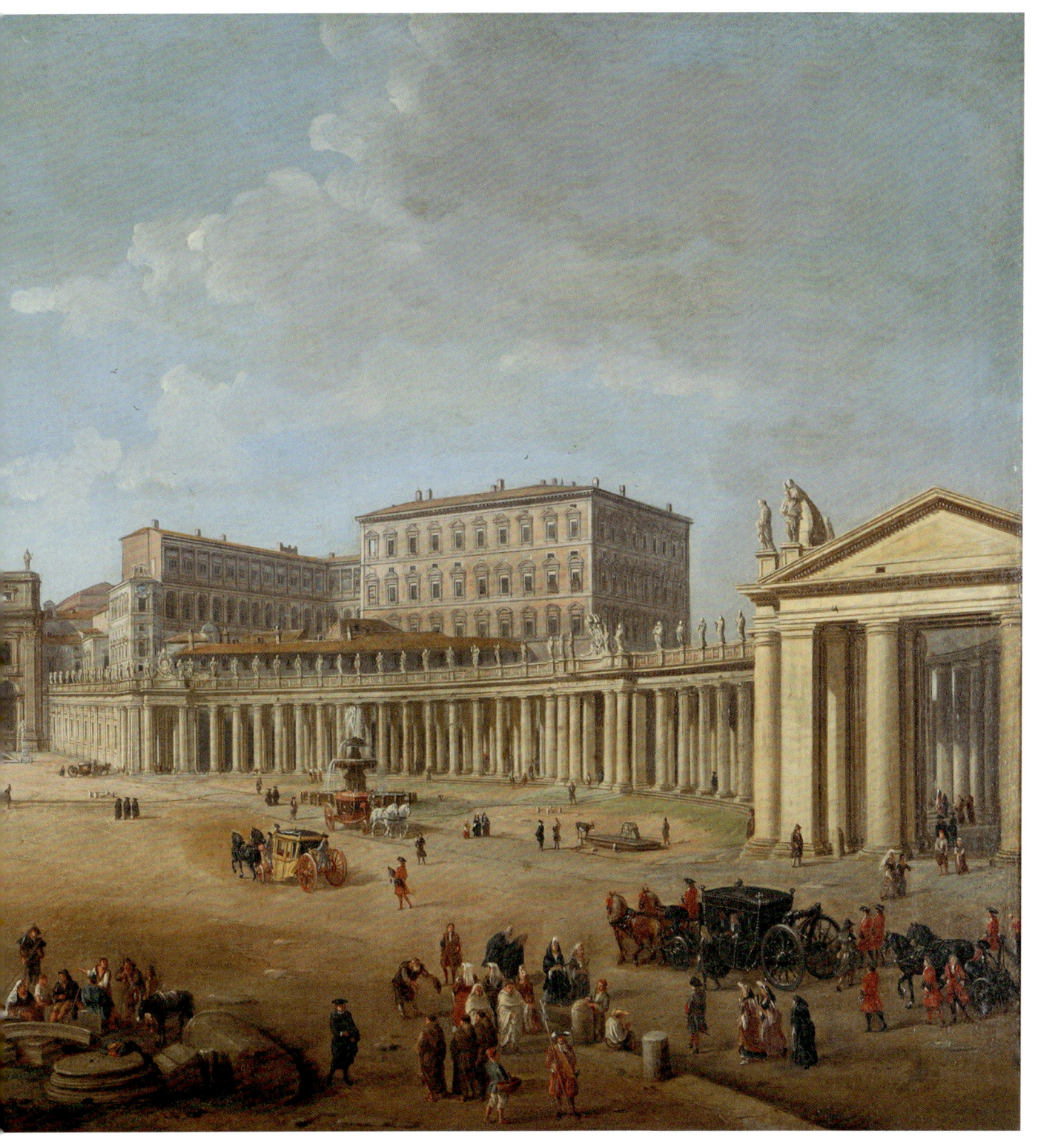

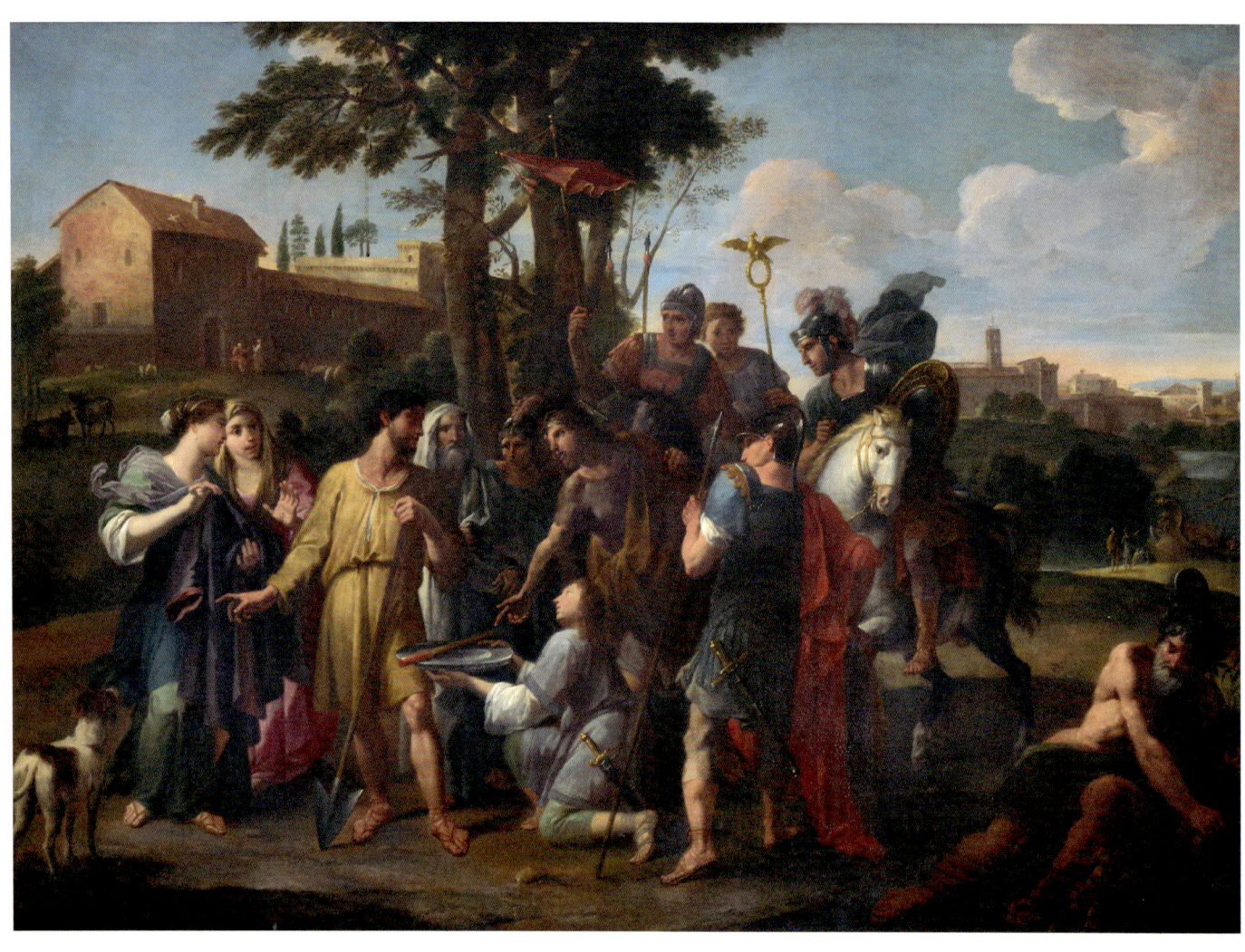

6

LUIGI GARZI

Cincinnatus at the Plough, 1716
Canvas, 182.8 x 21.9 cm

Holkham Hall

Although Luigi Garzi (1638-1721) is not a household name today, at the time that Thomas Coke (1697-1759) arrived in Rome in the second decade of the eighteenth century, he was one of the city's most sought-after painters. An accomplished painter of frescoes and altarpieces, Garzi was known for his formal elegance, creative originality and delicate use of colour. In 1680, he was appointed regent of the Congregazione dei Virtuosi al Pantheon, the papal academy of arts, and two years later he became director of Rome's painters' guild, the Accademia di San Luca. Garzi owed his fame mainly to large ecclesiastical commissions and together with Benedetto Luti, Sebastiano Conca, Andrea Procaccini and Francesco Trevisani – all painters Thomas would acquire paintings from – he was one of the favoured artists of Pope Clement XI (1649-1721).

Soon after his arrival in Rome in 1714, Thomas met William Kent (1605 1740), a British painter, dealer, and copyist who, on his return to England, would turn to architecture and play a key role in the construction of Holkham Hall. In Rome, Kent had introduced the young Thomas to much of the artistic milieu. This led to commissions to 'six of the best painters' in the city during Thomas's second visit to Rome in 1716.[53] In four of these paintings, Thomas requested to be included in the depicted scene as one of the historical figures.

This painting illustrates a scene from the life of Lucius Quinctius Cincinnatus (c.519-c.430 BCE), a Roman patrician who had retired from public service to live the simple life of a farmer. Summoned from his plough to return to his duties as a military leader, Cincinnatus won a quick victory over Rome's enemies. Eventually, he renounced power and its privileges to return to working the land. He is therefore regarded as a model of civic virtue and selfless leadership. Thomas is included in the centre of the composition as a kneeling figure presenting the baton to Cincinnatus. A preparatory drawing for the composition is also held in the Holkham collections.

As for the other Grand Tour commissions in which Thomas was portrayed, only one remains at Holkham: *The Elysian Fields* by Sebastiano Conca (1680-1764). In this work Thomas is depicted as Orpheus, playing the lyre. Two more works were sadly lost. These both illustrated episodes of civic virtue, like Garzi's painting. One, by Giuseppe Chiari (1654-1727), depicted the *Continence of Scipio*, and the other, by Andrea Procaccini (1671 1734), showed *Numa Pompilio giving the laws to Rome*. The account book of Thomas's valet attests to payments in 1716 for both the Garzi and the Chiari.[54]

The subjects of these commissions, carefully drawn from Roman history and mythology, show that Thomas really wanted to demonstrate his knowledge of ancient history and literature. They are tangible proof that he had indeed become the 'perfect virtuoso and great lover of pictures', as he proudly wrote to his grandfather in a letter dated 14 May 1714.[55]

MdP

7

ANONYMOUS

**The Head of the Goddess Roma mounted on a post-antique Bust,
130-140 CE (head), 18th-century additions**
White marble (head), rosso antico (bust), grey marble (base),
height 74.3 cm

―――――――

Holkham Hall

This small masterpiece is a depiction of the goddess Roma as a young woman.[56] Her delicate complexion and wavy hair exude a sense of femininity, which contrasts with the fortitude of the helmet. The distinctive Attic helmet is topped with the *lupa Romana* – the she-wolf who, in Roman mythology, fed the infant twins Romulus and Remus, believed to be the founders of Rome. This image of the she-wolf with the twins has been the symbol of Rome since 300 BCE. Marble and plaster restorations have been carried out on the head, the wolf, and the figures. Originally, feather plumes would have been positioned behind the figures, but these are now sadly missing – only three marks indicating their former placement remain today.

The bust is a later, possibly eighteenth century, addition of *Rosso antico* or *Marmor Taenarium* marble. The rich dark red heightens the drama of the portrait. It has been fashioned into an *aegis* – a type of breastplate with a scale pattern and in its centre a *gorgoneion*, a depiction of a Gorgon or Medusa, which was a protective symbol in Greek mythology. Anyone who looked upon such a creature would be instantly turned to stone. This style of breastplate was more commonly associated with Athena or Minerva, the ancient goddess of wisdom and warfare. The base in contrasting grey marble dates from the eighteenth century as well.

For many years, the bust was believed to have been purchased by Thomas Coke's (1697-1759) son, Edward, Viscount Coke (1719-1753), who undertook his Grand Tour between 1738 and 1740. However, this has recently been refuted with evidence hitherto overlooked.[57] The purchaser was Matthew Brettingham (1699-1769), who acted as an agent for Thomas Coke in the 1750s. His account book records the purchase of an antique marble head of Minerva from Bartolomeo Cavaceppi (1716-1799) in the spring of 1753, for the sum of 36 Roman crowns.[58] Cavaceppi was a well-known sculptor and restorer of antique statues in Rome, with much of his work attracting the eye of Grand Tourists. A further entry in Brettingham's account book, relating to the shipment of the bust to England, describes it as a 'Therme of a Minerva Good Antique and Marble'.[59] This suggests that restoration work had been done on the head and that the grey marble base had been added. The work was probably carried out by Cavaceppi, like other pieces Brettingham purchased for Thomas and the collection at Holkham.

Initially, the work was displayed in Thomas's London residence, Thanet House, far removed from the renowned collection of antique sculptures at Holkham Hall. It was later transferred there. In a printed guide to Holkham, the work was described as 'Antique busta of Roma'. Any suggestion that this was Minerva had been lost.[60]

LP

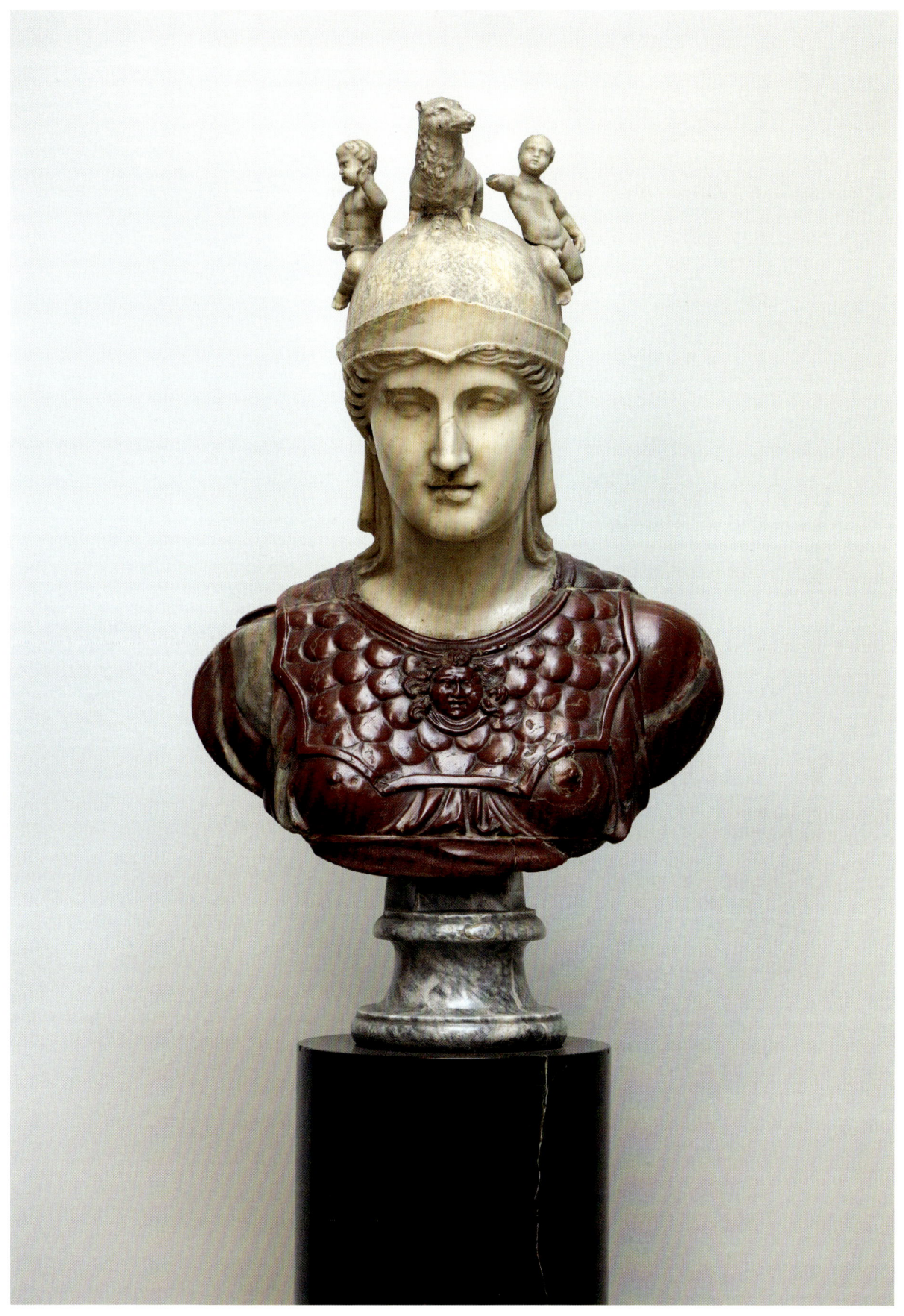

BUILDING THE LIBRARY AS A 'PERFECT VIRTUOSO'

Laura Nuvoloni

The Holkham volumes on display exemplify Thomas Coke's (1697-1759) Grand Tour acquisitions of manuscripts and early printed books.[61] They also represent splendidly the luxury books commissioned by Italian lords, intellectuals, professionals and merchants between 1450-1480. Most manuscripts were of Italian origin and included Leonardo da Vinci's (1452-1519) notes on water, known as the *Codex Leicester*, now in Bill Gates's possession. By the end of his European travelling in 1718, Thomas had assembled a collection of about 650 manuscripts and at least 103 books printed before 1501, the so-called incunabula.

Descending from a lineage of cultivated bibliophiles, Thomas showed a keen interest in literature at a very young age. His mother described him as 'more forward in his reading than any child of his age' in a letter to her father in November 1706.[62] Following the death of his parents in 1707, when merely nine years old, he became the beneficiary of two libraries: the magnificent library of Sir Edward Coke (1551/52-1634), Lord Chief Justice – rich in historical and legal treatises, works on natural science, and texts from Classical to contemporary authors – and the collection assembled by his parents, Edward (1679-1707) and Cary Coke (née Newton; 1680-1707). Their collection also featured novels and romances – often in translation from Latin or Italian – devotional texts, travel guides, geographical and scientific treatises, and publications on Roman antiquities and art.

Consequently, even before departing on the adventure of the Grand Tour in August 1712, young Thomas already had a remarkable library to his disposal. In June 1711 his private tutor Mr Wilkins described the boy as 'of great capacity [...] has applied himself extremely much in reading some of ye best Classick Authors & Latin as well as English poets'.[63] His studious attitude, though, was contrasted by an equally strong temperament. His guardians, anxious to direct the young teenager's energy, decided to send him on a Grand Tour abroad. Thomas's intellect and financial wealth, combined with the appointment of two learned bibliophiles, Dr Thomas Hobart (d.1727) and the Neapolitan Domenico Antonio Ferrari (1685-1744), as his tutors and governors, set the stage for a successful and educational Grand Tour. The young man would grow into a cultivated connoisseur and collector of art, as well as of manuscripts and books from the Middle Ages to his own days.

As soon as the party reached Rome in February 1714, Thomas began studying architecture and drawing. By May he had already purchased important drawings and paintings, so

as to write to his grandfather: 'I am become since my stay at Rome, a perfect virtuoso, & a great lover of pictures', and in January 1715: 'certainly one of the greatest ornaments to a gentleman or to his family is a fine library'.[64]

On 3 January 1715, two and a half years into his Grand Tour, Thomas attended the Military Academy of Turin – being educated in court life and military matters, as well as literature and history. He sent a letter to his grandfather to justify his recent expenditures on books and manuscripts: 'During my voyage round Italy I have bought several of the most valuable authors that have written in Italian or about the country, the reason that I incrouch so far on your kindness to me, & venter to put my guardians to that risk is, that if I missed the occasion of buying books while I am travelling, I should not be able to find several of the best of them, & it's impossible to buy them to my mind unless I myself am present'.[65]

In his first three years, Thomas mainly bought printed books and perhaps the odd manuscript of a classical text, such as Livy. However, during a ten-day visit to Lyon in November 1715, he acquired 47 manuscripts, mostly medieval, at the convent of the Discalced Augustinians, and proudly signed them all as 'T. Coke' in the right corner of the first page.

Among the acquisitions made in Lyon was 'The Third Decade' of Livy's *Ab urbe condita* (History of Rome; see cat. no. 8). It had been copied in Florence between 1465 and 1470 by the notary and scribe Giovan Francesco Marzi of San Gimignano (active c.1460-1494), and illuminated by an anonymous artist named the Master of the Naples Virgil (after a codex in the National Library of Naples).[66] Both the script and the 'white vine-stem' decoration of the border are characteristics of Italian manuscript-making and originate from codices dating from the eleventh and twelfth centuries. Their late Caroline script inspired the new '*all'antica*' handwriting of Florentine scholars; the 'white vine-stem' decoration is 'perhaps the single most recognizable distinguishing feature of Italian Renaissance illumination'.[67] The vignette at the beginning of the text depicts Hannibal kneeling before an altar, as instructed by his father Hamilcar, to swear an oath of eternal enmity towards Rome (fig. 1). The coffered arcade ceiling evokes both Renaissance funerary chapels and the ceiling of Holkham's Marble Hall (see p. 29, fig. 6).

If the Livy manuscript was among the first medieval codices Thomas acquired in Italy, the Italian translation of Pliny's *Naturalis Historia* – printed in Venice by the French engraver and printer Nicholas Jenson in 1476 (see cat. no. 9) – was probably one of the last he purchased before leaving

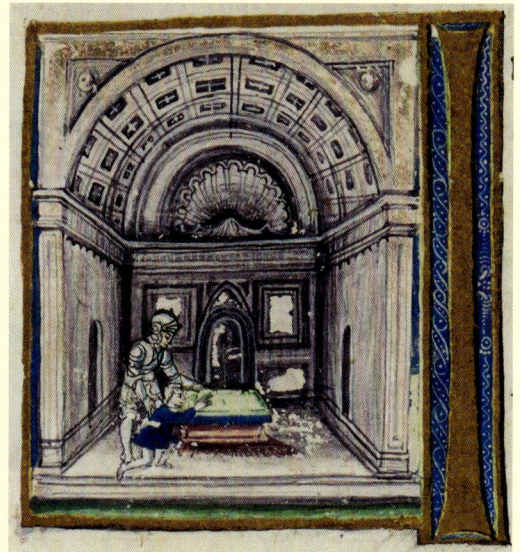

Fig. 1
Detail of Titus Livius, *Ab urbe condita*, 'The Third Decade',
Book 2 (cat. no. 8): Vignette painted in tempera and gold
at the beginning of the text, followed by the initial 'I' to
the right

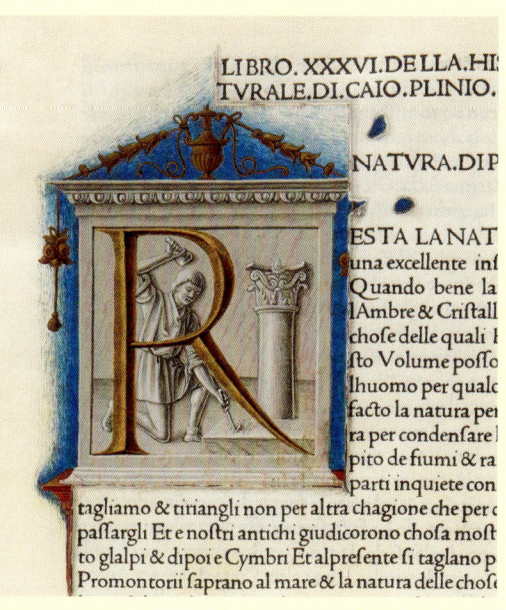

Fig. 2
Detail of Caius Plinius Secundus, *Naturalis Historia*,
Book XXXVI (cat. no. 9): Faceted initial R in gold,
historiated with the image of a sculptor at work;
behind him a half column with a Corinthian capital

the country in August 1717, never to return. One of only twenty copies printed on parchment, the book bears the arms of the Ridolfi family of Florence at the beginning of the text (Book II). It was possibly presented by Jenson to Giovambattista Ridolfi (1448–1514), the representative in Venice of the Florentine Strozzi Bank, which had financed the edition.[68] The illuminated frontispiece and the initials are decorated in the antiquarian style initiated by Andrea Mantegna (c.1431–1506) in the Veneto from the late 1450s (fig. 2). In fact, the initials are often referred to as *litterae mantiniane* after the illustrious Paduan artist. They are faceted, that is, painted as if three-dimensional, and cast in bronze and gold like the ancient inscriptions on imperial Rome monuments. The Corinthian entablature and capitals in the decoration of the books may have inspired those of the columns in the Statue Gallery and Marble Hall at Holkham Hall.

By the end of his Grand Tour, Thomas Coke had purchased books in the thousands. Their subject matter corresponded to and expanded the inherited collections, particularly with regards to classical literature, antiquities and the arts. Indeed, the Long Library was the first of the State Rooms to be built and used by Thomas to entertain his guests with readings from the classics.

After Thomas's death, his wife Margaret oversaw the completion of Holkham Hall according to his wishes, and brought his entire library there, exhibiting it in the South Tribunes, Statue Gallery and the Long Library. The manuscripts and some of his early printed books, kept in their crates since their arrival in England, were also brought to Holkham and placed in the Attic Library for the use of visitors and scholars.

Evidently the library played a pivotal role in transforming Thomas in the quintessential British 'virtuoso'. Holkham Hall should consequently be called 'Palace of the Arts and Learning', paraphrasing Adriano Aymonino's definition of it as 'Palace of the Arts'.[69]

8

Titus Livius, known as Livy (64/59 BCE-17 CE)
Ab urbe condita, 'The Third Decade', Books 21-30

Manuscript on parchment, with frontispiece and ten
book initials painted by hand in tempera and gold,
Florence, 1465-1470
Patron: a member of the Capponi family, probably
Bernardo di Niccola Capponi (1435-1497), his arms
painted in two medallions in the lower corners of the
frontispiece
Scribe: Giovan Francesco Marzi of San Gimignano,
Florentine notary (active 1460-1494)
Illuminator: Master of the Naples Virgil
238 fols, folio 325 x 220 mm
Holkham MS. 351.2, fol. 1 recto, frontispiece

―――――――

Holkham Hall

The border of the page is filled with winged putti, birds,
lions, golden medallions inhabited by female busts, battling
horsemen, musicians, a dancing couple, and the face of a
young man. May it be the artist or the patron?

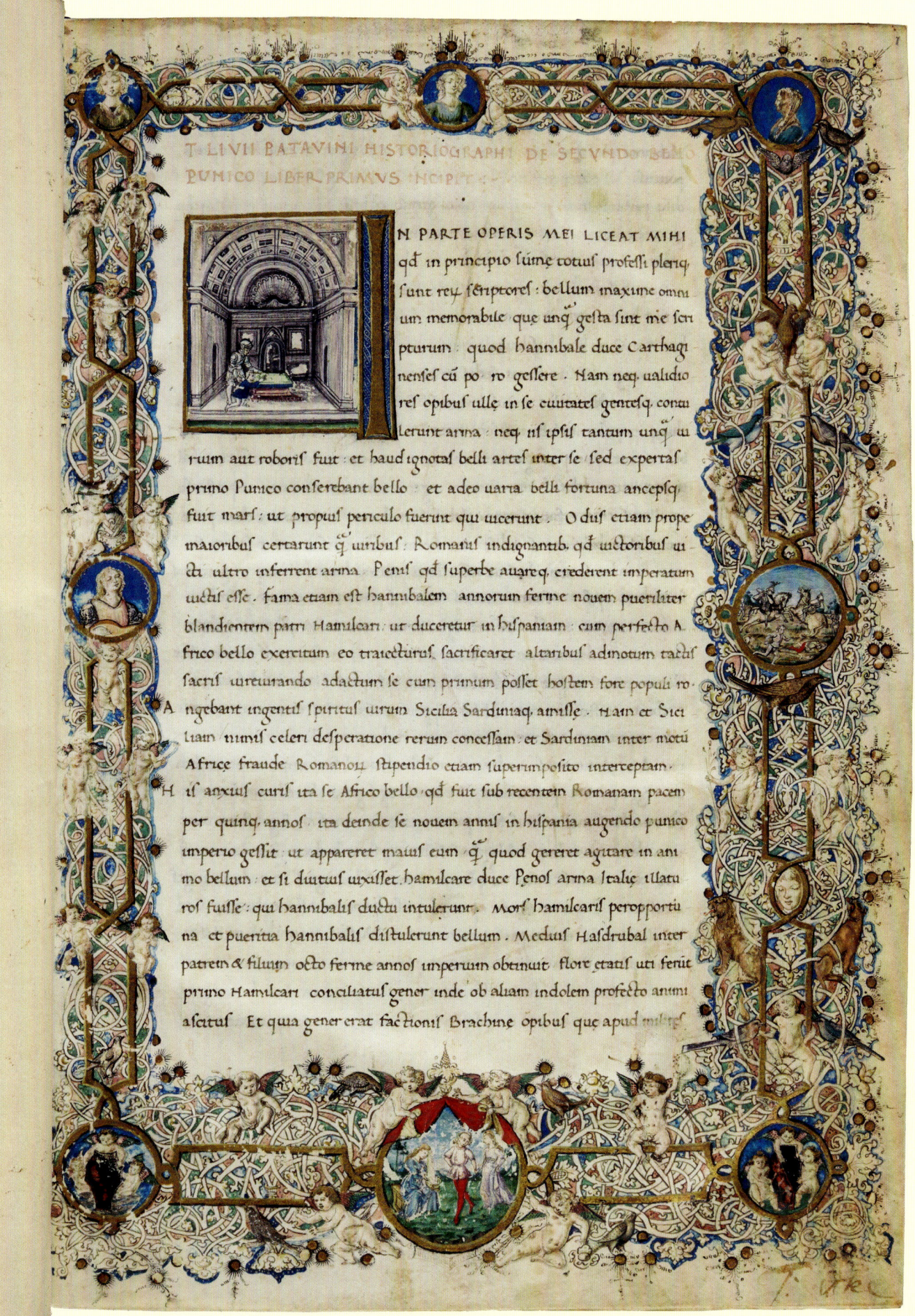

T. LIVII PATAVINI HISTORIOGRAPHI DE SECVNDO BELLO
PVNICO LIBER PRIMVS INCIPIT

N PARTE OPERIS MEI LICEAT MIHI
qd in principio sume totius professi pleriq,
sunt rei scriptores: bellum maxime omn
ium memorabile que unq, gesta sint me sen
pturum quod hannibale duce Carthagi
nenses cu po ro gessere. Nam neq, ualidio
res opibus ulle in se ciuitates gentesq, conu
lerunt arma neq, ipsis tantum unq, ui
rium aut roboris fuit: et haud ignotas belli artes inter se sed expertas
primo Punico conferebant bello: et adeo uaria belli fortuna ancepsq,
fuit mars: ut propius periculo fuerint qui uicerunt. Odiis etiam prope
maioribus certarunt q, uiribus: Romanis indignantib, qd uictoribus ui
cti ultro inferrent arma. Penis qd superbe auareq, crederent imperatum
uictis esse. Fama etiam est hannibalem annorum ferme nouem pueriliter
blandientem patri Hamilcari ut duceretur in hispaniam cum perfecto A
frico bello exercitum eo traiecturus, sacrificaret altaribus admotum tactis
sacris iureiurando adactum se cum primum posset hostem fore populi ro
angebant ingentis spiritus uirum Sicilia Sardiniaq, amisse. Nam et Sici
liam nimis celeri desperatione rerum concessam: et Sardiniam inter motu
Africe fraude Romanou stipendio etiam superimposito interceptam.
His anxius curis ita se Africo bello qd fuit sub recentem Romanam pacem
per quinq, annos: ita deinde se nouem annis in hispania augendo punico
imperio gessit: ut appareret maius eum q, quod gereret agitare in ani
mo bellum: et si diutius uixisset, hamilcare duce Penos arma Italie illatu
ros fuisse: qui hannibalis ductu intulerunt. Mors hamilcaris peropportu
na et pueritia hannibalis distulerunt bellum. Medius Hasdrubal inter
patrem & filium octo ferme annos imperium obtinuit: flore etatis uti ferut
primo Hamilcari conciliatus gener inde ob aliam indolem profecto animi
ascitus. Et quia gener erat factionis Brachine opibus que apud milites

9

**Gaius Plinius Secundus, known as Pliny the Elder
(23/24-79 CE)**
Naturalis Historia, **Italian translation by**
Cristoforo Landino (1424-1498)

Printed by Nicholas Jenson, Venice, 1476
Parchment, with frontispiece and 37 historiated book
initials painted by hand in tempera and gold
Patron: probably Giovambattista Ridolfi (1448-1514) of
Florence, his arms on the frontispiece
Illuminator: unknown
415 fols (unfoliated), parchment, folio 415 x 273 mm
Holkham BN 1985, Book II, frontispiece

Holkham Hall

The illuminated frontispiece to Pliny's Book II shows a *trompe-
l'oeil* image of the text as inscribed on a roll suspended to the
entablature of a marble pavilion with four Corinthian columns.
Its ledges are populated by putti playing heralds' trumpets
(*buisines*), holding crouched deer, or holding a half-eaten
apple. The initial 'E' to the text is set in a vignette inhabited by
a portrait of Pliny looking at an armillary sphere in his study,
with his books and apples for sustainment.

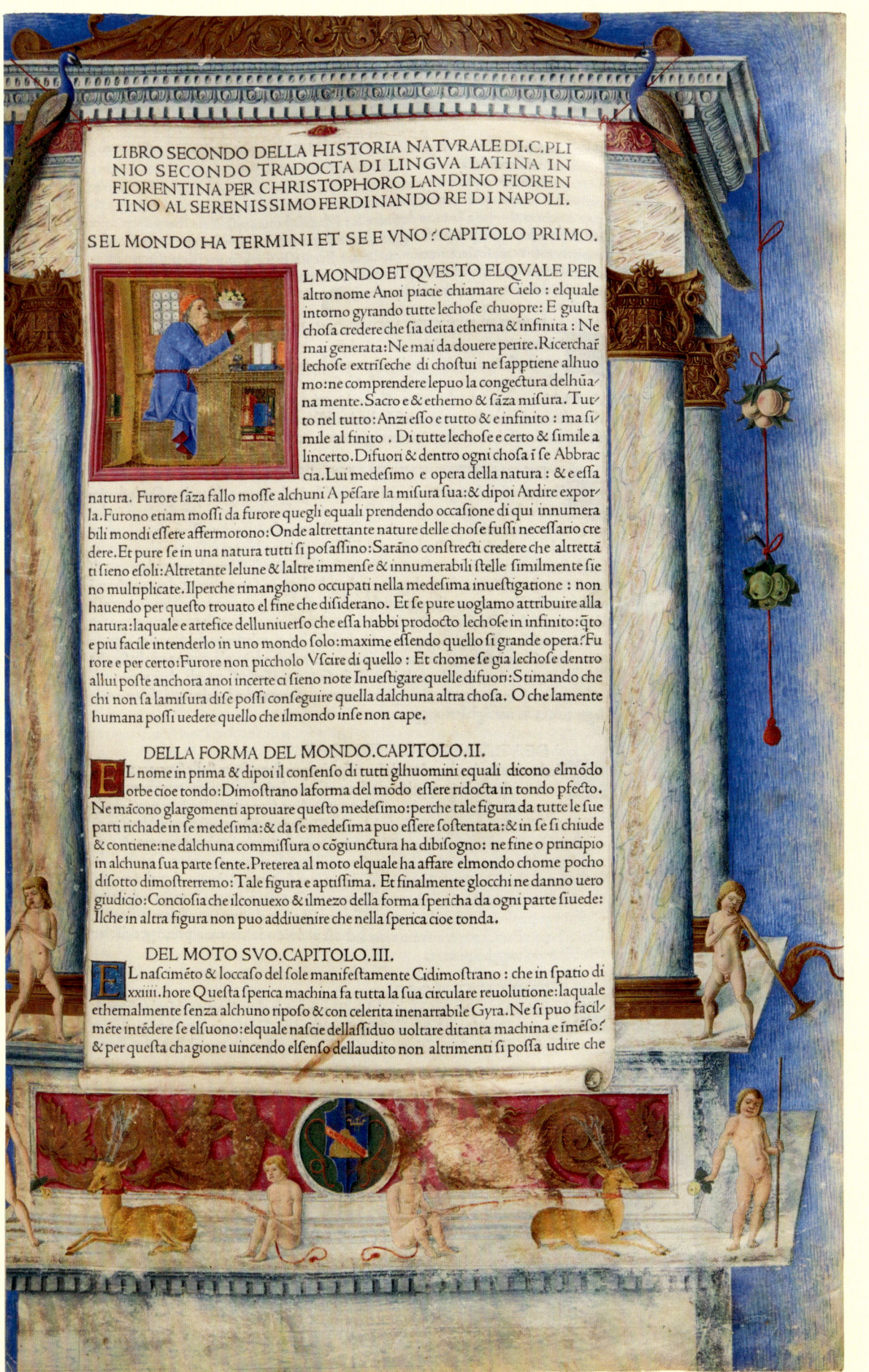

LIBRO SECONDO DELLA HISTORIA NATVRALE DI.C.PLI
NIO SECONDO TRADOCTA DI LINGVA LATINA IN
FIORENTINA PER CHRISTOPHORO LANDINO FIOREN
TINO AL SERENISSIMO FERDINANDO RE DI NAPOLI.

SEL MONDO HA TERMINI ET SE E VNO: CAPITOLO PRIMO.

L MONDO ET QVESTO ELQVALE PER
altro nome Anoi piacie chiamare Cielo : elquale
intorno gyrando tutte lechose chuopre : E giusta
chosa credere che sia deita etherna & infinita : Ne
mai generata : Ne mai da douere perire. Ricerchar
lechose extriseche di chostui ne sapptiene alhuo
mo : ne comprendere lepuo la congectura delhua
na mente. Sacro e & etherno & saza misura. Tut
to nel tutto : Anzi esso e tutto & e infinito : ma si
mile al finito . Di tutte lechose e certo & simile a
lincerto. Difuori & dentro ogni chosa i se Abbrac
cia. Lui medesimo e opera della natura : & e essa
natura. Furore saza fallo mosse alchuni A pesare la misura sua : & dipoi Ardire expor
la. Furono etiam mossi da furore quegli equali prendendo occasione di qui innumera
bili mondi essere affermorono : Onde altrettante nature delle chose fussi necessario cre
dere. Et pure se in una natura tutti si posassino : Saràno constrecti credere che altrettà
ti sieno esoli : Altretante lelune & laltre immense & innumerabili stelle similmente sie
no multiplicate. Ilperche rimanghono occupati nella medesima inuestigatione : non
hauendo per questo trouato el fine che disiderano. Et se pure uoglamo attribuire alla
natura : laquale e artefice delluniuerso che essa habbi prodocto lechose in infinito : qto
e piu facile intenderlo in uno mondo solo : maxime essendo quello si grande opera. Fu
rore e per certo : Furore non picchiolo Vscire di quello : Et chome se gia lechose dentro
allui poste anchora anoi incerte ci sieno note Inuestigare quelle difuori : Stimando che
chi non sa lamisura dise possi conseguire quella dalchuna altra chosa. O che lamente
humana possi uedere quello che ilmondo inse non cape.

DELLA FORMA DEL MONDO. CAPITOLO. II.

EL nome in prima & dipoi il consenso di tutti glhuomini equali dicono elmodo
orbe cioe tondo : Dimostrano laforma del modo essere ridocta in tondo pfecto.
Ne macono glargomenti aprouare questo medesimo : perche tale figura & le sue
parti richade in se medesima : & da se medesima puo essere sostentata : & in se si chiude
& contiene : ne dalchuna commissura o cogiunctura ha dibisogno : ne fine o principio
in alchuna sua parte sente. Preterea al moto elquale ha affare elmondo chome pocho
disotto dimostrremo : Tale figura e aptissima. Et finalmente glocchi ne danno uero
giudicio : Conciosia che ilconuexo & ilmezo della forma spericha da ogni parte siuede :
Ilche in altra figura non puo addiuenire che nella spericha cioe tonda.

DEL MOTO SVO. CAPITOLO. III.

EL nascimeto & loccaso del sole manifestamente Cidimostrano : che in spatio di
xxiiii. hore Questa sperica machina fa tutta la sua circulare reuolutione : laquale
ethernalmente senza alchuno riposo & con celerita inenarrabile Gyra. Ne si puo facil
mete intedere se elsuono : elquale nascie dellassiduo uoltare ditanta machina e imeso :
& per questa chagione uincendo elsenso dellaudito non altrimenti si possa udire che

FOLLOWING IN THE FOOTSTEPS OF THOMAS COKE'S GRAND TOUR

Lucy Purvis

The account book compiled by Edward Jarrett, *valet-de-chambre* of Thomas Coke (1697-1759), is an extraordinary document in the history of the Grand Tour (figs. 1 and 2).[70] Contained within its near 300 pages is the most comprehensive account of this young man's Tour across France, Italy, Germany and mainland northern Europe. What makes this particularly interesting is that this Tour was one of the longest – lasting six years – and among the earliest of the eighteenth century, from 1712-1718.

Orphaned at just 9, Thomas showed a great aptitude for learning and was particularly drawn to Livy and other classical authors. After the death of his parents, who were both bibliophiles, he went to live with his kinsman, Sir Edward Coke in Derbyshire. Thomas was only just 15 when he left England on his Tour. He was accompanied by his tutor Dr Thomas Hobart (d.1727), the Neapolitan bibliophile Domenico Ferrari (1685-1744), his valets Abraham and Edward Jarrett, and two grooms. Much later, on 9 May 1744, Thomas would rise to become Earl of Leicester, with a self-built temple to the arts at Holkham, Norfolk.

Thomas's *valet-de-chambre* Edward Jarrett was to prove a very able accountant on the continent. He described the daily transactions in such minutiae that his account book provides one of the best accounts of how a Grand Tourist made his way across Europe. Jarrett juggles the different currencies with ease, converting where necessary and providing an accurate account of the monies. His spelling is variable, but the entries can be deciphered. Hobart reported to Thomas's guardians, outlining their progress which in turn ensured there was a smooth supply of funds for the itinerant group.

The entries in the account book can be broadly split into two categories: the humdrum (domestic, consumables, travel, personal expenditure) and the transformative (visits, acquisitions, education) to turn Thomas into a *connoisseur*. It is apparent that Jarrett had more confidence in describing the first category. Entries covering day-to-day matters are full and detailed, for example washing of clothes, accommodation, and oil and wig powder. Staying abreast of the latest fashion trends was clearly important to Thomas and there are frequent accounts of purchases of cloth, lace and trimmings and then details of payments made to tailors and seamstresses. For example, during their first visit to Rome Jarrett enters on 1 May 1714: 'Paid for gray Cloath for a coat and briches, and for gold lopes [loops] and edging and silke linding [silk lining]. Paid for Black damask for a wastcoat and buttons, making the sute of clothes'. This can be contrasted with one of the last and most extravagant clothing purchases in Paris on 13 May 1718: 'Paid to Mr Allvian for lace 2147 [livres] 10 [sols]'.[71] It wasn't only Thomas that needed suitable attire, his servants too had new appropriate livery and there are multiple entries for 'great coats, wast coats, britches' for them.

Thomas's party had left England with a coach and four horses. The account book records post stations used to hire additional horses, farriers' accounts for shoeing, and frequent entries for repairs to the *chaise* – an additional carriage used by Thomas. From this, it can be assumed that the road network was rutted, and axles could buckle easily. Sometimes extra assistance was needed with the chaise, for example, on 3 November 1713 whilst travelling towards Mont Cenis, Jarrett entered 'Gave to a man that helped the shaise up a hill'. The following day they crossed over to Susa in Italy: 'Paid to the marons for carrying over Mount Senis to Susa'. Their luggage was hauled by mules. Later entries show how they travelled in boats and how purchases were sent home in ships.

There are almost daily entries for foodstuffs, and rarely a day goes by without a 'Paid for chocolate today'.[72] Meals were taken in taverns while travelling, and at other times cooks were employed – something Jarrett records along with purchases of wine (of various types), bread, butter, and tea. There are also entries for 'pocket money', which would have been used by Thomas for small fripperies. This is contrasted by the charitable entries such as 'given to a poore' woman or fellow, which regularly appear. The need to have personal unaccounted purchases and caring for those less fortunate would feature throughout Thomas's life and can be seen in later account books when he is back in England.[73]

The principal aim of Thomas's Grand Tour was to complete his education under the tutorship of Hobart. Hobart, himself a bibliophile, was an experienced 'Bear Leader', he had recently returned from the continent leading a Grand Tour for Viscount Cornbury in 1710-1711.[74] The account book records how Hobart set about a comprehensive curriculum with supplementary tutors to cover subjects such as mathematics, languages, music and the gentleman-making pursuits of fencing, horse riding and dancing. These shaped Thomas, who was a keen scholar, to become the *virtuoso* that returned to England.[75] The account book includes details of the academies he attended. On 7 December 1712, in Angers, Jarret writes: 'Paid for my master first month riding at the academy' followed by 'paid for stirrups'.[76] Two years later, when in Turin, there is an entry on 24 December 1714: 'Paid for my master entering in the academy'.[77] It is clear from a letter home that Thomas did not enjoy his time in Turin, instead he wanted to be able to travel freely and acquire books. He wrote that he was worried attending would mean missing 'the occasion of buying books while I am travelling. I should not be able to find several of the best of them, and it is impossible to buy them, to my mind, unless I myself am present and certainly, one of the greatest ornaments to a gentleman or to his family is a fine library'.[78]

Thomas also had a musical bent. He took flute lessons in Aix-en-Provence and regularly visited the opera in Turin and Rome. When in Venice on 23 January 1713 he bought two opera scores and on the following day 'paid for a box of the opera of St John Christostome'.[79] The next evening Jarrett notes: 'paid for a box for the first night at the opera of St Angelois'.[80] He was also interested in musical instruments. While in Angers, he bought 'two flutes and a flagiolet [recorder]' and in the following entry Jarrett notes: 'paid for a trompet marine that was broke'.[81] There are no details about any subsequent repair. Later in Messina on 29 April 1716, Thomas bought three harpsichords and interestingly Jarrett notes the purchase price in Sicilian Crowns and then its equivalent in Roman Crowns.[82]

Jarrett records on 1 June 1714: 'Paid Mr Kent'.[83] This is the first reference to William Kent (1685-1748), a man who would play an important role at Holkham. Kent, an Englishman in Rome, worked initially as a painter in the leading studios of Giuseppe Bartolomeo Chiari (1654-1727) and Benedetto Luti (1666-1724) and acted as an agent, before developing an interest in architecture. After his return to England, Kent was instrumental in establishing Palladian architecture, schemes for coherent interior design and landscape architecture, all three of which were evident at Holkham Hall.[84] Kent enjoyed Thomas's patronage and there are further entries for payment to him when acting as his agent. For example, on 6 June 1716 Jarrett settles Kent's 'expenses

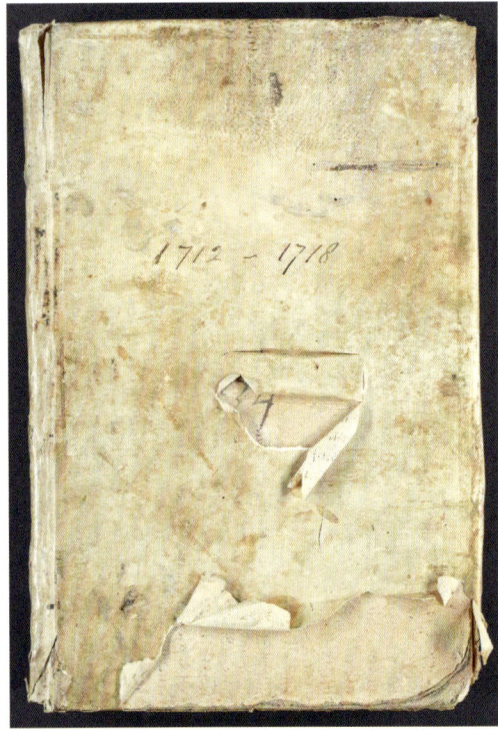

Fig. 1
Account book of Thomas Coke, kept by his
valet-de-chambre Edward Jarrett, recording
his expenses in Europe, 1712-1718

Fig. 2
Page from the account book kept by Edward Jarrett,
Rome 17 July 1716. The top includes entries for a book
of prints and a 'view of the Colosseum'

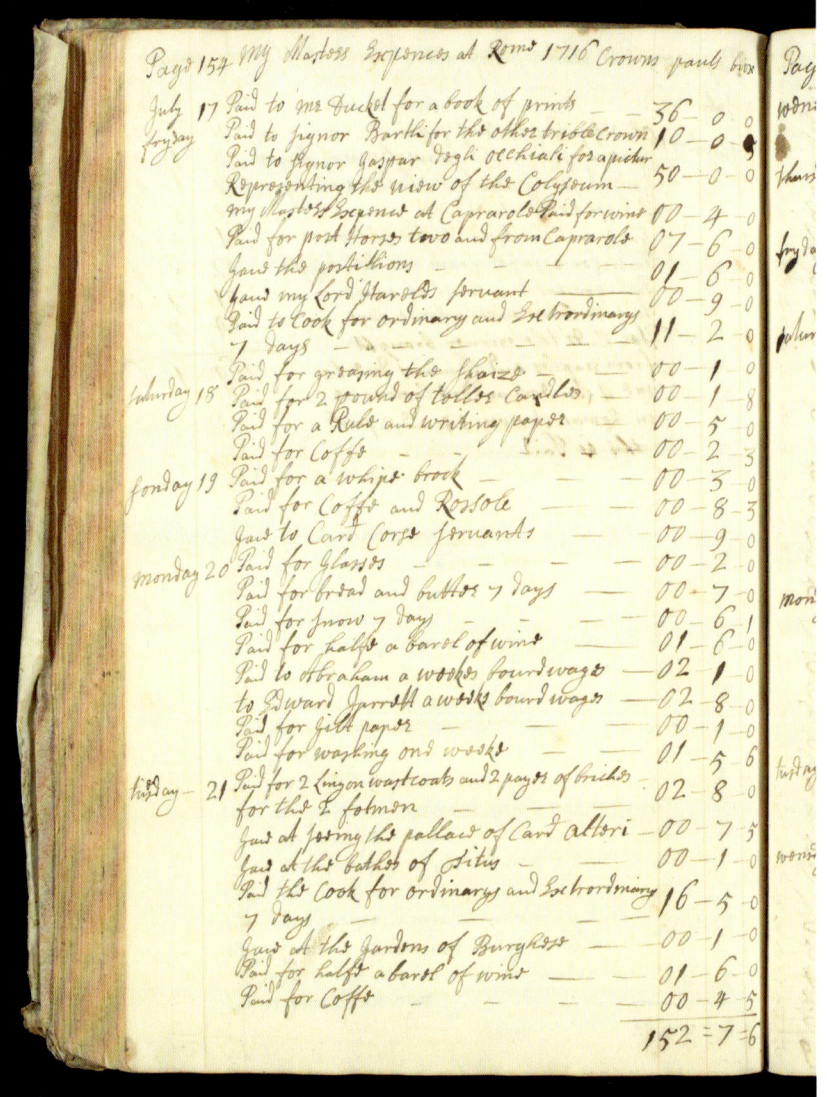

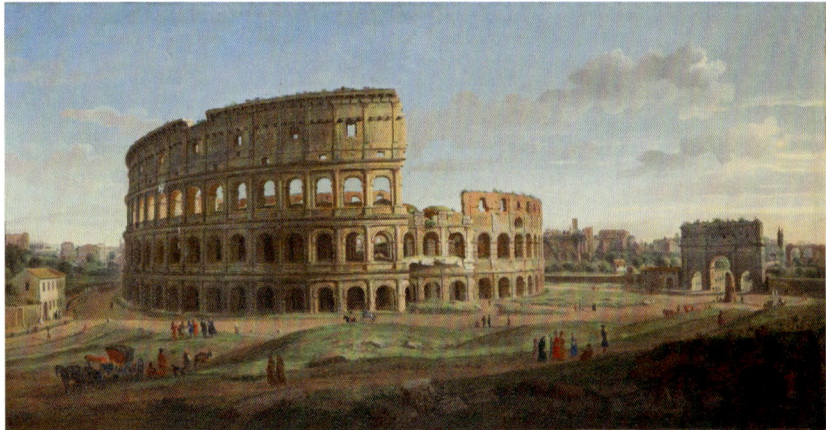

Fig. 3
Caspar van Wittel, *View of the Colosseum, Rome*,
1716. Canvas, 61 x 114.3 cm. Holkham Hall

of his journey to Naples and for pictures and drawings that he bought for my master at severale times'.[85] But their relationship was not just transactional, it was built on friendship and shared interests. Poignantly, when Kent was taken ill in Modena, it is Thomas who paid for Doctor Pamazzinni's bills, with Jarrett noting that they were for 'Mr Kent'.[86]

Perhaps the most important aspect of Thomas's education can be seen when in Rome. At just the age of sixteen, Thomas has his first foray into architecture. A certain Signor Giacomo was paid 33 pauls [Paolos, a Roman coin] a month in May and June 1714, and on 1 June 28 pauls 'paid for instruments to larne architecture' is recorded.[87] On each of his three extended visits to Rome, Thomas took between seven and eight months of formal architectural lessons and with Giacomo they visited the palaces of the greatest Roman families.[88]

Thomas's interest in architecture and the antique wasn't restricted to just Rome. Everywhere he travelled there are details of payments made to visit and draw in the principal estates and residences. Seeing antique marbles, Classical buildings, and architecture inspired by the Italian architect Palladio (1508-1580) would be shaping his ideas for designing Holkham Hall. Thomas wanted to make his own collection of marbles and with Kent acting as his agent he acquired some fine examples.[89] The first that Jarrett records is on 11 September 1716: 'paid for a bust of Luci Verius [emperor Lucius Verus]'.[90]

Guided by Dr Hobart and his own love of the classics, Thomas's purchases of books and manuscripts can be partially traced in the accounts. These were clearly harder for Jarrett to describe and frustratingly there are various entries for 'boxes of books' or 'paid for a book'. Thomas also commissioned for copies to be made of the first three decades of Livy's *Ab urbe condita* (see cat. no. 8). On 13 April 1717, there are three crucial entries, and the details given suggest Jarrett knew the importance that Thomas put on this purchase: 'Paid to Doctur Biscioni for collating that manuscript of Titus Livius', 'Paid for paper to copy a manuscript', 'Paid in part to Doctur Salvini for collating the manuscript of Titus Livius'.

Like many Grand Tourists, Thomas bought and commissioned art. On his second visit to Rome, his focus was on buying, and Jarrett attempts to record in detail items obtained at this time. For example, on 17 July 1716, he notes: 'Paid to Mr Ducket for a book of prints [...] Paid to Signor Gaspar deli Occhiali [Italian nickname for Caspar van Wittel (c.1653-1736)] for a pictur representing the view of the Colyseum' (fig. 3).[91]

Shortly after the party returned to England, Edward Jarrett can be found working as a house steward, an upper servant, again itemising Thomas's personal expenditure and household expenses in London and Holkham.

Through Jarrett's comprehensive accounts we gain a real insight into the mundane and extraordinary days that Thomas Coke encountered on his Grand Tour. Unlike correspondence or diaries that survive for other tourists, the account book provides a chronological and locational record without opinion or speculation, which makes it a crucial source in understanding the lives of these young men when travelling beyond their shores.

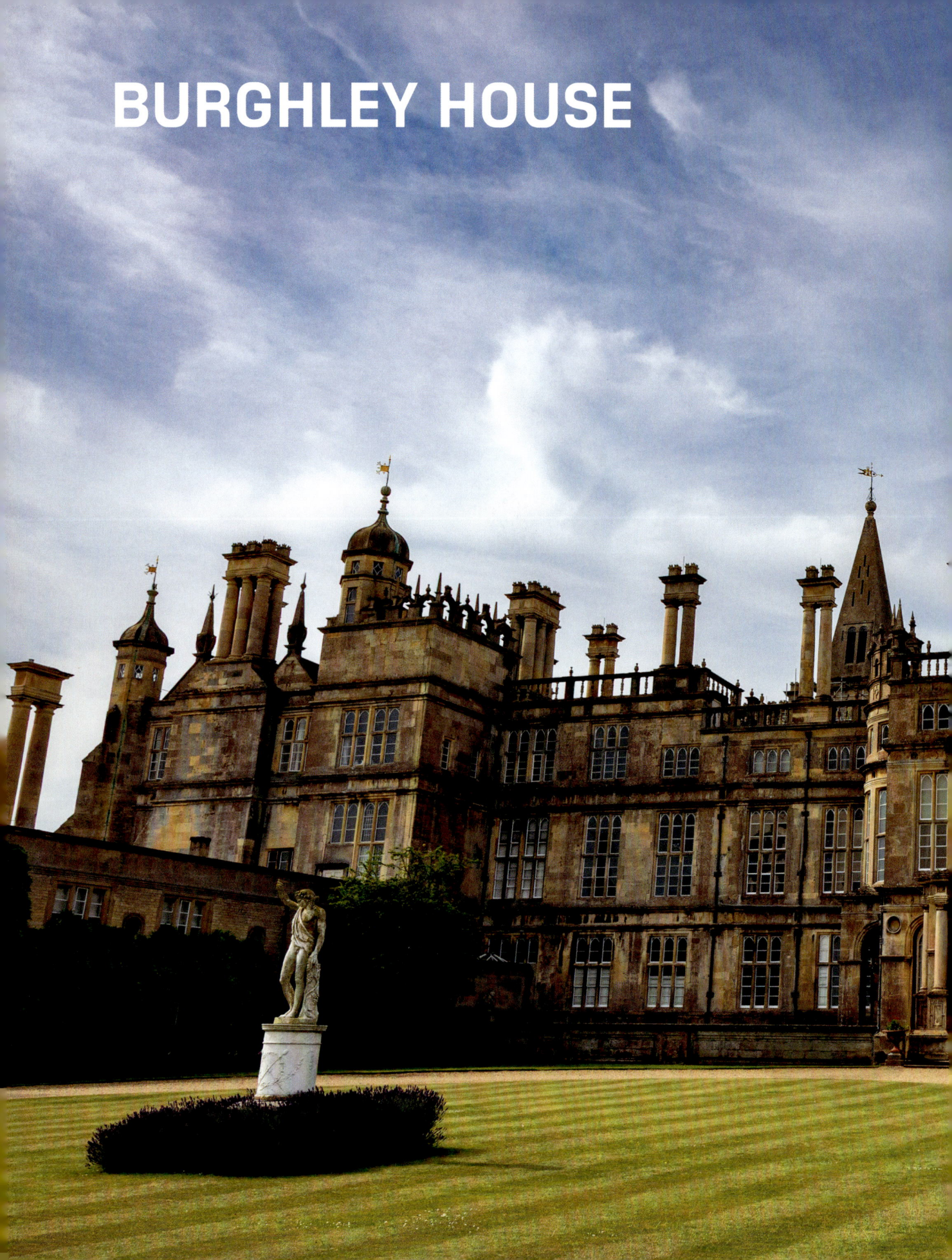

BURGHLEY HOUSE

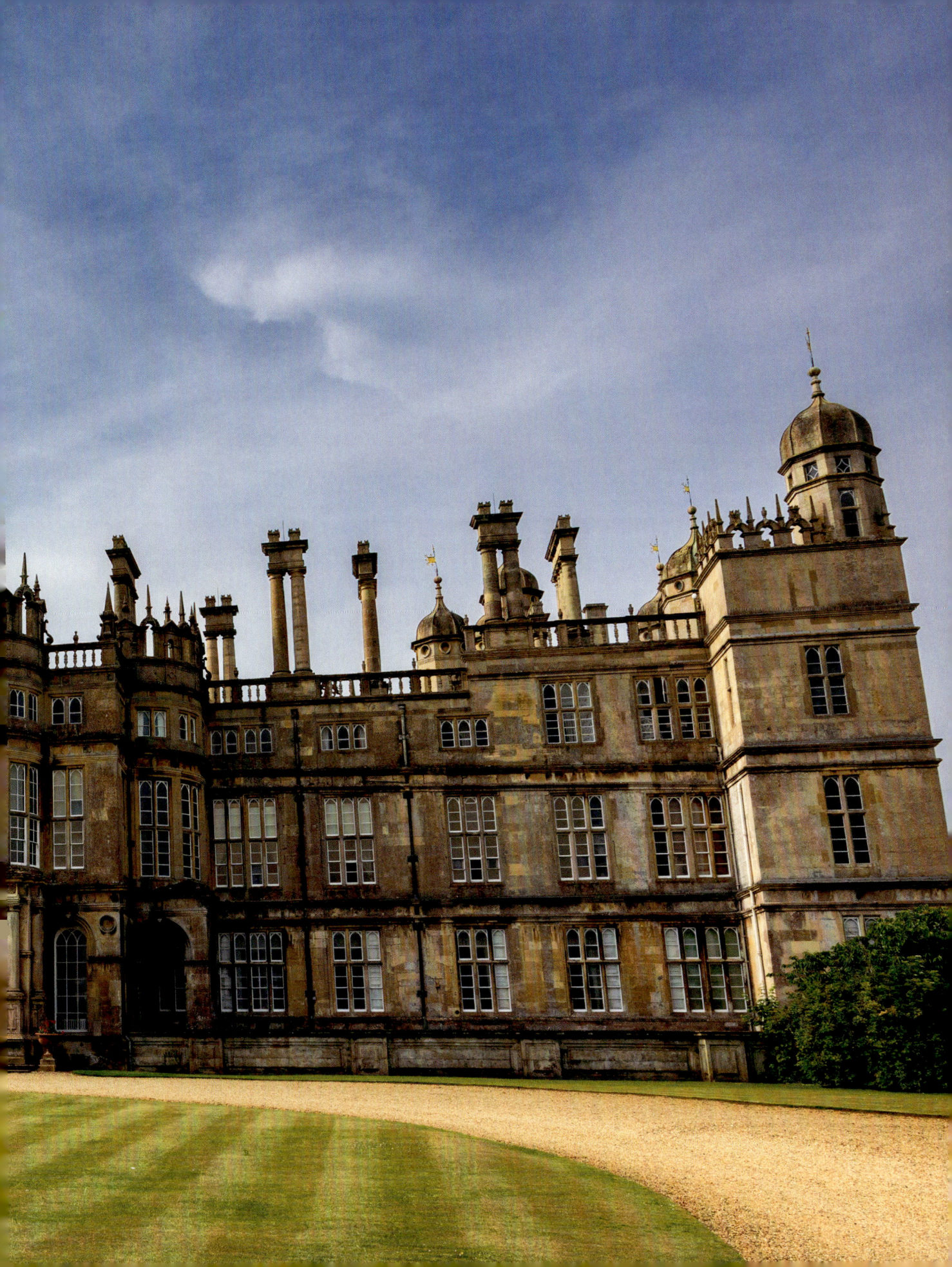

BURGHLEY HOUSE
THE TRAVELLING EARLS

Jon Culverhouse

Burghley, the most remarkable surviving 'prodigy house' of the first Elizabethan Age, was designed and built by Sir William Cecil, the 1st Baron Burghley (1520-1598). William was Queen Elizabeth's (1533-1603) most trusted advisor; he was involved in every aspect of government, both domestic and foreign, and was one of the most powerful men in England. He built three great houses: Exeter House on the Strand in London; Theobalds, an immense palace where he entertained the Queen and Court; and Burghley, which he intended as a seat for the dynasty that he was founding. Neither Exeter House nor Theobalds have survived; Burghley remains, architecturally almost as he left it at his death (fig. 1).

There are no records of the contents or furnishings of Burghley at that time. One can only imagine oak furniture, tapestries hanging in the two immense galleries, and portraits of William's contemporaries, family and friends. William died in 1598, leaving Burghley to his elder son Thomas Cecil (1542-1623), who was created 1st Earl of Exeter on 4 May 1605. His younger son Robert Cecil (1563-1612) was created 1st Earl of Salisbury on the same day. No developments to the house are recorded until the mid-seventeenth century when, in 1678, John Cecil (c.1648-1700) succeeded to the title and became the 5th Earl of Exeter.

John Cecil, 6th Baron Burghley, 5th Earl of Exeter (c.1648-1700)

A child of the interregnum, John was educated at St. John's, Cambridge. In 1670, he married Anne Rich (c.1649-1704), daughter of William Cavendish, 3rd Earl of Devonshire (1617-1684) and widow of Charles, Lord Rich (1643-1664; figs. 2 and 3). A modern-thinking man with a similarly minded and extremely wealthy wife, the young couple wasted no time in setting the modernisation of Burghley under way. Teams of masons began the reconstruction of the two Long Galleries into suites of smaller rooms. On the ground floor the earl specified two suites of apartments in the Continental style.

Over the next fifteen years, most of the eminent English artists and craftsmen of the time found employment with him. This included famous portrait painters such as William Wissing (c.1656-1687) from The Hague, who died in 1687 while working at Burghley, as well as the German Gottfried Kneller (1646-1723) and the Netherlandish painter Peter Lely (1618-1680). Antonio Verrio (c.1636-1707), the Italian decorative painter brought to England by Ralph Montagu (1638-1709) in 1672, came to Burghley after he had painted ceilings and other works for King Charles II (1630-1685) at Windsor. With intermissions, he lived at Burghley and Stamford from 1686 to 1697, painting the five George Rooms and other areas. The Frenchman Jean Tijou (active 1689-1712) designed and forged the Golden Gates on the west front and his son-in-law Louis Laguerre (1663-1721) executed the decorative wall paintings of the Bow Room in 1697. Matthew Prior (1664-1721), the poet, was tutor to one of John's sons. John Vanderbank (d.1717) was weaving tapestries for Burghley some years before receiving the Royal Wardrobe appointment, and many examples of hangings from his workshops are still in Burghley House. Internal decoration was undertaken by the ubiquitous woodcarver Grinling Gibbons (1648-1721) and his followers. Gibbons himself was paid £100 in 1683-1685 for undefined work, although authorities have suggested that this was for the overdoor trophies in the First George Room. A small school of carvers, including Jonathan Mayne, Thomas Young, Joel Lobb and Samuel Watson all carried out work in Gibbons's style, carving door jambs and overdoors, swags and drops, mouldings on panelling and elaborate cornices above. There was also a huge expenditure on textiles, particularly intricate *passementerie* and embroidered hangings; between 1678 and 1700 the upholsterers Francis Lapiere and Peter Dufresnoy were paid more than £1,000 for their work.

As the new staterooms and family apartments were completed, they were filled with the most fashionable decorative objects. The Continental passion for collecting Chinese and Japanese items, imported by the Dutch and British East India Companies, was enthusiastically embraced by the Exeters. The inventory of the contents of Burghley House that was drawn up in 1688 contains numerous references to blue and white and polychrome ceramics, often displayed upon or alongside lacquer chests. It represents a very early record of oriental porcelain in a British collection (fig. 4). Burghley must have been a busy, even chaotic scene. The earl was not politically active and did not maintain a presence at Court. His interests lay in European fashion and collecting fine art to fill his great house.

In 1679, the Exeters set off on their first Grand Tour of Europe, heading for Paris and Italy. The Royal '*passe*' granted for their journey records that they were accompanied by their young son John, a chaplain, two gentlemen soldiers as bodyguards, nineteen servants and 30 horses. A key member of the party was the Steward, Culpepper Tanner, whose extensive notes of occurrences and expenses survive. The company was grossly over-equipped; a large tent, heavy cooking pots and utensils, two carriages and quantities of unsuitable woollen clothing ensured a slow progress. They wintered in Paris, taking the opportunity to buy tapestries from Jean Jans the Younger's (1644-1723) Gobelins workshop and furniture from Pierre Gôle (c.1620-1684), *ébéniste* to the French King Louis XIV (1638-1715). As the weather improved, they travelled south via Tours and Lyon, and crossed into Italy, arriving in Venice just before Christmas, 1680.

This first journey seems to have been devoted more to sightseeing than to the purchase of paintings, although Tanner's notes refer to John buying a painting by Livio Mehus (1627/30-1691) and a fine version of the *Adoration of the Magi* from Carlo Dolci (1616-1686). John also established connections with bankers, art dealers and shipping agents, obviously in anticipation of future purchasing.

The second journey to Italy of 1683-1684 is well-recorded by Tanner, whose notes show that John was becoming an experienced traveler; he bought a light *callashay* (open coach) in France, and was accompanied by Tanner, two soldiers, a chaplain and four servants. The party arrived in Florence in October and was welcomed into the Anglophile court of Cosimo III, Grand Duke of Tuscany (1642-1723). With visions of his redesigned house in mind, John set about purchasing paintings. He bought two huge works, *The Death of Seneca* and *The Rape of Europa,* from Luca Giordano (1634-1705), who went on to sell him thirteen more pictures, most of which remain at Burghley. Dolci's earlier sale of an *Adoration* was followed by the acquisition of eight further works by him, including *Christ Consecrating the Elements*, often considered his masterpiece. In Venice, John bought from Pietro Liberi (1614-1687), Jaques van de Kerckhoven (called Jacopo di Castello in Italy, c.1637-1712), Johann Carl Loth (1632-1698) and Antonio Zanchi (1631-1722). The buying spree continued in Bologna and Genoa. The sheer volume

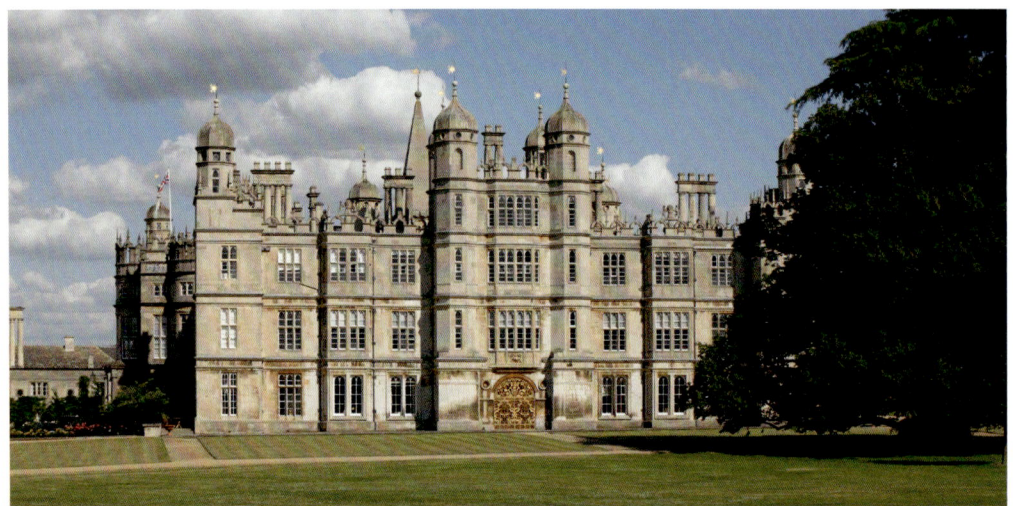

Fig. 1
View of Burghley House,
Lincolnshire, from the west

Fig. 2
Peter Lely, *Portrait of John,
5th Earl of Exeter (1648–1700)*,
c.1675–1685. Canvas, 120.6 x
94 cm. Burghley House

Fig. 3
Peter Lely, *Portrait of Anne,
Countess of Exeter (1649–1703)*,
c.1675–1685. Canvas, 120.7 x
94 cm. Burghley House

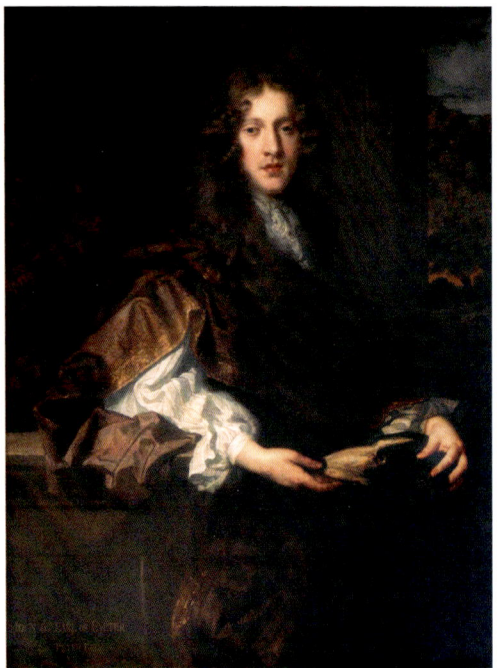

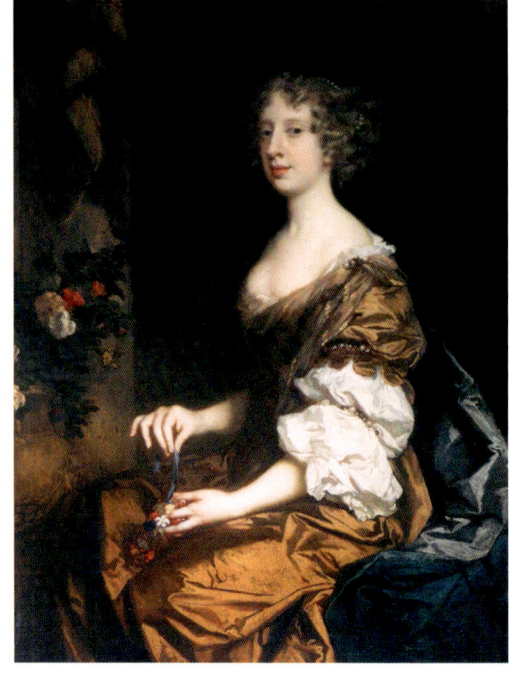

Fig. 4 →
The Blue Silk Dressing Room at
Burghley House, with precious
Chinese and Japanese porcelain
and lacquerwork

Fig. 5
The 3rd George Room at
Burghley House

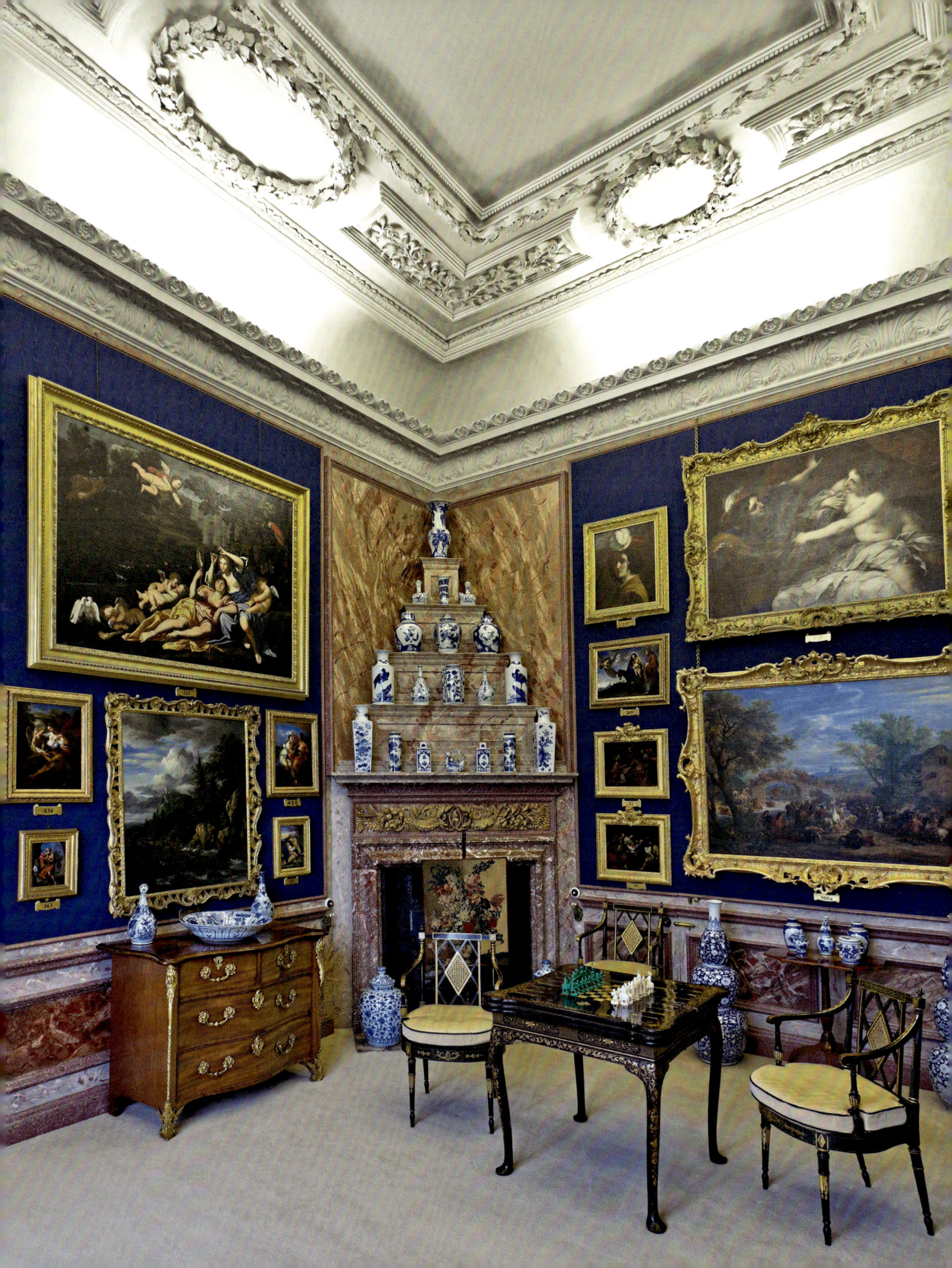

of paintings purchased was remarkable; more than 300 between 1679 and 1700. In his book *Patrons and Painters*, the art historian Francis Haskell noted that 'No Englishman had ever commissioned contemporary Italian paintings on such a scale before; few were ever to do so again'. The redoubtable Tanner arranged for the works to be packed in stout boxes for shipping to England, usually from Leghorn (Livorno).

At the same time, further additions were being made to Burghley House from another source as well. In England, Anne's mother, Elizabeth, Countess of Devonshire (1619-1689) died in 1689. She made the astonishing bequest to her daughter of the entire contents of her rooms at Chatsworth. This included a variety of silver and silver gilt objects such as a 'Dressing plate, Guilt plate and Chamber plate', as well as 66 'Oyle colour pictures', 35 'Water Colour pictures' (mainly portrait miniatures by the finest limners), 67 items of jewellery, 130 'Objects of Virtue' (small luxury products), and 155 pieces of 'China garnished with silver gilt', 'Lesser China' and 'Plain China'. In addition, it encompassed diverse '*Household goods*', among which were 6 state beds, many chairs, 4 cabinets, quantities of fabrics, a marble fireplace, 2 marble window sills, and even a silver lock and key. This amazing accumulation, truly worth a King's ransom, must have trundled down the Great North Road in a convoy of wagons, to be amalgamated into a house already crammed with great objects. An astonishing inheritance indeed.

Whilst the '*passe*' for another journey to Italy in 1693 survives, there are no other records of that trip. John's final Tour began in the autumn of 1699, once again in the company of his wife Anne. Their party arrived in Rome just before Christmas, in time for the Jubilee celebrations. They had established contacts during previous visits to the Holy City, so they now wasted no time buying works from, among others, Francesco Trevisani (1656-1746) and Giuseppe Chiari (1654-1727). The couple also met the French sculptor Pierre Etienne Monnot (1657-1733), from whom they commissioned a considerable group of sculptures, including busts of themselves as Roman Emperor and Empress. Their largest commission from Monnot was a massive funerary monument. Unfortunately, the need for this came all too soon.

John died outside Paris on his way home, Anne survived him by only three years. Their debts were huge; the family finances did not recover for years. However, many of the purchases made by this remarkable couple remain at Burghley, forming the basis of one of the finest collections of seventeenth century Italian art in private hands.

Brownlow Cecil, 10ᵗʰ Baron Burghley, 9ᵗʰ Earl of Exeter (1725-1793)

In 1724, the 9ᵗʰ Earl's father, also named Brownlow (1701-1754), married Hannah Sophia Chambers (1702-1765), the daughter of an immensely wealthy Derby merchant. Her dowry began the rescue of the family finances from the considerable debts incurred by the 5ᵗʰ Earl.

Brownlow Cecil, the great-great-grandson of John, succeeded to the title in 1754, becoming the 9ᵗʰ Earl of Exeter. In 1748 he had married Letitia Townshend (1726-1756), daughter and heiress of the banker and politician Horatio Townshend (c.1683-1751). The writer and politician Horace Walpole (1717-1797) states that on her sudden death in 1756, she 'left her lord the use of £70,000 during his lifetime'. Thus, sufficient capital was once again available for Burghley House.

The 9ᵗʰ Earl retained Lancelot 'Capability' Brown (c.1715/16-1783) as landscape designer and architect to design and oversee a complete transformation of the park and gardens, and to carry out lesser alterations to the structure of the house. Inside, Brownlow completed the suite known as the George Rooms, which had been initiated by John, but left abandoned after his death in 1700 (fig. 5). It is apparent, both from records and from designs used, that the earl admired and respected his ancestor's tastes.

In 1763, with works at Burghley well underway, Brownlow set off for Italy. He travelled in the company of William Patoun (d.1783), a historian and seasoned Continental traveller. In Italy, Brownlow visited Florence, Naples and Rome. In each city he was welcomed into fashionable society, meeting a number of art *cognoscenti*, including Angelica Kauffman (1741-1807), with whom he was considerably enamoured. He bought her portrait of the actor and playwright David Garrick (1717-1779), sat for his own portrait, and subsequently acquired twelve more of her paintings (figs. 6 and 7; see cat. no. 10). Other purchases, which remain at Burghley, included *Jacob Receiving the Bloody Coat of Joseph* by Guercino (1591-1666) and *Virgin and Child* by Marco d'Oggiono (1457-1524), bought from the Barberini Palace as by Leonardo da Vinci (1452-1519).

Whilst visiting the Barberini Palace, Brownlow met Nicolaus Mosman (1727-1787), a soldier, who was drawing a painting that hung there. Brownlow greatly admired his work. On enquiry as to the artist's circumstance, he was told by Mosman that he had, 'deserted his vixen of a wife and enlisted into a foreign regiment as a common man'. Brownlow purchased his discharge from the army and employed him to make drawings of various fine paintings for which, at that time, no engravings existed. The drawings, sent back to Burghley over many years, were bound into volumes, used by Brownlow as a record, and extensively annotated by him. Mosman was paid 5 shillings a day and later half a guinea. Brownlow told the sculptor Joseph Nollekens (1737-1823) that the books had cost him a total of £2,000. The drawings, more than 270 in number, fill four volumes and were donated by the earl to the British Museum in 1789.

Brownlow returned to Italy in 1768, for the second and last time. In Venice, he acquired three excellent paintings by Paolo Veronese (1528-1588) – *St. James, St. Augustine* and *Zebedee's Wife Petitioning Our Lord* – all from the decaying church of S. Jacopo on the island of Murano. His most remarkable purchase, from Signor Vitturi and recorded in the earl's diary as 'bought in his gondola at night', was Jacopo Bassano's (1510-1592) glorious *Adoration of the Magi* (fig. 8). In Rome, Brownlow bought a considerable number of paintings from the famed Barberini Collection, including Artemisia Gentileschi's (1593-1652) superb *Susannah and the Elders* (fig. 9). In his purchases, Brownlow was advised by the antiquarians

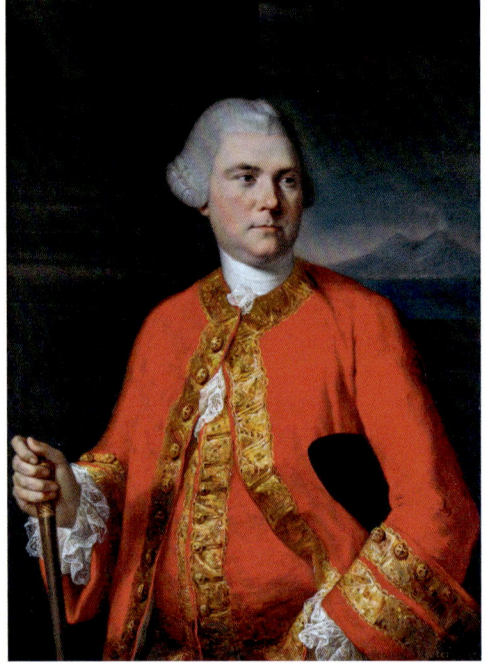

Fig. 6
Angelica Kauffman, *Portrait of Brownlow Cecil, 9th Earl of Exeter (1725–1793)*, 1764. Canvas, 101.5 x 74.5 cm. Burghley House. (cat. no. 10)

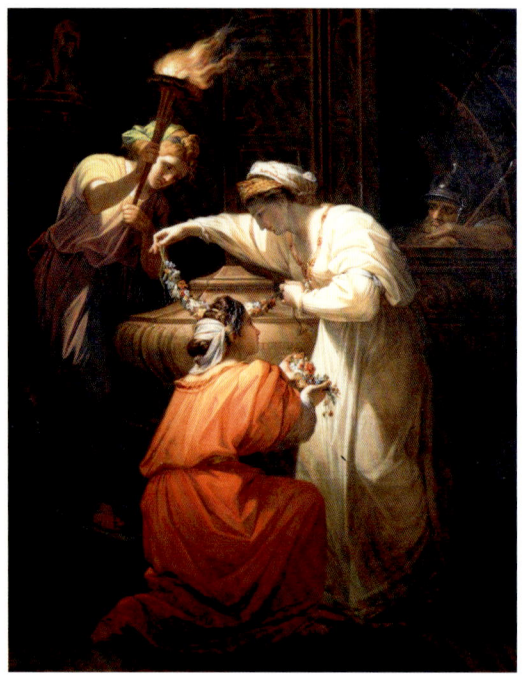

Fig. 7
Angelica Kauffman, *Cleopatra decorating the Tomb of Mark Anthony*, 1764. Canvas, 125.5 x 105 cm. Burghley House

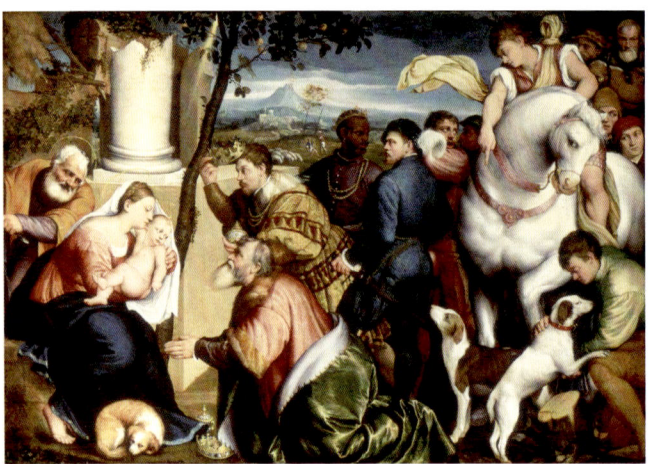

Fig. 8
Jacopo dal Ponte, called Jacopo Bassano, *The Adoration of the Magi*, before 1538. Canvas, 149 x 224 cm. Burghley House

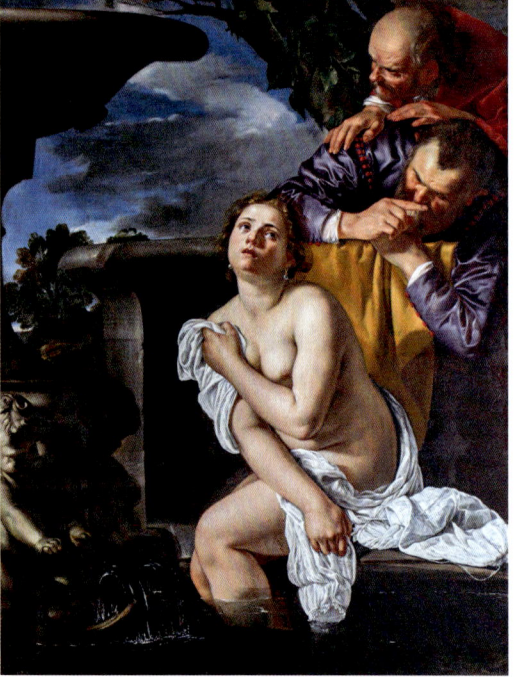

Fig. 9
Artemisia Gentileschi, *Susannah and the Elders*, 1622. Canvas, 161.5 x 123 cm. Burghley House

James Byres (1733-1817) and Thomas Jenkins (c.1722-1798). With their guidance, he bought paintings by Domenichino (1581-1641), Pietro Fabris (active 1740-1792; see cat. no. 12), Sassoferrato (1609-1685), and Pier Francesco Mola (1612-1666), as well as several excellent watercolour views of Italy by Giovanni Battista Busiri (1698-1764) and the German brothers Jacob Philipp (1737-1807) and Johann Gottlieb Hackert (1744-1773).

Brownlow collected a wide variety of sculptures, both antique and contemporary. He commissioned reworked marbles and a fine fireplace from Giovanni Battista Piranesi (1720-1778) and micro-mosaics from Cesare Aguatti (see cat. no. 17). Other typical Grand Tour souvenirs included hardstone boxes (see cat. no. 24) and two pairs of table-tops made from polished samples of volcanic lava. After his return to England in 1769, he was presented by Pope Clement XIV (1705-1774), apparently in exchange for a telescope, with a jewel-like *Madonna and Child* by Orazio Gentileschi (1563-1639).

At home, the scale of Brownlow's spending was astonishing. In the mid-1750s, he commissioned plates from John Parker and Edward Wakelin, which altogether amounted to more than 5,000 ounces of silver – one of the greatest English services of the eighteenth century. For fine furniture, he strongly patronised Ince & Mayhew and, later, Fell & Newton. Many exemplary pieces from both workshops remain at Burghley House, forming part of one of the finest private collections in England.

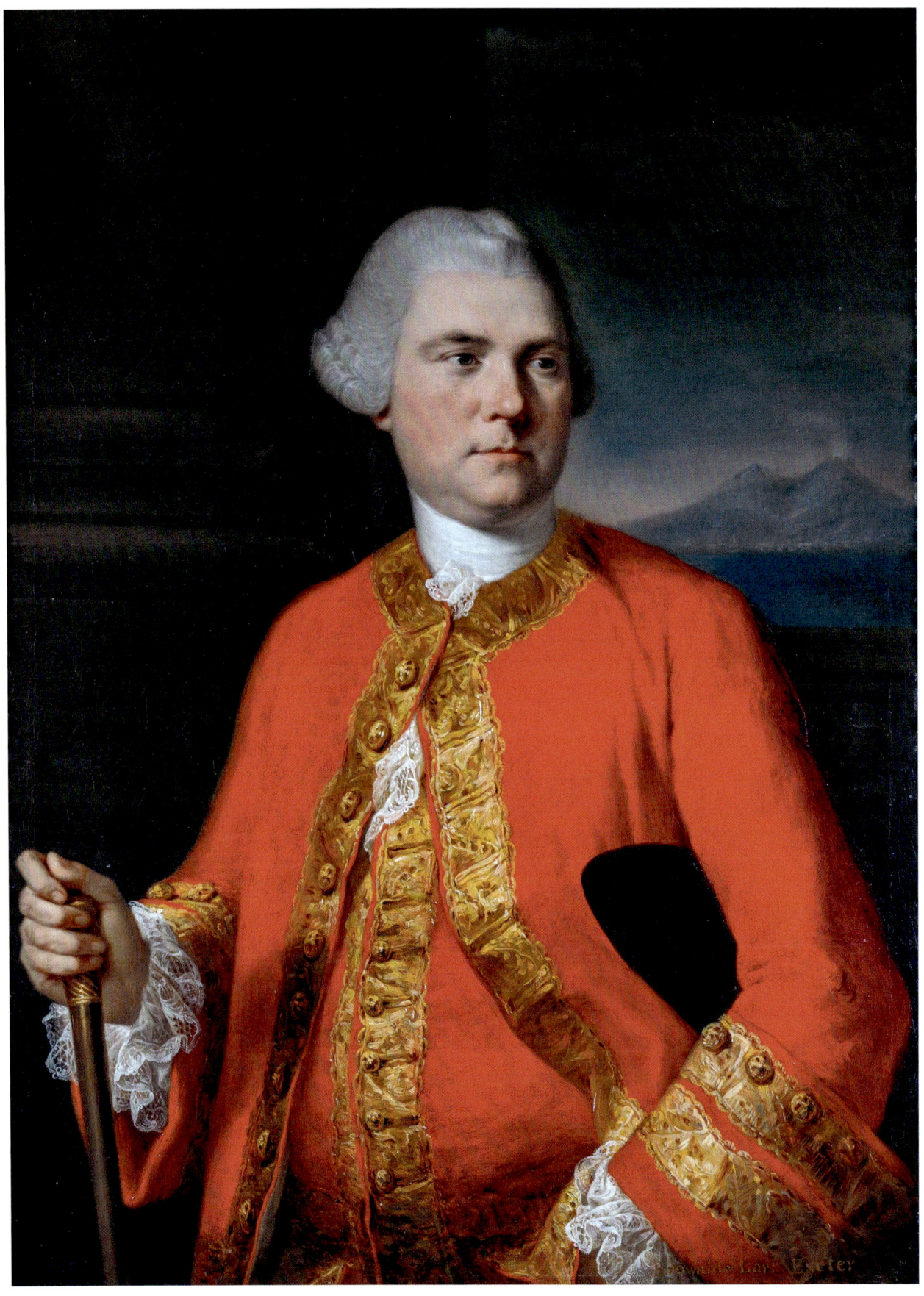

10

ANGELICA KAUFFMAN

Portrait of Brownlow Cecil, 9th Earl of Exeter (1725-1793), 1764
Canvas, 101.5 x 74.5 cm
Signed and dated: *Angelica Kauffman fecit at aua Napolina/ Ao 1764*

Burghley House

Brownlow Cecil, 9th Earl of Exeter, first travelled to the Continent at the age of 38. He had been a childless widower since the untimely death of his wife seven years earlier. In July 1763, he informed his friend, the writer and politician Horace Walpole (1717-1797), that he would soon be leaving for France and Italy and was planning to be away for at least two years. After arriving in Italy, he probably lost no time in travelling on to Naples, a popular destination for foreign travellers in the second half of the eighteenth century. Its attractions included not only the excavations at Herculaneum (from 1738) and Pompeii (from 1748) but also Vesuvius, then a very active volcano. In Naples, the British ambassador William Hamilton (1730-1803), a collector and volcanologist, put Cecil in touch with the Swiss-Austrian artist Angelica Kauffman (1741-1807), who painted his portrait in early 1764.[92] She portrayed the English nobleman wearing a fashionable grey peruke wig and a striking red coat trimmed with gold braid. By depicting the bay of Naples with the smoking Vesuvius in the background, Kauffman turned it into a typical Grand Tour portrait, a souvenir to take home. Every Grand Tourist in Naples made an excursion to the volcano, which never failed to provide a spectacle (see cat.no. 12). Brownlow Cecil became one of Kauffman's most important patrons, eventually acquiring at least fourteen of her paintings and an extensive collections of prints after her work. In addition to portraits, Kauffman's oeuvre consists of landscapes and history paintings executed in an elegant style reminiscent of Raphael (1483-1520).[93]

When Kauffman painted this portrait at the age of 22, she was already a superstar with countless admirers (see cat. no. 11). Born in the Swiss city of Chur as the only child of the painter Johann Kauffman (1707-1782), this child prodigy had caused a furore at the age of 9 with her first pastel portraits. She spent much of her life in Italy, which she first visited between 1754 and 1757, a period in which she attracted attention not only as a portrait painter, but also as a singer.

In the years 1758-1759 and 1762-1766 she sojourned again in Italy, as usual in the company of her father. Evidence of her success is the fact that, in June 1762, she was given her own studio in the Uffizi in Florence, where she made copies of paintings from the famous Medici collections housed there. In 1763, she visited Rome for the first time and made her first history painting there. History painting topped the hierarchy of painting genres, but it was generally deemed an inappropriate pursuit for women. Such biases seem not to have applied to Kauffman, however. From Rome she travelled to Naples, where, the following year, she painted not only Brownlow Cecil's portrait but also, among other works, the likeness of the renowned German archaeologist Johann Winckelmann (1717-1768), who played a key role in nearly all the important excavations taking place at that time.[94]

Kauffman spent the years between 1766 and 1781 in England, where she became one of the founders of the Royal Academy of Arts (see cat. no. 11). Back in Italy, she continued her extremely successful career, having meanwhile married the Venetian painter Antonio Zucchi (1726-1795). In Rome, she lived in a palazzo in the 'English ghetto' near the Spanish Steps, where her open house was *de rigueur* for every self-respecting Grand Tourist. In 1786, at the start of his Italian journey, Johann Wolfgang von Goethe (1749-1832) ended up almost immediately in Kauffman's salon and declared that making her acquaintance was one of the most worthwhile experiences of his trip. In the words of a contemporary, the whole world was 'Angelica-mad', and that was certainly no exaggeration. She died in 1807 in Rome, where she was given an extraordinary funeral, at which her paintings were carried in a long procession by members of the Accademia di San Luca. A year after her death, a bust of the 'divine Angelica' was installed in the Pantheon next to the bust of Raphael.[95]

AvS

11

NATHANIEL DANCE

Portrait of Angelica Kauffman (1741-1807), 1764
Doek, 83 x 69 cm
Signed and dated on the portfolio: *Angelica Kauffman, painted at Rome 1764 by N. Dance*

———

Burghley House

Angelica Kauffman was 22 or 23 years old when her portrait was painted by the English artist Nathaniel Dance (1735-1811). Her name and that of the portraitist, as well as the year 1764, are written on the portfolio that she holds, upright, on her lap. Kauffman had spent the first two months of that year in Naples, where she had painted, among other works, the portrait of Brownlow Cecil, 9ᵗʰ Earl of Exeter (1725-1793; see cat. no. 10), during his first Grand Tour. The earl, who would become one of the most important collectors of Kauffman's work, was so impressed by her that he also acquired this portrait, painted shortly after she returned from Naples to Rome in the spring of 1764.

Kauffman, who looks at us over her shoulder, was portrayed by Dance in her professional capacity as an artist: she has her portfolio at the ready, prepared to start work immediately. Such portfolios were used by artists as sturdy supports for loose sheets of paper while working outdoors.[96] In her right hand Kauffman holds her copper stylus, which contains a piece of chalk or other drawing material. Elegantly clad in a pink dress that features wide sleeves trimmed with three layers of lace, she also wears a fur stole and a hairband with floral decorations.

Dance, a native of London, began his career as a history painter but was most successful as a portraitist. Together with his brother, George Dance, he was long active in Italy, where he earned a living painting the portraits of English Grand Tourists. He specialised in group portraits of gentlemen posing in the midst of Roman ruins, of which he made as many copies as there were sitters, so that everyone had a painting to take home.[97]

Dance had become acquainted with Kauffman in Rome in early 1763, and the following year he painted this engaging portrait of her. Kauffmann was a hugely popular painter in her day, and according to various contemporaries, she and Dance were lovers. The English diarist Joseph Farrington (1740-1821) wrote the following about Dance: 'At Rome he became acquainted with Angelica Kauffman and became so enamoured of her, she encouraging his passion, that when he came to England whither she also came.'[98] Kauffmann followed Dance to London in 1766. The couple became engaged, but the relationship foundered when she befriended Joshua Reynolds (1723-1792; see cat. no. 27). Kauffman's tumultuous love life – which finally calmed down after her marriage in 1781 to the Venetian painter Antonio Zucchi (1726-1795) – was the focus of much interest in her time, for she was celebrated as both a painter and a muse. In the fifteen years she spent in England, Kauffman, despite her penchant for history painting, was chiefly active as a portraitist, which was not unusual for a painter who lived by her brush. In 1768, she became, along with fellow painters such as Dance and Reynolds, a founder member of the Royal Academy, modelled after the renowned Accademia di San Luca in Rome, of which both Dance and Kauffman had been members. Later in life, Dance entered politics and became a Member of Parliament.

In 2024 the Royal Academy honoured Kauffman with its first retrospective exhibition of her work.[99] The compelling portrait that Dance painted in 1764 of the young Kauffman hangs in Burghley House near the portrait of Brownlow Cecil, thus testifying to the admiration Cecil felt for the most famous female artist of the eighteenth century.

AvS

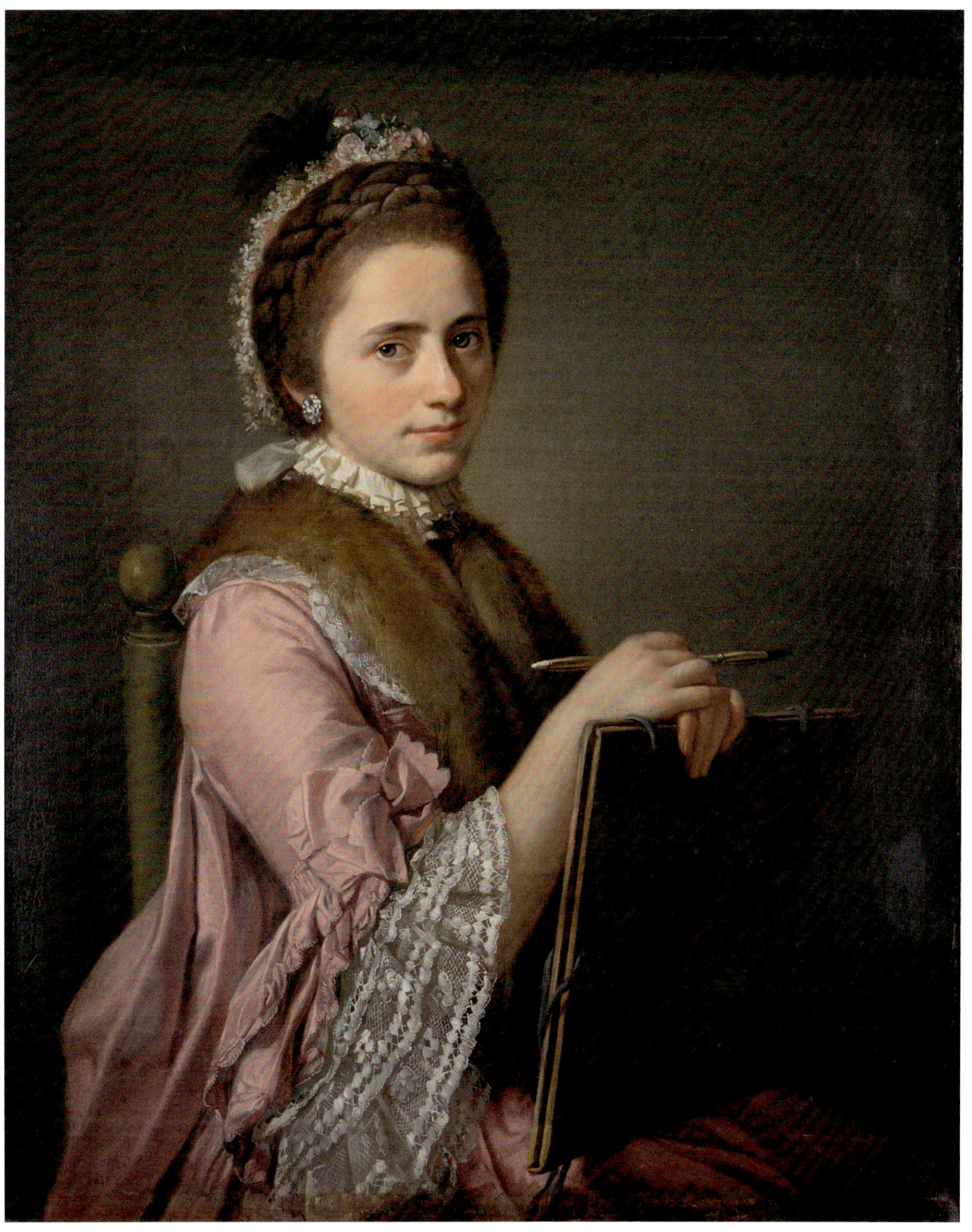

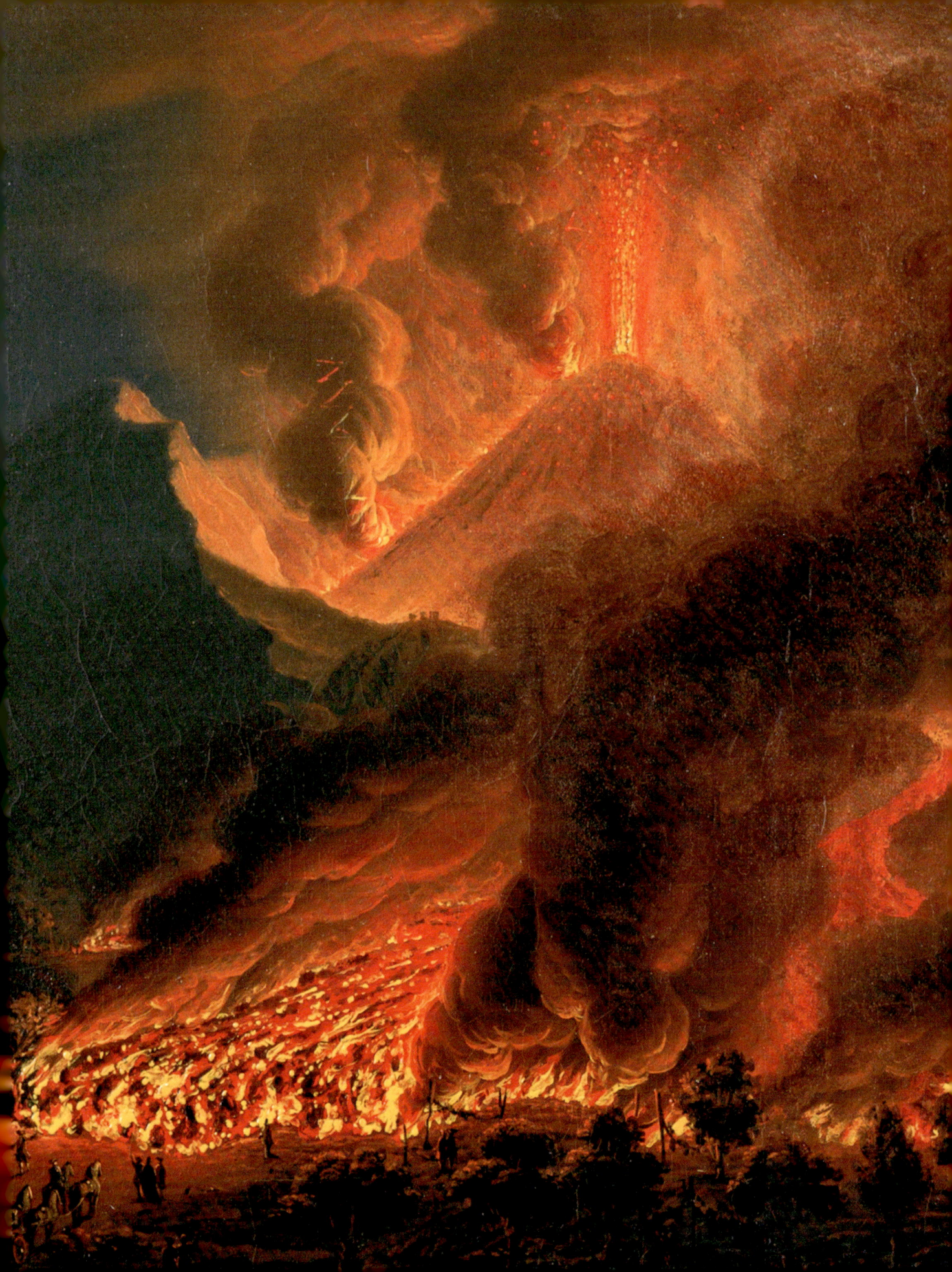

12

PIETRO FABRIS

The Eruption of Vesuvius in 1767
Canvas, 39 x 69 cm

Burghley House

The reverse of this painting by Pietro Fabris (active 1740-1792) bears an autograph inscription by Brownlow Cecil, 9th Earl of Exeter (1725-1793): 'Eruption of Mount Vesuvius in 1767'. This refers to the violent eruption that lasted from 19 to 27 October 1767, one of a series that started in 1631 and lasted until the end of the eighteenth century, marking an extremely active period in the history of this volcano.[100] Cecil bought this painting – probably directly from Fabris, an English-Italian artist resident in Naples – during his second and last Grand Tour to Italy in 1768-1769.

The son of a Venetian theatre designer, Fabris grew up in England, and his fluency in English stood him in good stead throughout his career. He was chiefly known for his life-like illustrations in the vulcanological publications of the English diplomat, collector and geologist William Hamilton (1730-1803), who served as ambassador to the court of the Kingdom of Naples and Sicily from 1764 to 1800. Fabris went on countless excursions with Hamilton, who commissioned him to document Vesuvius, Etna and the volcanic island of Lipari off Sicily. The versatile Hamilton fulfilled a key function for the English Grand Tourists who visited Naples. He introduced these foreigners to the right circles, made sure they did not miss any of the important cultural attractions, and took them to Vesuvius to climb the volcano under his expert guidance.[101] Between 1776 and 1779, Hamilton wrote a series of scientific letters to the Royal Society in London about his pioneering geological research, later published in the series *Campi Phlegraei* (flaming fields), for which Fabris produced the illustrations. The artist also made derivatives of his prints in the form of paintings of volcanic eruptions, which were undoubtedly much in demand by Grand Tourists in search of eye-catching souvenirs.

The painting discussed here gives a good impression of the great excitement caused by this spectacular natural phenomenon. It depicts a steadily approaching stream of lava, the sight of which is truly terrifying. Small groups of spectators, who have approached the red-hot mass of lava, stand near their carriages, pointing and gesturing excitedly, apparently insensitive to the fear their horses must have felt. It looks extremely dangerous, but for many Grand Tourists the first-hand experience of such a fiery spectacle was the high point of their journey. Brownlow Cecil was in England when Vesuvius erupted in 1767. No doubt he had climbed the volcano on his first trip to Naples a couple of years previously. It was not for nothing that Angelica Kauffman (1741-1807) had depicted the smoking volcano in the background of his portrait (see cat. no. 10). Together, Kauffman's portrait and Fabris's painting illustrate the sense of adventure that the Grand Tour held for someone like Cecil.

AvS

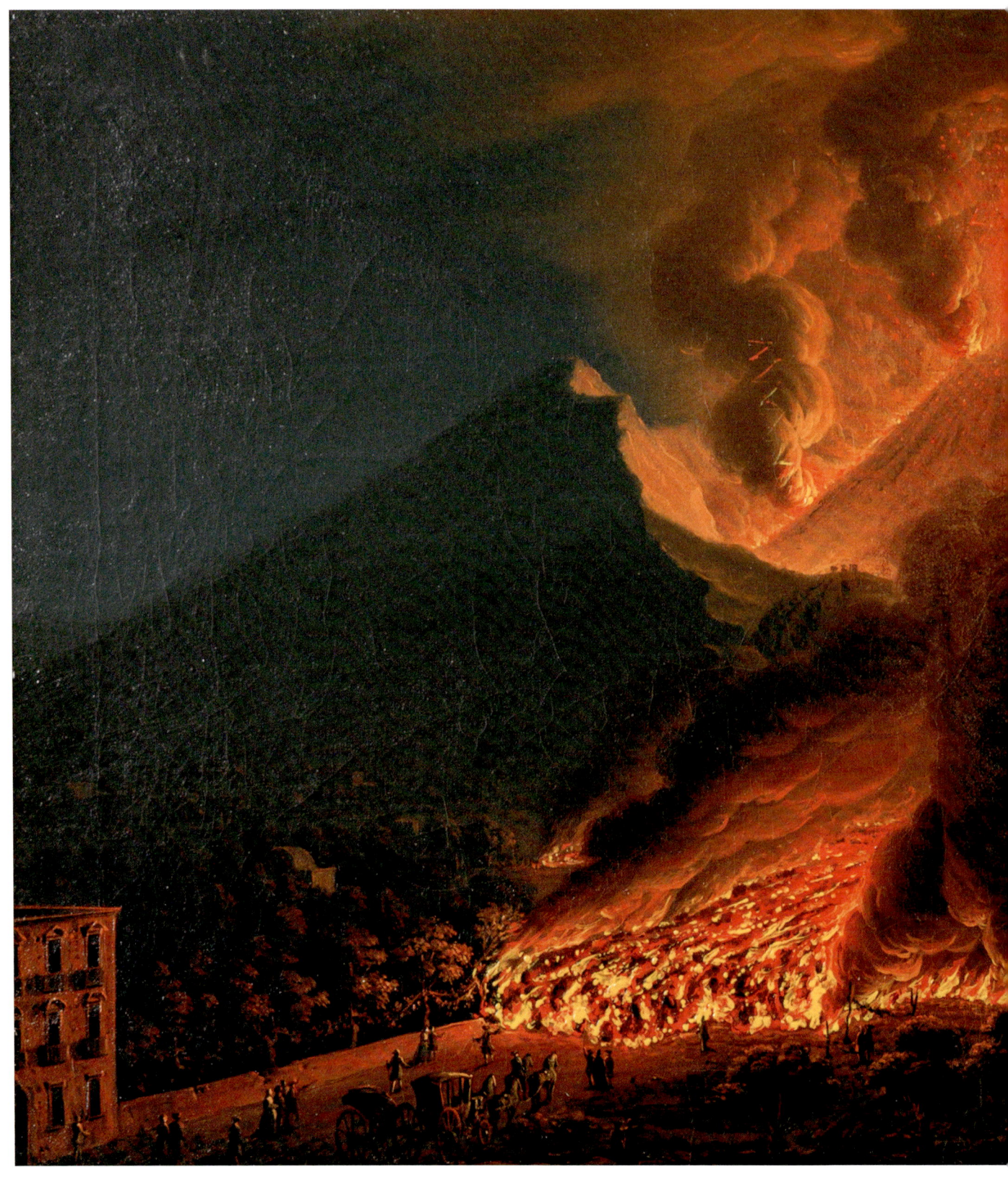

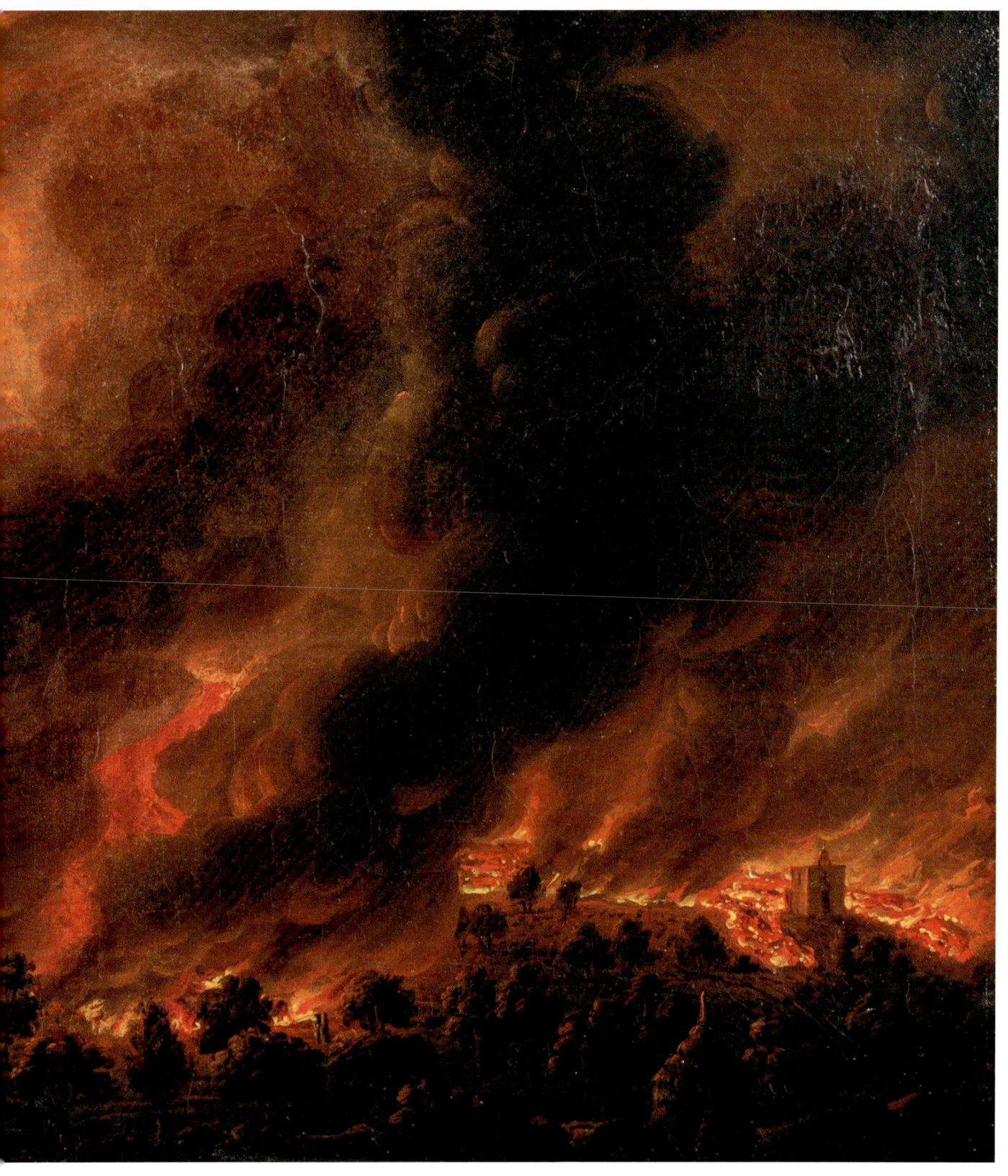

13-14

PAOLO VERONESE

Saint Peter, c.1585
Saint Paul, c.1585
Canvas on panel, 29 x 15 cm (each)
Inscription on the back: *Palo* [sic] *Veronese pinxit*

Burghley House

Brownlow Cecil, 9th Earl of Exeter (1725-1793), was known for the bookkeeperly precision with which he recorded expenses and other practical matters. We often find, for example, on the backs of paintings he acquired on his journeys to Italy, inscriptions in his hand that provide interesting background information about the acquisition. On the reverse of these small paintings by Paolo Veronese (1529-1588) he wrote: 'St. Peter & St. Paul small life by P. Veronese from Mr. Hamilton at Rome a present'. The person referred to is Gavin Hamilton (1723-1798), a well-known Scottish painter and art dealer active in Rome, who was a focal point in Italy for English Grand Tourists in search of paintings and the Roman antiquities that were still being unearthed at numerous excavations in the eighteenth century. Hamilton acquired many of the paintings he traded in Rome from the Barberini collection, which was the source of these two works by Veronese. The heiress Cornelia Costanza Barberini-Colonna was forced to sell large numbers of paintings to pay off her gambling debts. The manner in which Brownlow acquired these two paintings – as 'a present' – shows how highly Hamilton valued him as a client.

The Verona-born Paolo Caliare, thus called Veronese, spent almost his entire career in Venice, where he became, together with Titian (c.1488/90-1576) and Tintoretto (1518-1594), a prominent standard-bearer of the colourful Venetian School of painting of the late Renaissance. When Brownlow visited Venice in June 1769, during his second Tour of Italy, he succeeded in acquiring a number of costly paintings by this very sought-after master, which had belonged to the destitute church of San Jacopo on the island of Murano. The works in question are two organ shutters with life-size portrayals of Saint James and Saint John, and the central panel of an altarpiece with a representation of Salome, wife of Zebedee, beseeching Christ to favour her sons, John and James.[102] The panel came to hang in the chapel of Burghley House – apparently there was no objection to its Catholic character.

Hamilton must have done Brownlow a very great favour by giving him these costly paintings. Both apostles are portrayed barefoot and standing. Peter, the first bishop of Rome and therefore a key figure in the dissemination of Christianity, holds an opened book and is recognisable by his attribute, the keys to the kingdom of heaven. Paul, whose biblical writings were also important in spreading the Christian faith, is portrayed clutching a book under his left arm and using his right hand to support a sword, the means of his beheading and martyrdom. The small size of the canvases suggests that they were studies for large-scale likenesses of these two saints.

AvS

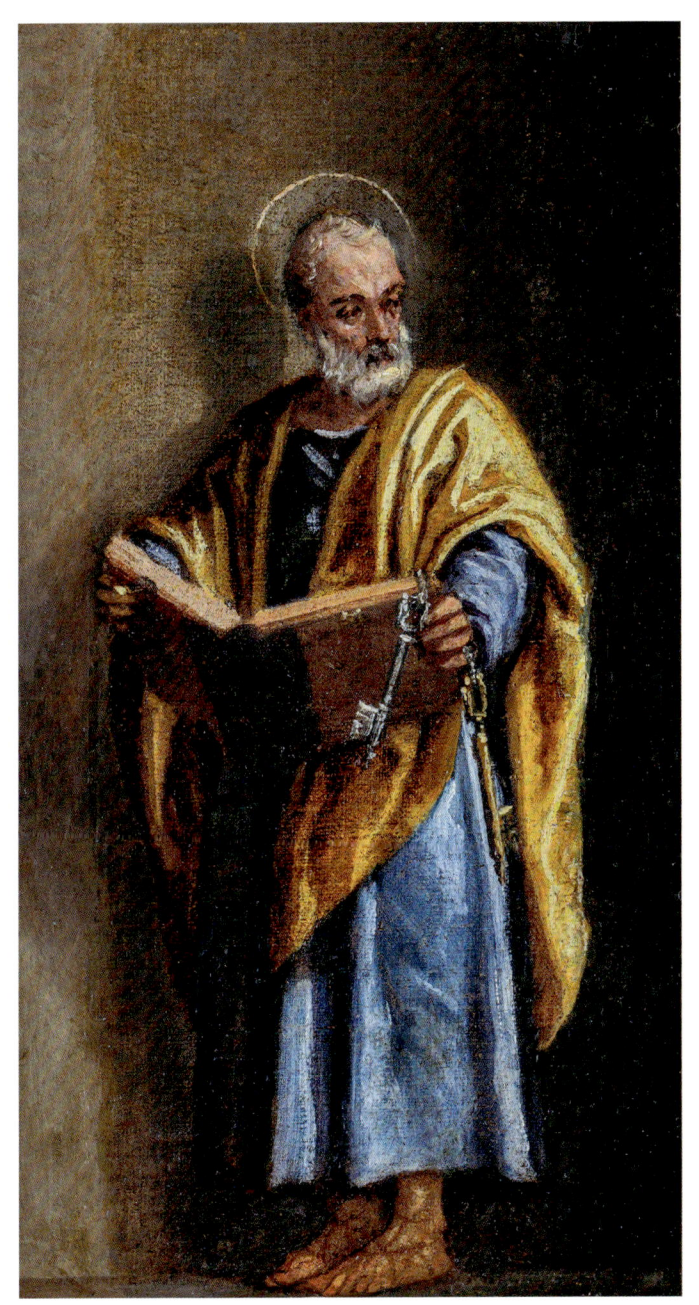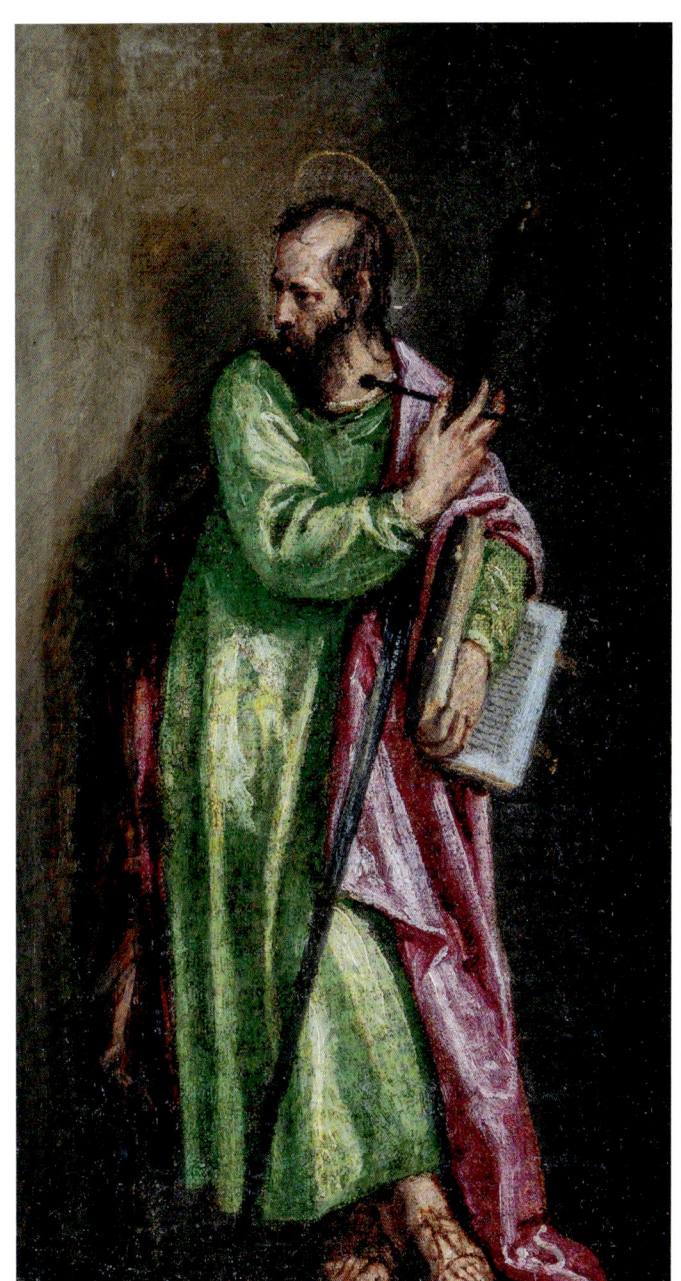

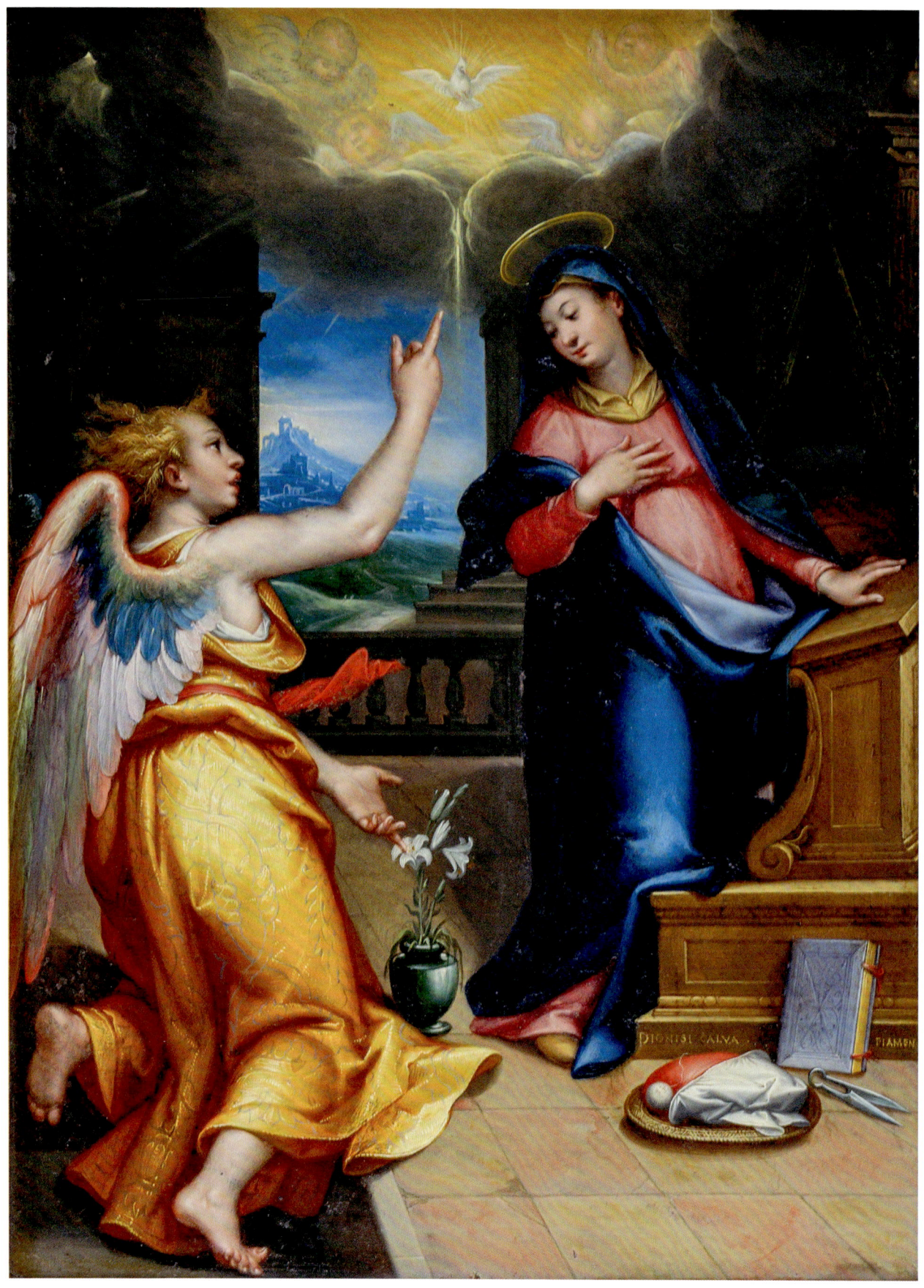

15

DENYS CALVAERT

Annunciation, c.1585
Copper, 37.5 x 29 cm
Signed on the prie-dieu: *DIONISI CALVA. FIAMENGO*

———

Burghley House

The back of this painting bears an inscription in which Brownlow Cecil, 9th Earl of Exeter (1725-1793), noted that he acquired this work in Bologna from a certain 'Abbé Fiori'. Unfortunately, this abbot cannot be identified.[103] Cecil made two Grand Tours to Italy. Following in the footsteps of his great-great-grandfather, John Cecil, 5th Earl of Exeter (c.1648-1700), he purchased paintings and other costly souvenirs that are still to be found in the collection of Burghley House. In contrast to his ancestor, however, Brownlow Cecil not only bought the work of contemporary Italian painters but also acquired works by older masters. A fine example of the latter is this late sixteenth-century painting by the Flemish-born artist Denys Calvaert (c.1540-1619).

With a keen eye for life-like detail reminiscent of his Flemish origins, Calvaert painted this Annunciation on a small copper plate. The angel who announces the birth of Christ flies in from the left in such haste that he almost loses his balance. Pointing with his right hand to heaven, the source of his divine message, he uses his left hand to focus attention on a vase of white lilies, which symbolise Mary's virginity. Mary, her hand on her heart, turns with full acceptance towards the angel. The wicker basket with sewing, the scissors next to it and the book – a Bible or a prayer book – point to her virtuous activities, which the angel has interrupted. Above the scene float four angels and the Holy Spirit in the form of a white dove. A landscape is visible in the background.

Little is known about Calvaert's early life. He was probably born around 1540 in Antwerp, where he was trained by the landscape painter Christiaen van Queborn (c.1521-1578), by whom no work survives. Calvaert's most important biographer, Carlo Cesare Malvasia (1616-1693), relates in his *Felsina Pittrice. Vite dei Pittori Bolognesi* (1678) that the artist went to Italy after completing his training. At some point after 1557, he arrived in Bologna, where, apart from an interval in Rome, he continued to work for the rest of his life. By the last quarter of the sixteenth century, Calvaert had developed into one of the most successful painters in the city. Around 1575, he founded a painters' academy, where he trained such famous masters as Guido Reni (1575-1642) and Domenichino (1581-1641), who, following his example, also took to painting on copper.

Calvaert's oeuvre mainly consists of religious scenes: large altarpieces painted to commission and a considerable number of small works on copper. In the first half of the sixteenth century, various Italian artists began to paint on copper, after which the technique was embraced in the second half of the century chiefly by Northern painters working in Italy.[104] The smooth surface of the copper plate makes it possible to work with great painterly refinement, and the bright colours produce a jewel-like quality that is beautifully exemplified by this small painting.

AvS

16

CARLO DOLCI

The Adoration of the Shepherds, c.1630
Copper, 18 x 12 cm

Burghley House

This small work, painted on a copper plate by the Florentine artist Carlo Dolci (1616-1686), is a precious jewel. First recorded in the 1688 inventory of Burghley House as a 'Nativity of Christ', it is one of the six paintings in 'ebony frames' that were hanging at that time in 'My Lady's closet'. It was acquired in Florence by John Cecil, 5th Earl of Exeter (c.1648-1700), during one of his four Grand Tours, which he usually made in the company of his wife, Countess Anne Cavendish (c.1649-1704). The small painting does not represent the Nativity of Christ, however, but rather the Adoration of the Shepherds.[105]

In the dark of night, Mary shows her child to one of the shepherds, who have received the divine message of the birth of the Messiah. With Joseph at her side, Mary lifts the swaddling cloth in which the child is wrapped. The divine light radiating from the infant illuminates the darkness. Dolci's representation reduces the famous story to its core. He portrays only one of the shepherds, who kneels in adoration at the manger and touchingly kisses the baby's foot. The lamb lying next to him, in front of the manager, recalls the Lamb of God and prefigures the child's death on the cross for the redemption of all humankind. Research carried out during a restoration revealed that the paint contains ground gold leaf, which enhances the rich luminosity of the paint surface.

In the seventeenth century, Dolci, who was known for his piety, was regarded as one of the greatest painters of Italy. His reputation ebbed away in the centuries after his death, but today he is once again held in high esteem. In his day, Dolci was a favourite painter of the Medici family in Florence and was admired for his brilliant palette and the intense religiosity of his scenes. Much of his production consists of small paintings intended for private devotion. In this case, Dolci deviated from the traditional iconography of the popular theme by portraying only one shepherd instead of a group of them. The viewer is urged to empathise with this humble man in his worship of the child.

John Cecil bought art on a grand scale on his trips to Italy. He acquired more than 300 paintings by contemporary Italian masters, including at least eight works by Dolci. We can only guess at the part played by Cecil's wife, Anne, in his passion for collecting abroad. Indeed, recent research has shown that wives exerted a much greater influence than previously thought on their husbands' purchases of art and the decoration of their houses. The fact that this beautiful little painting ended up in the countess's quarters in Burghley House suggests that she played an important role in its acquisition.

AvS

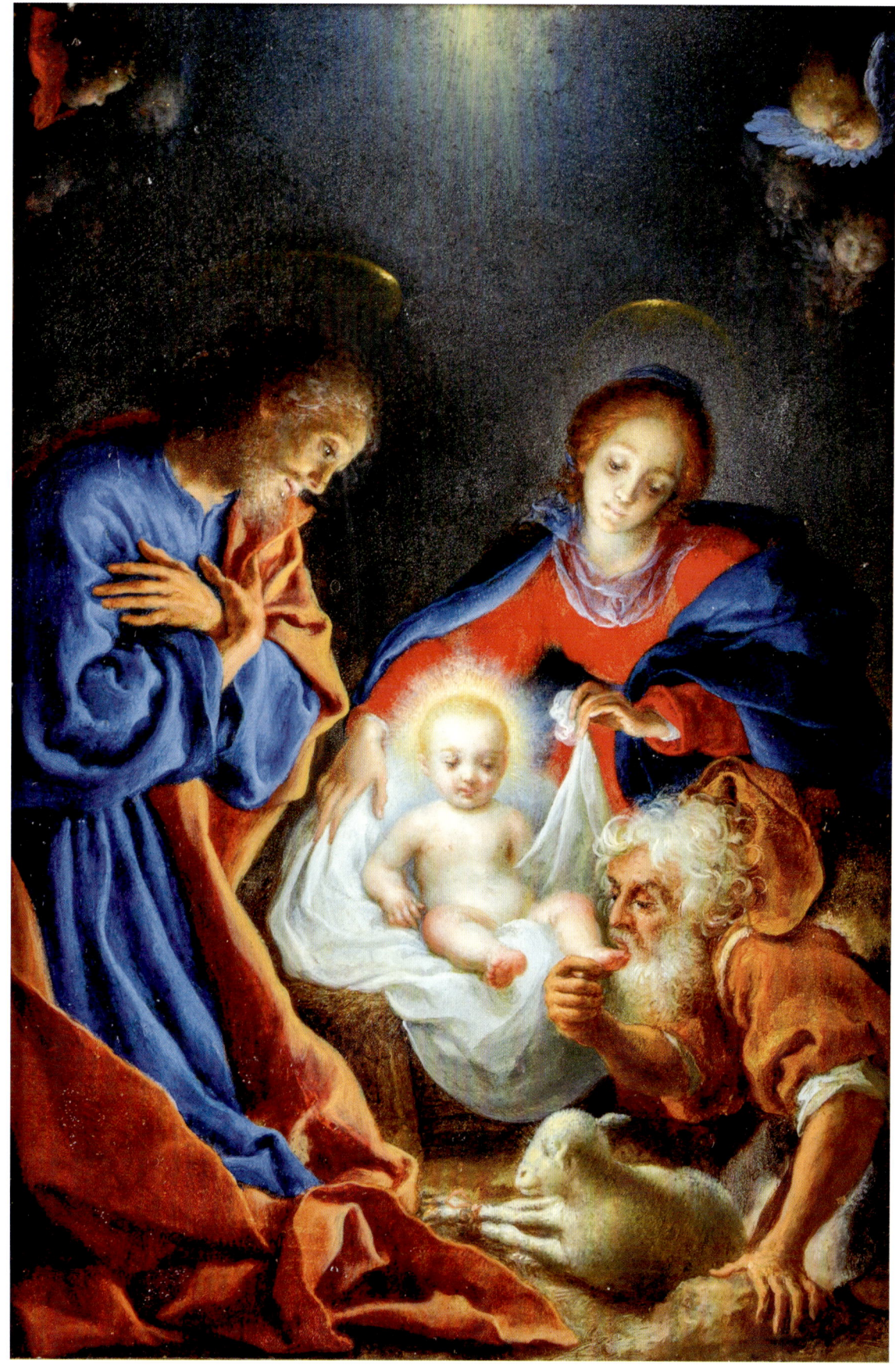

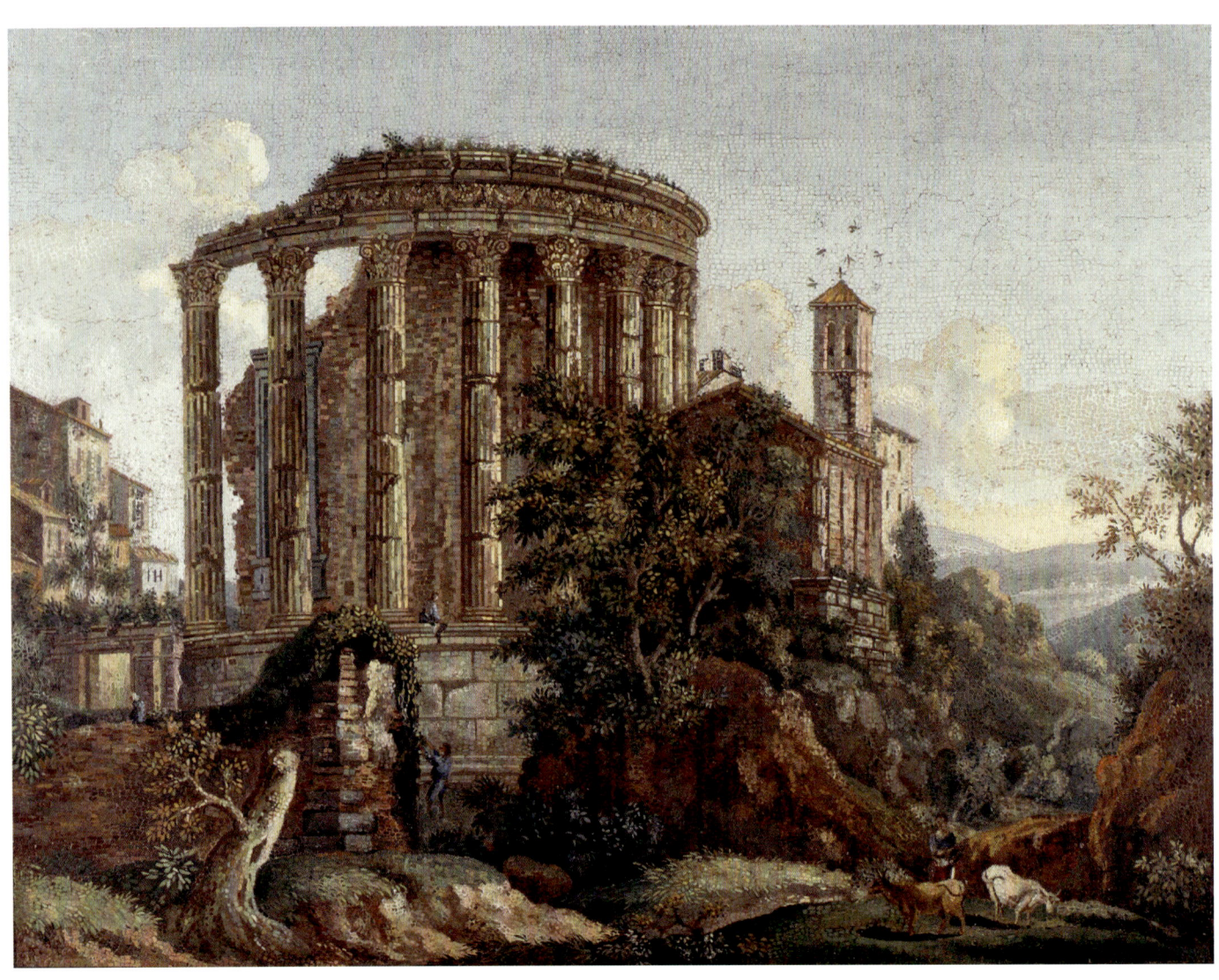

17

CESARE AGUATTI

Micro-mosaic of the Temple of Vesta, 1774
42 x 54.5 cm
Signed and dated on the gilt wood frame:
Cesare Aguatti Romano 1774

Burghley House

This mosaic of the famous Temple of Vesta in Tivoli (1st century CE) is one of a pair hanging at Burghley House. The other portrays the ruins of the Colosseum. In a letter to Brownlow Cecil, 9th Earl of Exeter (1725-1793) from Rome, dated 11 March 1775, the British antiquary and dealer Thomas Jenkins (1722-1798) writes: 'The Minerva ordered as a Companion to Your Lrdp.s Colleseo will most assuredly make an Excellent Mosaick, the Person that Makes it has by him one of the Sibils temple at Tivoli somewhat larger than your Picture which will Cost 150 or about £75 but 'tis really wonderfully fine. He is certainly the best workman that ever was in Mosaick'.

Jenkins's letter is confusing and probably indicates that he was trying to persuade the earl to purchase a ready-made mosaic of the Sybil's Temple, but that the earl instead decided to commission this piece from Cesare Aguatti (active late 18th century). Another identical version by Aguatti is in the Vatican Museums, dated 1774 and mounted in a bronze frame bearing the papal coat of arms.[106]

The development of the micro-mosaic technique has been attributed to two mosaicists, Giacomo Raffaelli (1753-1836) and Aguatti, who both worked in the Vatican Mosaic Studio and began producing mosaics on a miniature scale around 1770. The micro-mosaic process begins by melting and stretching glass into long canes called *filati*, which are broken into tiny lengths. A base is then covered with a paste which assists in holding the glass pieces in place while the image is constructed. Tweezers are used to place the glass fragments to create an image that may be made up of thousands of pieces. Made in a wide variety of colours and shapes, it is not just the placement of the *tesserae* (pieces) which is integral to achieving a clear final image but also the choice of their colour and shape. Once the final design has been achieved, the micro-mosaic is pressed with a wooden block to ensure each piece is firmly in place. Wax is then poured over the top to fill any gaps and the surface is lightly sanded and polished.

Micro-mosaics became one of the most sought-after souvenirs of Rome, particularly by aristocrats making the Grand Tour.

JC

18

JOSEPH NOLLEKENS

Head of Medusa, 1762-1764
White marble, 54.5 x 44 x 18 cm

Burghley House

This bust portrays an unusually gentle-looking Medusa. Her hair, normally shown as a mass of writhing snakes, is restrained to just two serpents that form a surround to her face. However, the hint of teeth behind parted lips gives a slightly menacing look to her classical features. The bust is a copy of a famous Roman sculpture known as the *Rondanini Medusa*, which at the time was in the Palazzo Rondanini in Rome. It is now in the Glyptothek in Munich, having been purchased by the art-loving King Ludwig of Bavaria (1786-1868) from the heirs of the Marquis Rondanini.

Joseph Nollekens (1737-1823) was born in London, the son of an expatriate Flemish artist. In 1750, he was apprenticed to Pieter Scheemakers (1691-1781), a successful Flemish sculptor. He travelled to Rome in 1762, where he was employed by Bartolomeo Cavaceppi (c.1716-1799), whose workshop specialised in the restoration and copying of antiquities. Cavaceppi's studio was extremely popular with young aristocrats making their Grand Tour, many of whom made purchases from his stock of sometimes imaginative 'antiques'.

Nollekens sold this bust to Brownlow Cecil, 9th Earl of Exeter (1725-1793) in 1764. The Earl also bought from him a magnificent marble copy of *A Boy carried by a Dolphin* and several other sculptures. These are recorded in an export licence of 27 June 1766.[107] Upon its arrival at Burghley House, the sculpture of Medusa was placed on the mantelpiece in the 3rd George Room. A small cavity was carved out from the wall to accommodate the projection at the back of the sculpture. It remains in place there today.

JC

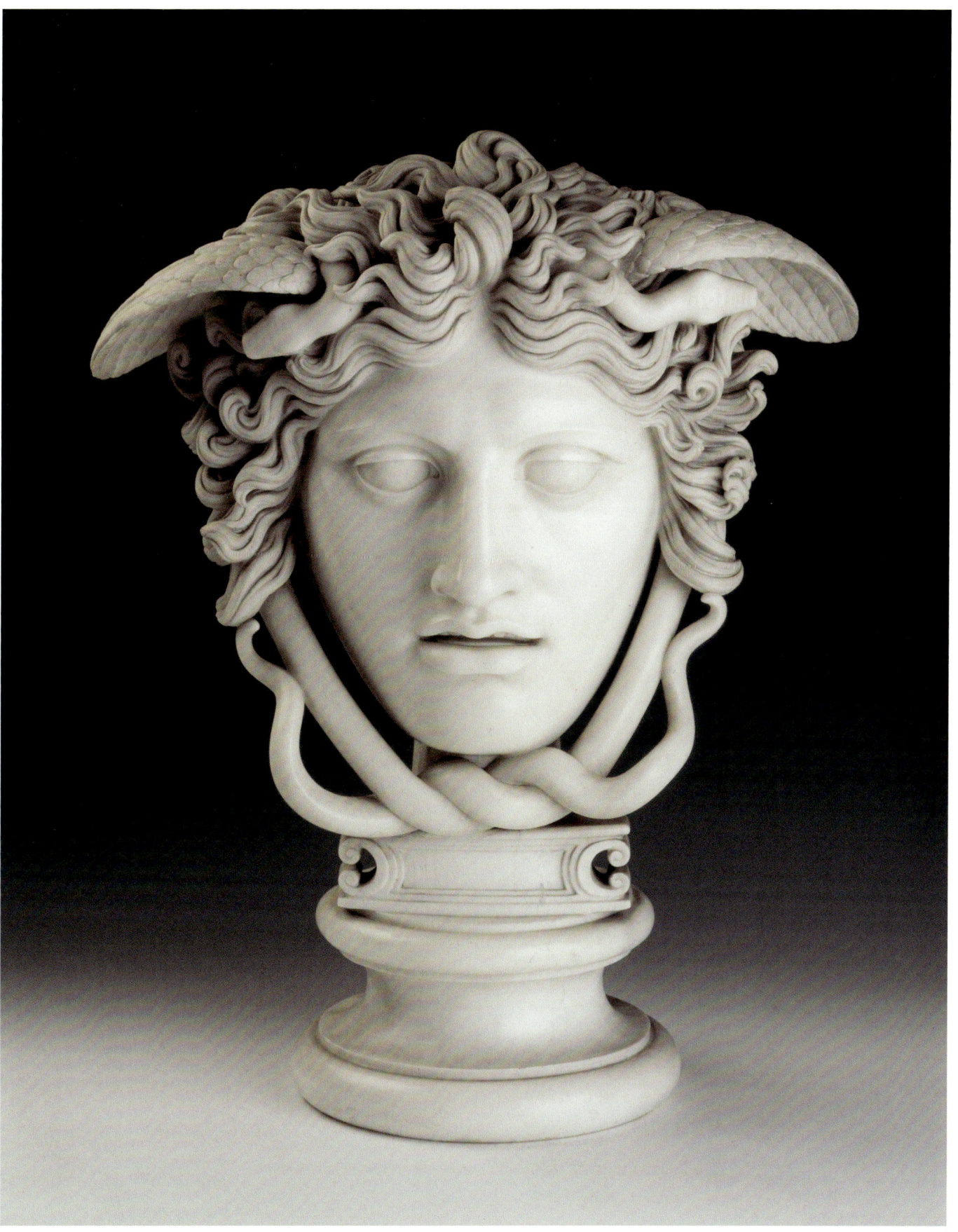

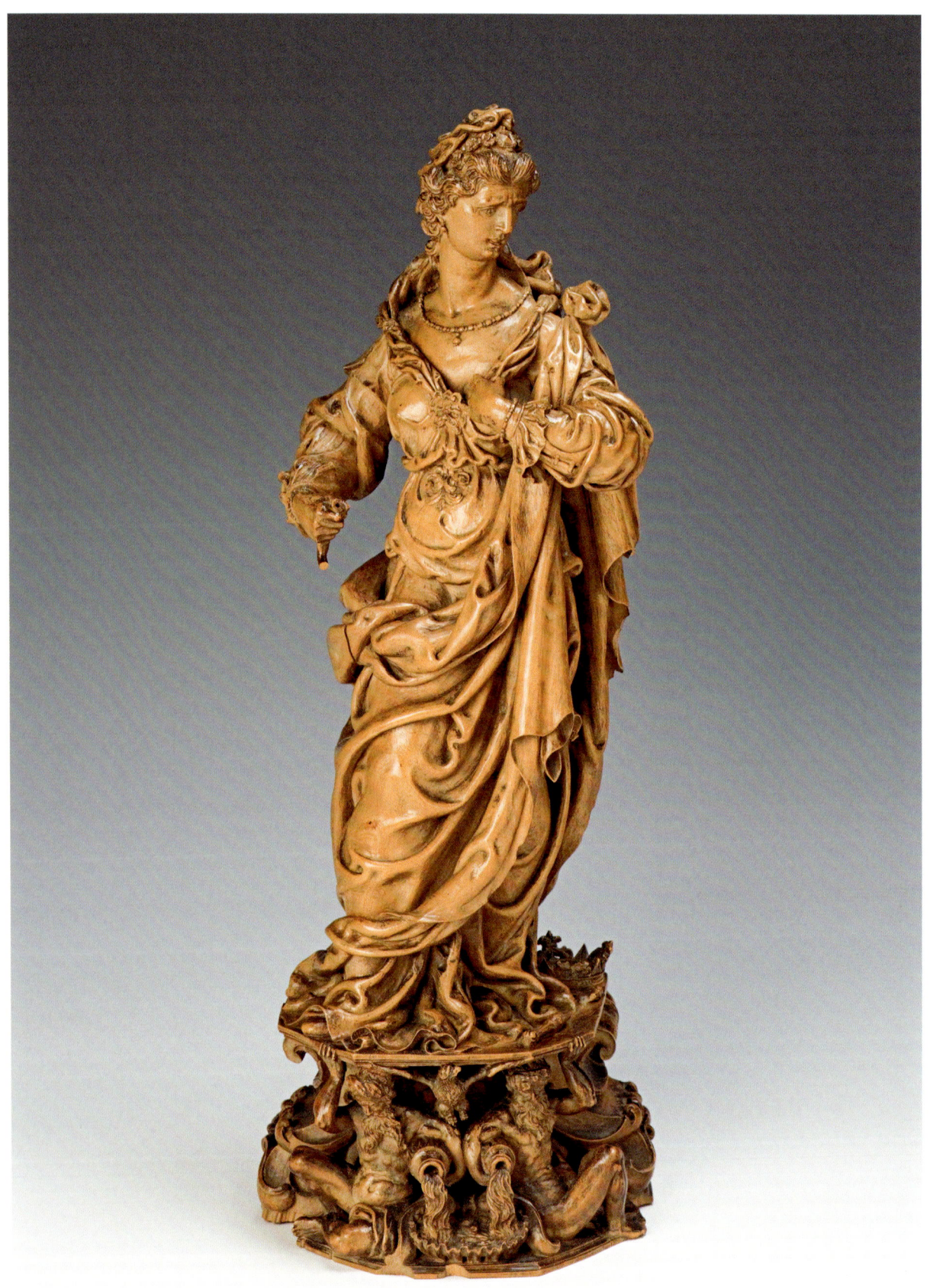

19

ANONYMOUS GERMAN ARTIST IN ITALY

Cleopatra, mid-17ᵗʰ century
Boxwood, 37 x 15 cm

––––––––––

Burghley House

This boxwood figure is one of a set of eight, probably made by a German craftsman working in Italy. They were purchased by John Cecil, 5ᵗʰ Earl of Exeter (c.1648-1700) during either his Tour of 1679 or that of 1684, as all of the group are recorded at Burghley House in the inventory of 1688. The statuettes average 37 cm in height and are crisply carved with heavy undercutting at the plinths. Each base bears, within a cartouche, a minutely carved scene relevant to the deity or personage represented in the figure above. The plinth of *Cleopatra* has bearers delivering water from amphorae in a reference to the Nile. The bird with outstretched wings is probably an ibis, another allusion to Egypt. Her broken crown lies at her feet.

Other figures in the group represent Pallas Athena, Lucretia, Venus, Cicero, Alexander, Catalina and Mars. The 1688 inventory records them clearly:

'My Ladyes Dressing Roome – 2 figures carved in Box being a Cleopatra & an Pallace by –. My Ladyes Closett – 2 figures in Box a Venus, a Lucretia by –. The Best Bedd Chamber – 4 carved figures in Box a Alexander, …'.

It is amusing to note that the countess delicately retained the female figures for her own private apartments whilst the male figures were relegated to a guest room.

Two of the bases bear original carved inscriptions or marks, subsequently mutilated with a gouge. On the *Alexander* the inscription '*A.27. D. Gennaie incominciata questa figura*', suggests 'From the 27ᵗʰ D[ay] of January commenced this figure'. On the *Pallas Athena* appears '*A. primo Aprile*', the first of April.

The Victoria and Albert Museum in London exhibits two similar wood statuettes, a *Caesar* and an *Alexander*. Both have finely finished plinths with cartouche scenes and display the same mannerism in the treatment of the figures. The bases on these examples have been extensively gouged, one in a very rough fashion. Former curator of sculpture of the Victoria and Albert Museum, Dr Charles Avery, records that he has examined a further pair, a *Bacchus* and a *Marine Venus*, related in general terms to the others, but apparently of a much later date and with less elaboration of the plinths. These were said to be part of a now scattered set of six which had a possible North Italian provenance.[108]

JC

20-21

ANONYMOUS NORTH GERMAN ARTIST IN ITALY

***St Peter and St Simon the Zealot*, 17th century**
Amber, height 11 cm, including pedestals

Burghley House

The question of the religious beliefs of the 5th Earl and his Countess has been discussed at length and often. They lived during a time when Catholicism, whilst not forbidden, was frowned upon in England. The earl was not political, spending most of his time away from London. A child of the Interregnum, he had learnt, from seeing the properties of others seized as punishment for dissent, that maintaining a low profile was a wise course of action for Catholics. Extended European travels fitted well with this belief.

The dramatic fashion of the portrayal of religious scenes, so favoured by the Catholic Church, is reflected in so many of the Exeter's purchases that there can be little doubt of their approval of this ideal. Their final journey, which began in 1699, was timed to bring them to Rome for the Jubilee celebrations of 1700. Their documented itinerary records that they were well-received by the Pope.

The purchase of these two small figures, beautifully carved in amber, follows the trend of their purchases of religious artworks. St Peter is shown carrying the keys to Heaven whilst St Simon holds his attribute, a saw. He was martyred for his belief by being sawn apart. The style of the carving is North German, however, as with the boxwood figure of Cleopatra (see cat. no. 19), many German artists were working in the more lucrative Italian market during this period.

JC

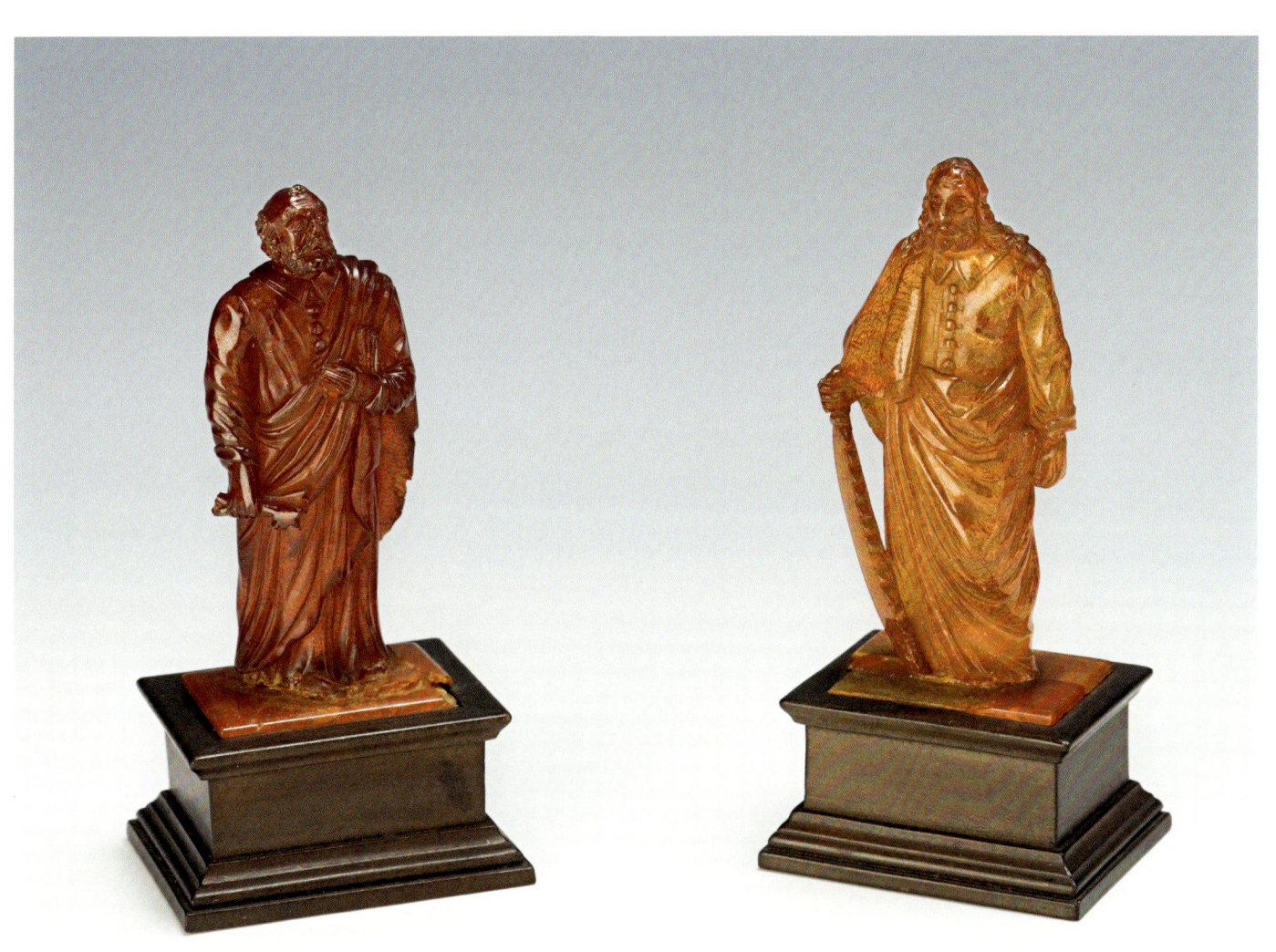

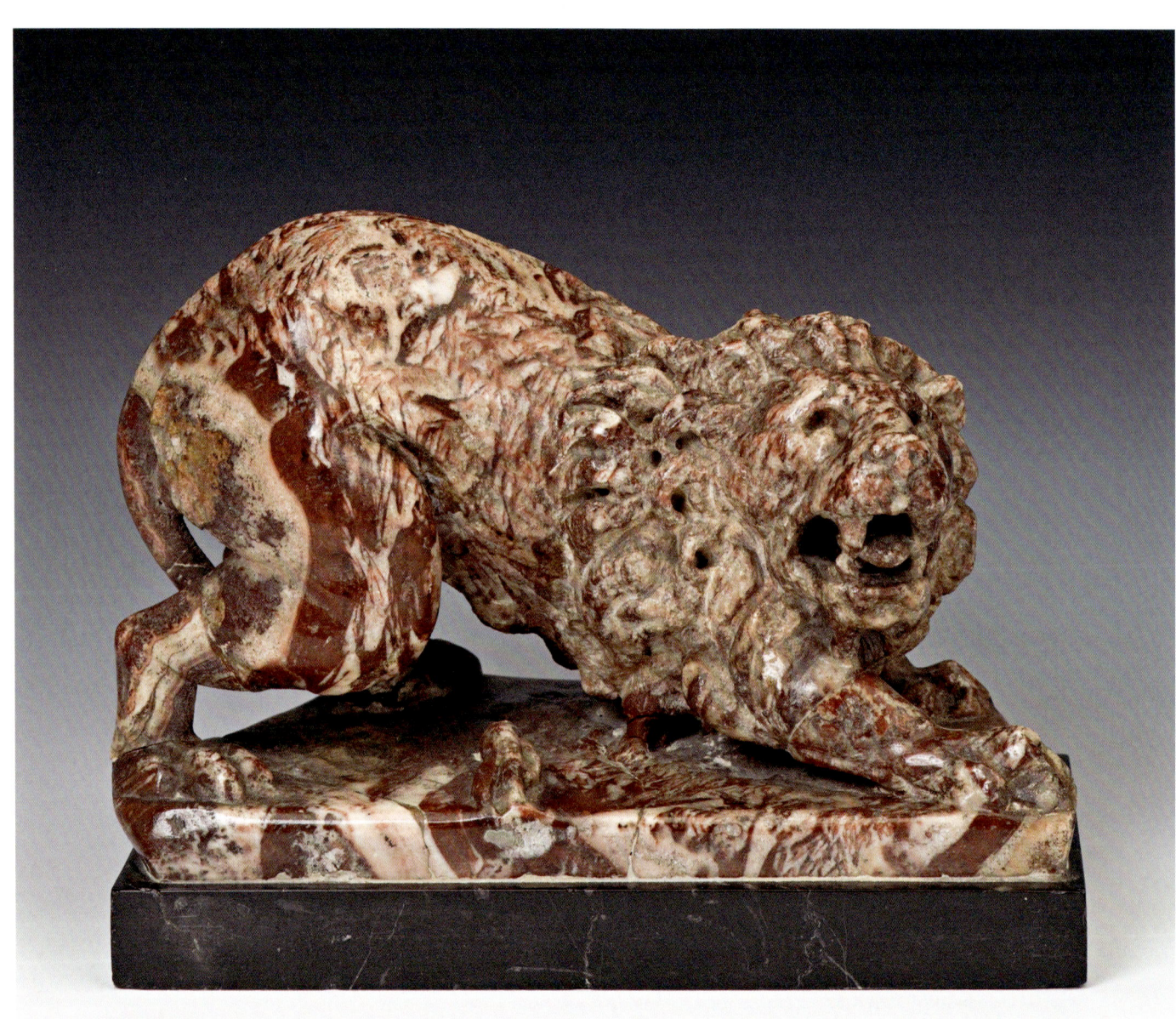

22

ANONYMOUS

A Crouching Lion, **probably 18th century**
Pink marble, 16.5 x 23 cm

Burghley House

This piece was purchased in Italy by Brownlow Cecil, 9th Earl of Exeter (1725-1793) during his second Grand Tour. The earl left England in 1768 and reached Rome in March 1769, where he quickly became part of the fashionable set of aristocratic travellers that were courted by antiquaries such as James Byers (1733-1817) and Thomas Jenkins (1722-1798). This piece was bought from Jenkins as having been excavated from the ruins of the port of Ostia nearly half a century earlier. It is listed in the inventory of Burghley House that was commenced by the earl in 1763: 'the dining room, 4 George room ... Fig. of a Lion Marble found at Ostia 1725 upon ye chimney'. However, it may be a fake made in one of the prolifically active studios that flourished in Rome, specialising in the production of such items for Grand Tourists. The most famous studio was that of Bartolomeo Cavaceppi (c.1716-1799).

Ostia was an ancient seaport situated some 25 kilometres from Rome at the mouth of the river Tiber. As the main port serving Rome, it became an important and populous city during the first and second centuries CE, when it had a population of 100,000. After the fall of the Roman Empire, the harbour gradually became unusable due to the build-up of silt and sand, and was abandoned as a commercial port. The site was first quarried for marble during the eighteenth century, after which the Vatican authorities began serious excavations seeking antiquities in the early nineteenth century. In the twentieth century, Benito Mussolini (1883-1945) undertook massive excavations there until prevented by the escalation of World War II.

JC

23

ANONYMOUS, ITALY (CASTELLI)

Majolica Trembleuse, c.1720
Glazed earthenware, 18 x 18 cm

———————

Burghley House

The manufacture of tin-glazed earthenware is thought to have originated in Mesopotamia in the tenth century. The technique gradually spread westwards into Europe and was widespread by the fifteenth century, as European pottery gradually developed from utilitarian wares toward decorative objects. Spanish potteries produced splendid lustreware that attracted many wealthy Italian patrons. Export of these pieces via traders based on the island of Majorca led to them becoming known as 'majolica' in Italy. Italian potters soon began producing similar pieces using a bright palette of yellow, blue, green, purple, and red, painting in the *'istoriato'* (storytelling) style. In such pieces, biblical, mythological and historical scenes are painted with a realism (including the use of perspective) quite unlike any previous pottery decoration.

The main centres of production in Italy were Faenza and Urbino in the north, and Castelli near Naples.

This *trembleuse* (a saucer with a central cavity to hold a cup) is decorated with a mythological scene of the Titan Oceanus astride a sea monster and wielding his trident, with to his right Thetis, a sea goddess and the mother of the Greek hero Achilles.[109] The source for this illustration is the left half of an engraving by an anonymous artist after Hendrick Goltzius (1558-1617).[110]

Brownlow Cecil, 9th Earl of Exeter (1725-1793) was a keen collector of majolica, purchasing more than thirty examples during both of his Tours.

JC

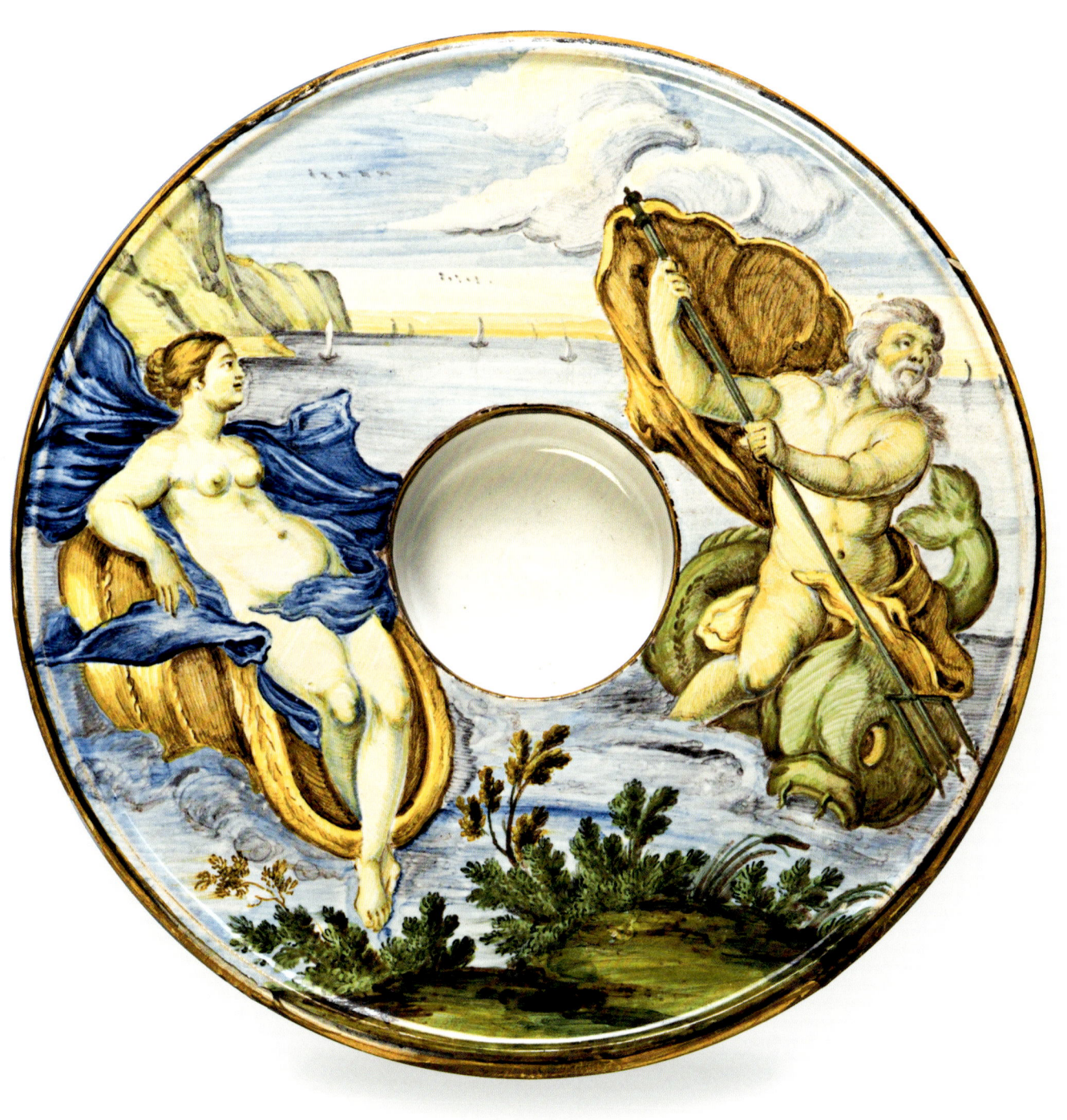

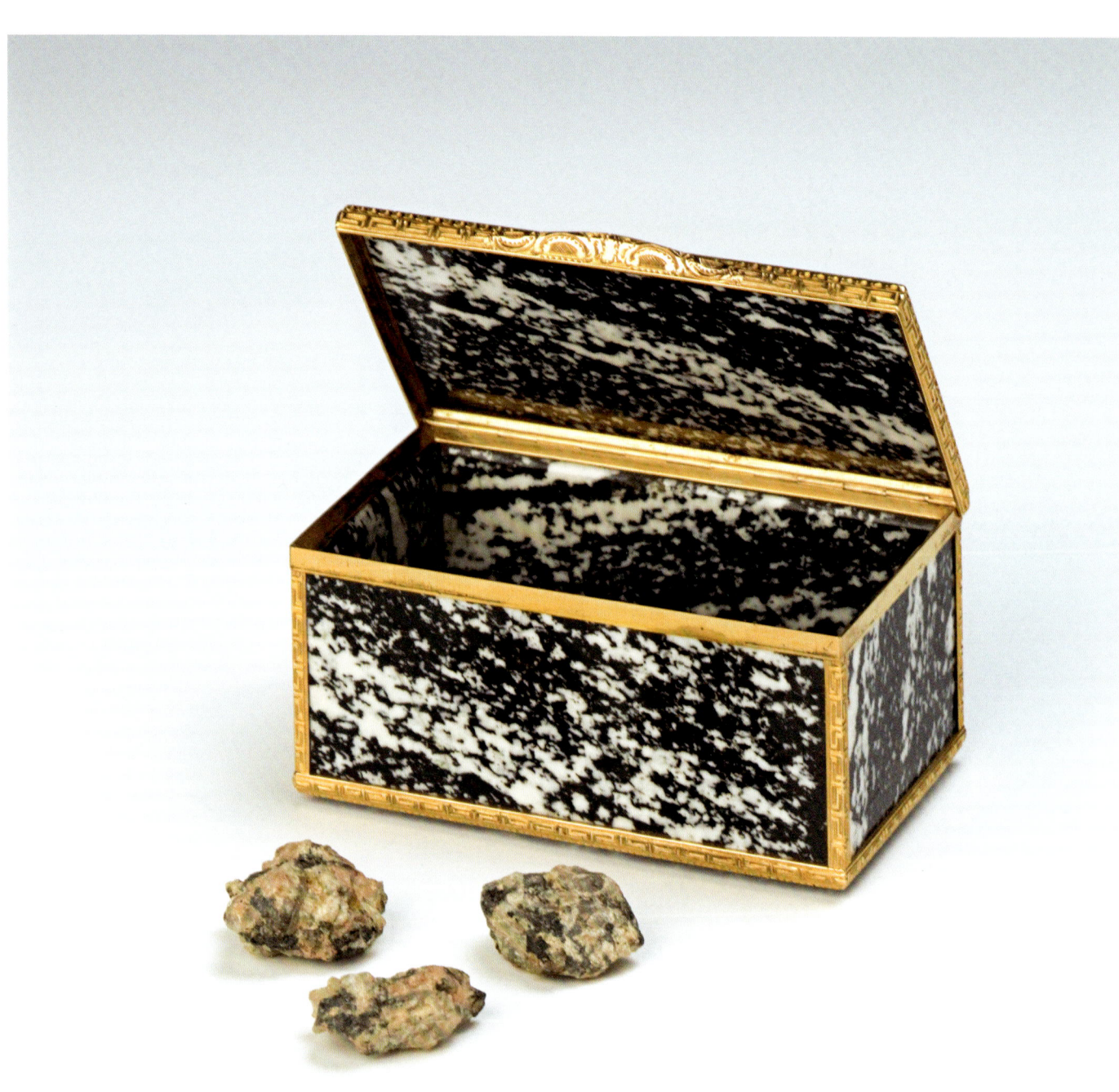

24

ANONYMOUS, ITALY

Snuff box with rocks, before 1767
Hardstone (black and white polished lava), gold,
width 7.5 cm

―――――――

Burghley House

This small box is typical of the type used to contain snuff: powdered tobacco that was inhaled as a mild stimulant by eighteenth century gentlemen. Made from small panels of black and white polished lava and mounted with gold banding and clasp, it contains three small stones and a note written in in the hand of Brownlow Cecil, 9th Earl of Exeter (1725-1793): 'This snuff box is made of Lava from the Island of Iskia near Naples; also containing three Pieces of Pompey's Pillar – A present from Capt. Bell of Lincolnshire, January 20th 1767 – He received them from Major Budgard, who had them from the Captain of the ship, who received them from the Sailors who drank a bowl of punch on the top of the Pillar'.

This charming provenance of the rock fragments is interesting. Pompey's Pillar is a remarkable ancient monument (c.300 CE): a single, monolithic column of red granite quarried in Aswan, Egypt, which stands in Alexandria on Egypt's northern coast. Including its base and capital, the column measures nearly 27 metres in height and originally supported a colossal seven-metre porphyry statue of the Roman emperor Diocletian. Its coastal location has always attracted tourists, particularly sailors, who are occasionally recorded as climbing the column using rope ladders, a remarkable feat. Several such ascents are mentioned in naval records of the eighteenth and nineteenth centuries, and they usually involved raising a flag and drinking a toast from the summit.

JC

25

ANONYMOUS INDO-PORTUGUESE ARTIST

Essence Bottle Carved in the Form of a Pine Cone,
17th century
Organic material, garnished with gold wire, height 7.8 cm

—————

Burghley House

Culpepper Tanner was the steward of John Cecil, 5th Earl of Exeter (c.1648-1700) and accompanied him on all his Continental trips. He was responsible for day-to-day matters whilst travelling and recorded any small expenses incurred by the party: payments to Italian servants, tolls, stabling and feed for the horses, grease for the wheels of the carriage and wagon, and the like. These notes were written, often obviously in haste and sometimes using rudimentary Italian. They remain in the archive at Burghley House and give a fascinating insight into the parties' progress.[111] They frequently visited well-known tourist sites, particularly those of religious significance, and often purchased fruit and iced drinks from roadside stalls in true tourist fashion. The notes also record more serious acquisitions:

> 'To Carlo Marat   600   0,   To Phillippo Laro   100   0,
> To Scyllo   074   0
> To Gimignano   104   0,   To Sigr Davide   125   0
> [David de Koninck]'.

Amongst the many exotic souvenirs purchased by the earl and his party, Tanner frequently records expenses for 'essences' and exotic potions such as 'Balsam Apoplecticum' and 'Venice Treacle'. On one occasion, he mentions an essence as being contained 'in a small flask in the shape of a pinecone'. This flask, garnished with gold wire, fits this description.

JC

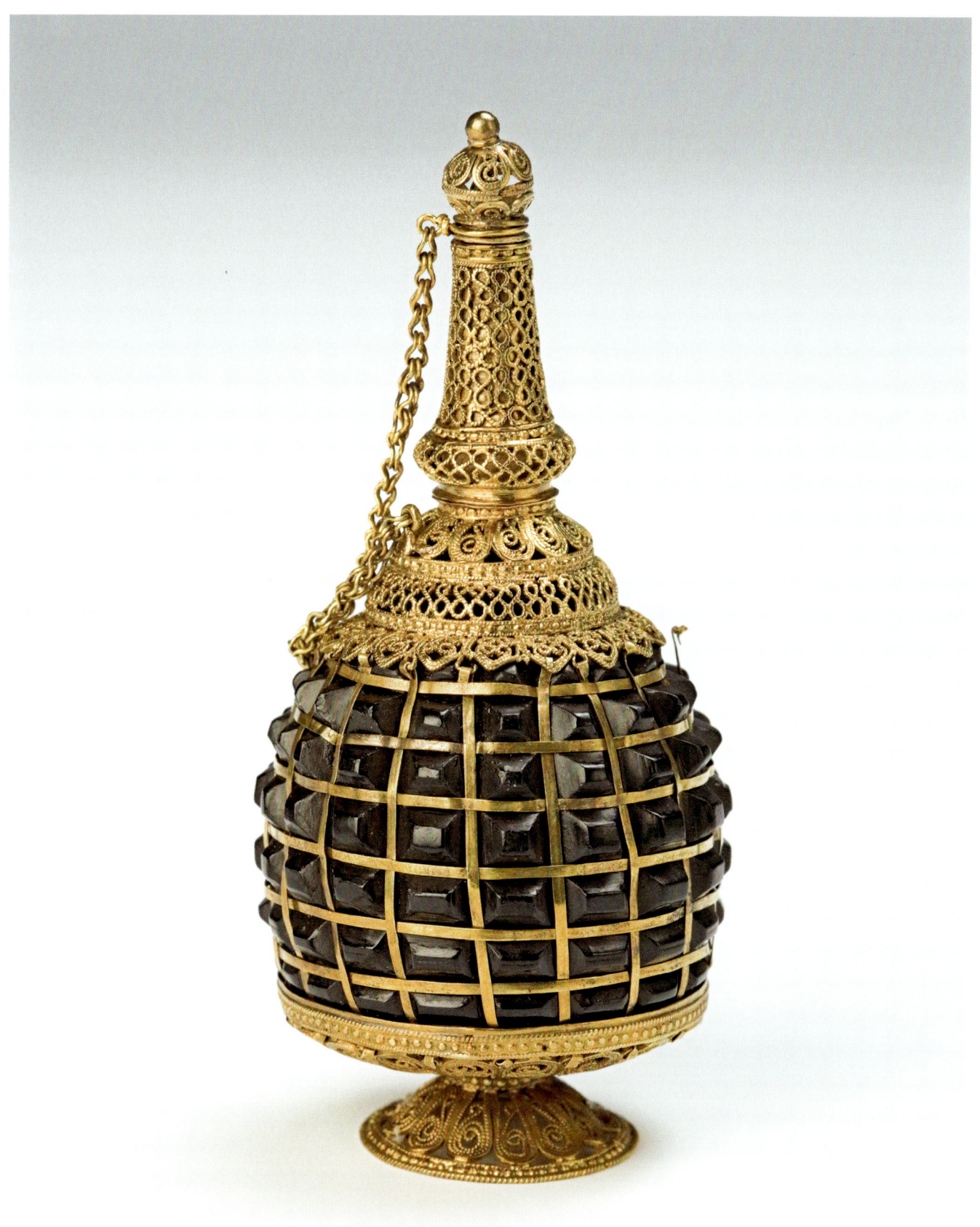

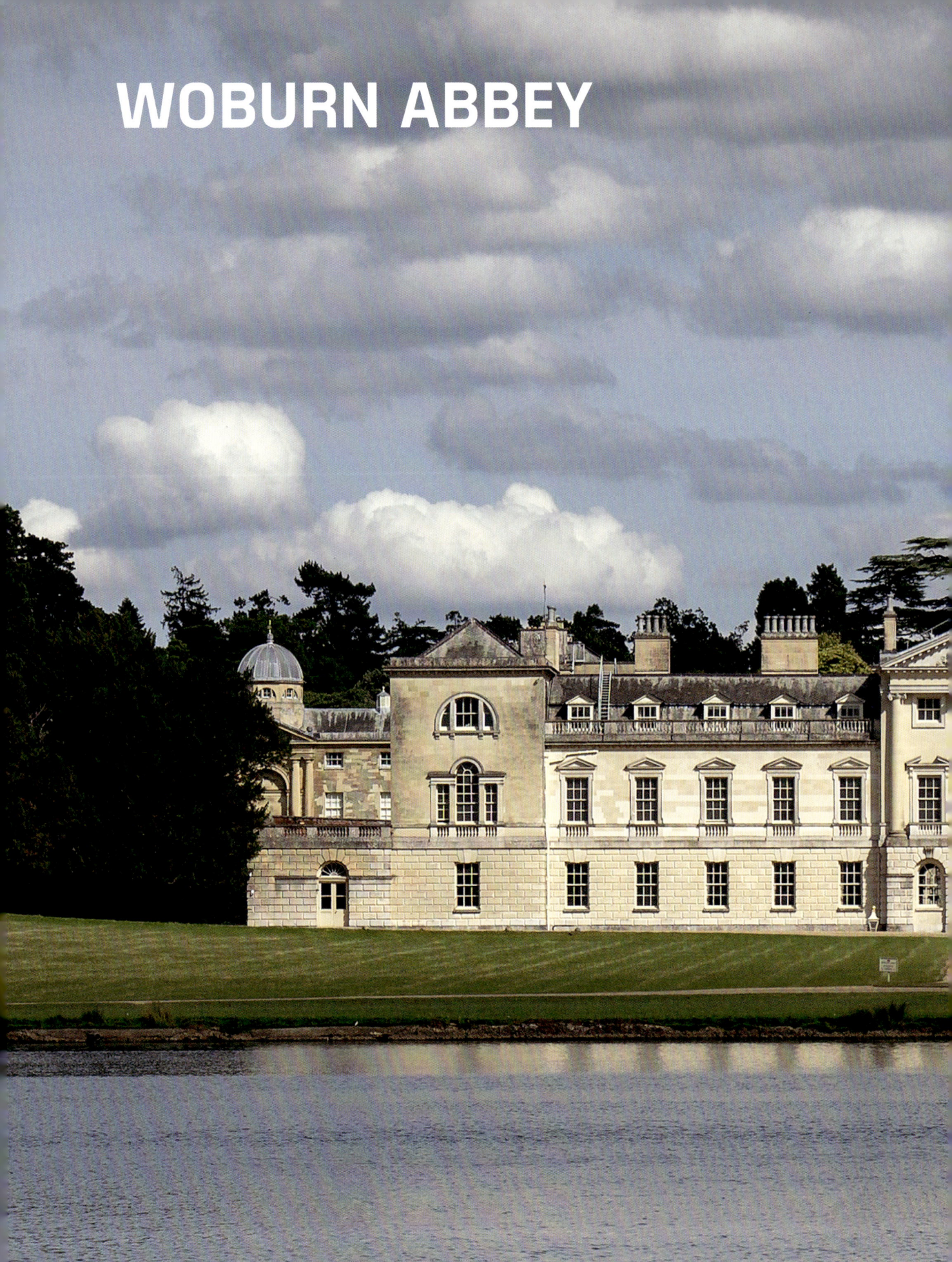

WOBURN ABBEY

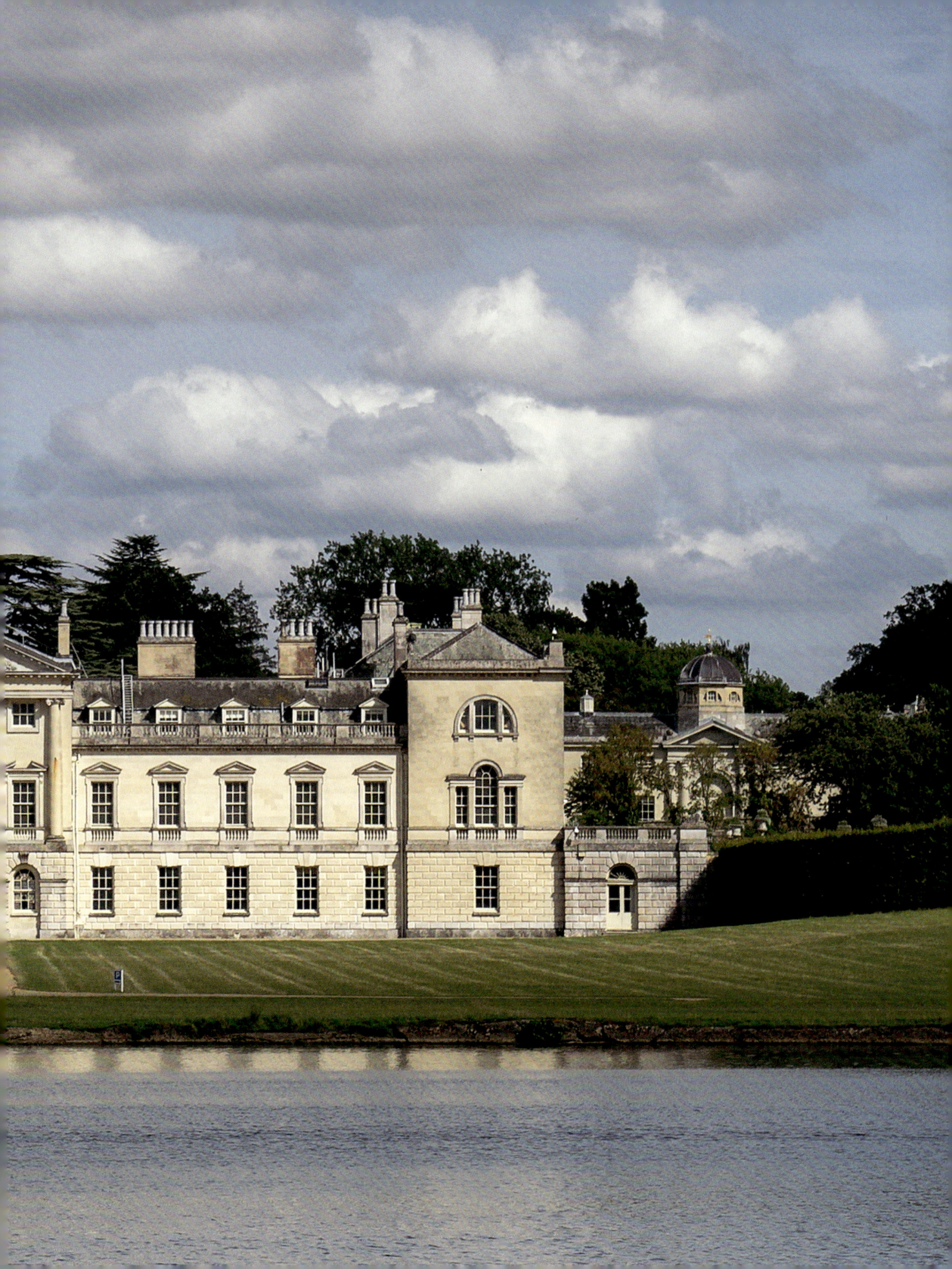

JOHN RUSSELL, 4TH DUKE OF BEDFORD, FRANCIS RUSSELL, MARQUESS OF TAVISTOCK, AND THE GRAND TOUR
WOBURN ABBEY AND ITS COLLECTION

Matthew Hirst

Lord John Russell (1710-1771), the younger brother of Wriothesley Russell, 3rd Duke of Bedford (1708-1732), embarked on a Grand Tour in 1728 – perhaps with a nascent expectation, though no guarantee, of inheriting the Bedford title and estates, which only became certain when his brother died without issue in 1732. John's son, Francis Russell, Marquess of Tavistock (1739-1767), embarked on his Tour in 1762 with the full expectation of an inheritance – an expectation never fulfilled due to his sad and early death at the age of 27, shortly after returning home. Both men are recognised for making a significant contribution to Woburn Abbey (fig. 1) and its collection, in part as a result of their Grand Tour travels.

John became the 4th Duke of Bedford shortly after returning home from Italy (fig. 2; see cat. no. 26). Before inheriting, he had already demonstrated a predilection for building and in 1730 he purchased the family estate of Stratton Park, Hampshire, from his elder brother. With the assistance of the architect John Sanderson (active 1730-1774), he embarked on an ambitious new house in the neo-Palladian style, inspired by the Italian Renaissance architect Andrea Palladio (1508-1580). Subsequently much altered, and then demolished in 1803, it is today only known from a small series of design drawings, and the published engravings in *Vitruvius Britannicus*, a publication on British architecture from 1767 (fig. 3). This substantial country residence featured a suite of State Rooms and a 'Great Gallery' of 30 by 7 metres, which occupied the entire east wing and terminated in a large Venetian window at each end. The plan reveals limited fenestration on the long external wall, suggesting that it was conceived principally as a gallery for the display of pictures, and perhaps as the original intended home for the views by Canaletto (1697-1768) John had acquired in Venice (see cat. nos. 30 and 31). By the time the Canaletto paintings were arriving in England, from 1732, John had inherited the Bedford title, and attention was turned to developing other areas of his estate. The paintings were displayed in Bedford House, Bloomsbury, for the next 50 years.

At Woburn Abbey, the family's principal seat, Sanderson was invited in 1733 to survey the existing structures, which largely comprised former monastic buildings remodelled in the seventeenth century. Sanderson proposed various ambitious designs for the new house, but these were ultimately set aside in favour of Henry Flitcroft's (1697-1769) schemes in 1747. Though Sanderson's architectural schemes were not realised, he did have success acting as agent for John, acquiring eight marbles by the Flemish sculptor Laurent Delvaux (1696-1778) on his behalf. The sculptures replicate famous antique and Renaissance models that John may have seen first-hand in Rome, such as the *Crouching Venus*, *Frowning Caracalla Bust* and Gianlorenzo Bernini's (1598-1680) *David*.[112]

The architectural scheme that Flitcroft proposed for Woburn Abbey largely replaced the surviving monastic accommodation, creating a new range of state apartments on the west side of the site, curtailed at each end by the buildings put up in the 1630s by Francis Russell, the 4th Earl of Bedford (1587-1641). This preserved the

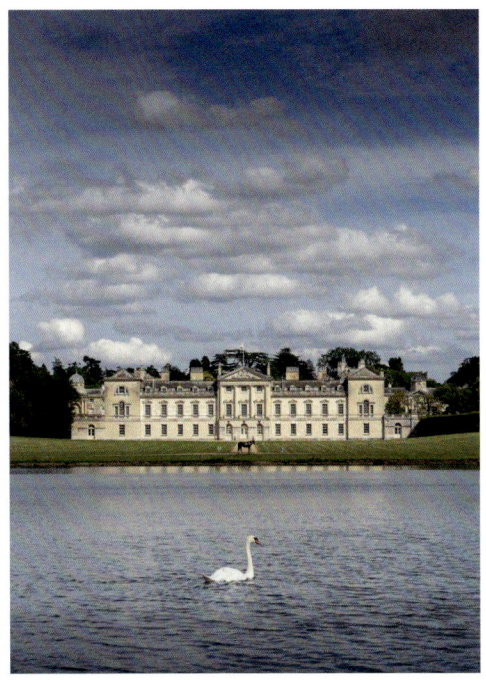

Fig. 1
Woburn Abbey, Bedfordshire,
View on the west façade

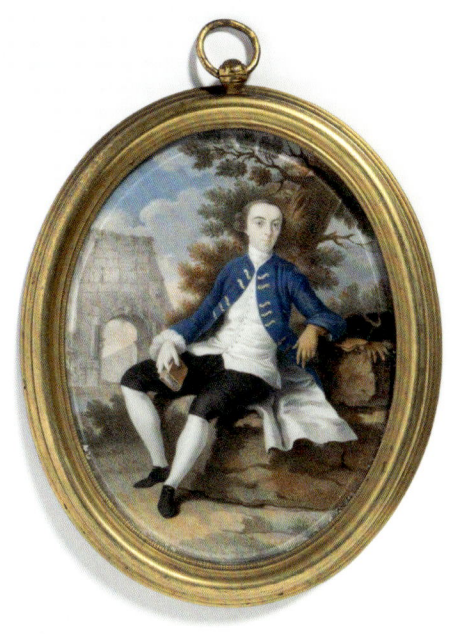

Fig. 2
Orsola Urbani (attributed to), *Portrait of a Man
traditionally identified as Lord John Russell, later
4th Duke of Bedford (1710-1771)*, c. 1730. Watercolour
on ivory, 15,4 x 12 cm, Woburn Abbey. (cat. no. 26)

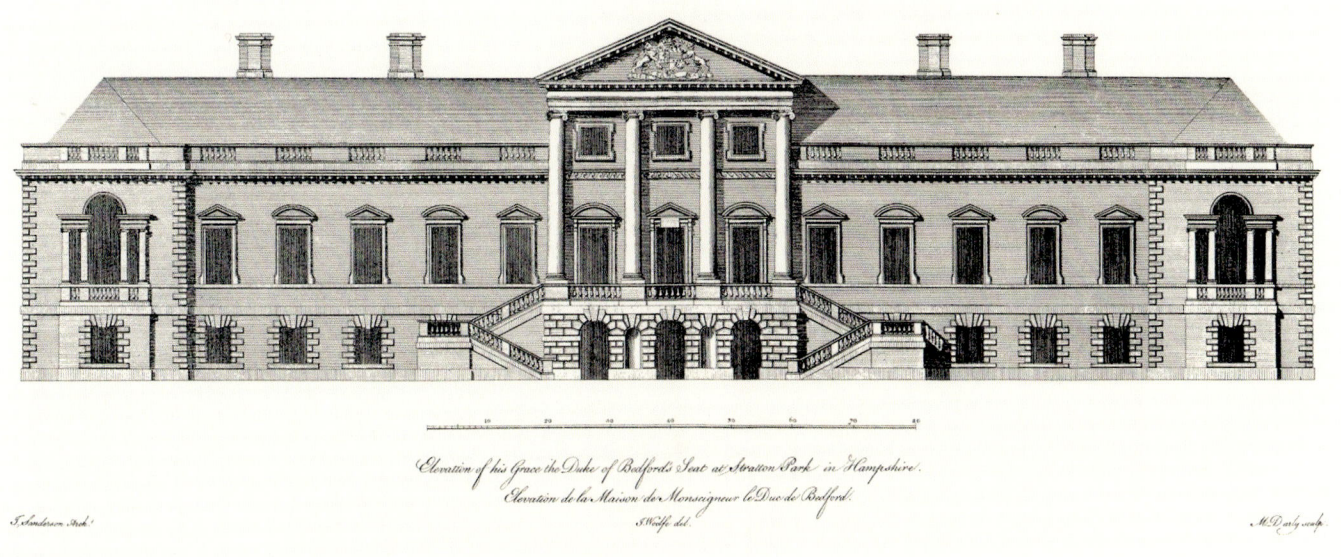

Fig. 3
Colen Campbell, *Elevation of His Grace the Duke
of Bedford's Seat at Stratton Park in Hampshire*,
in: *Vitruvius Britannicus, or the British Architect
1715-1717*

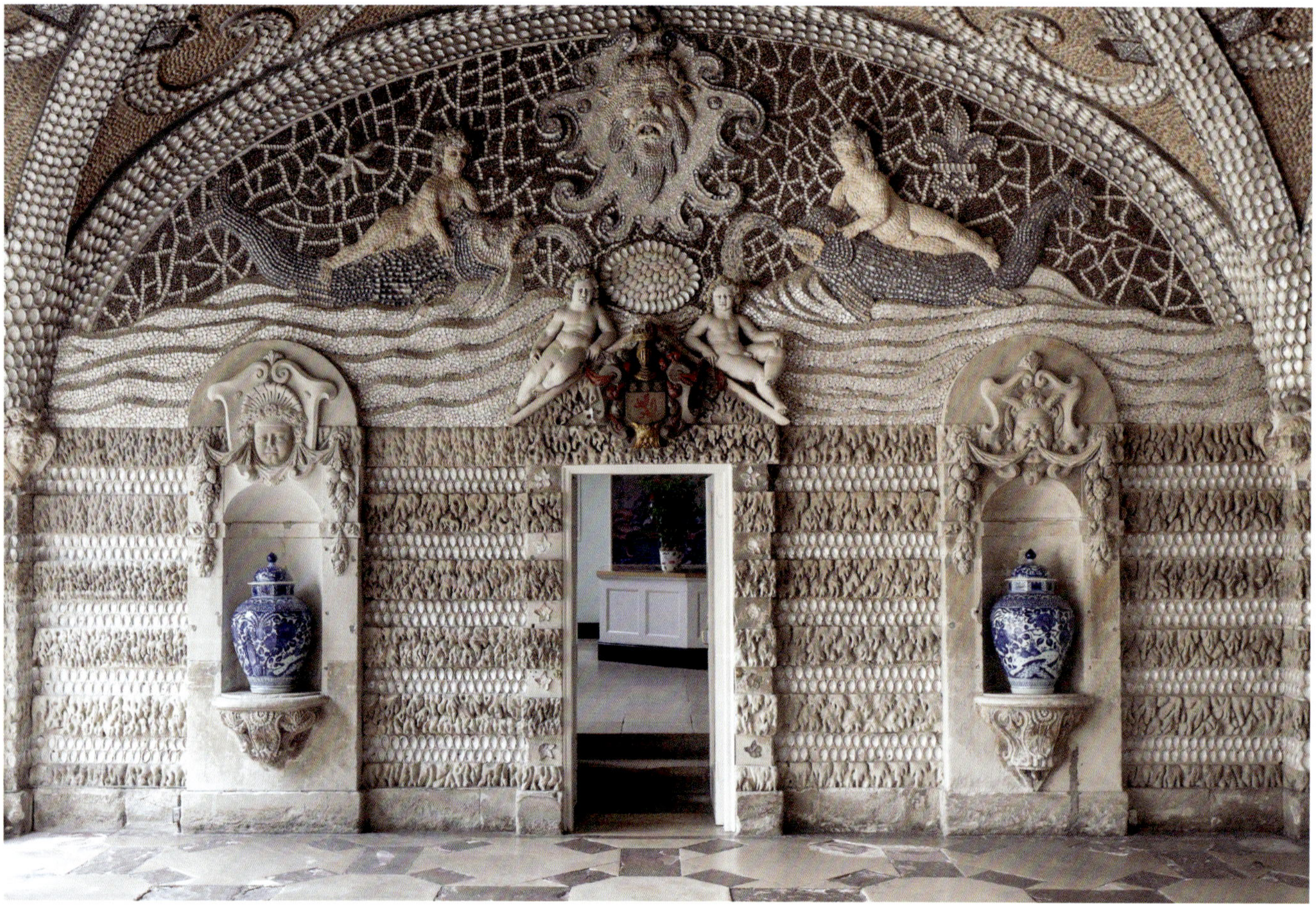

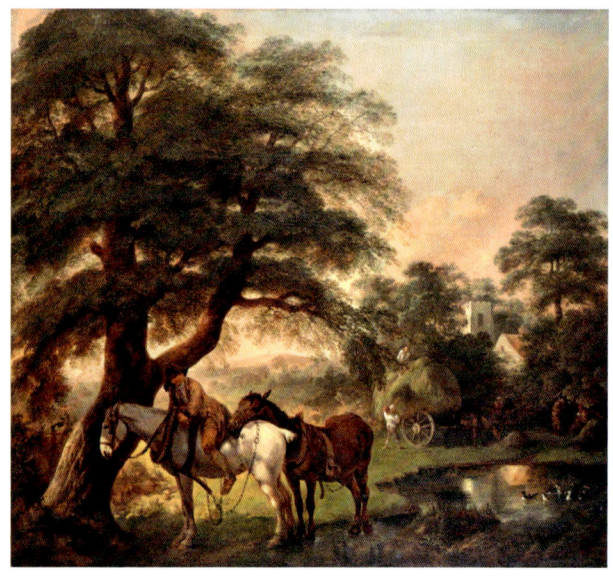

Fig. 4
The Grotto Apartments on the North Side
of Woburn Abbey

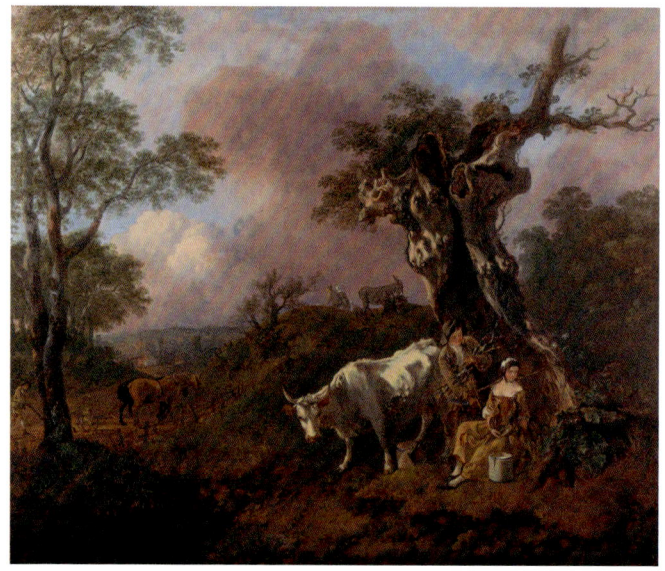

Fig. 5
homas Gainsborough, *A Wooded Landscape*, 1755.
Canvas, 92 x 102 cm. Woburn Abbey

Fig. 6
Thomas Gainsborough, *The Milkmaid*, 1755.
Canvas, 108.6 x 129.5 cm. Woburn Abbey

important Grotto Apartment (fig. 4) on the north side (which still survives today) and the 4th Earl's Library and garden loggia on the south.[113] Flitcroft swept away the range of kitchens that had subdivided the central court of the Abbey and originally formed one side of the cloister, and refaced the enlarged court on each side. The east range was remodelled, converting the last surviving monastic fabric, including the former Chapter House, into domestic service accommodation and stabling.

The building project is documented both formally, in an incredibly detailed series of account books and vouchers, and informally, in John's pocketbooks.[114] A prolific note-taker, the Duke recorded thoughts and tasks ranging from the purchase of fine art to the repair of fences as he went about his daily business in the 1740s to 1760s. Delightfully for the historian today, he fastidiously scored through each entry once it was complete. There is scant evidence of his activity prior to this period, especially during his Grand Tour, save for a curious earlier pocketbook listing an ambitious itinerary and various cash withdrawals.[115]

In order to furnish the walls of his new Palladian country house, John continued to acquire paintings in the 1740s and 1750s, both on the art market in London and while travelling. [116] For example, in 1741, while touring in the Netherlands, he acquired Peter Wouverman's *View of Pont Neuf* for £20.[117] Exposure to art on the Continent fostered a demand for similar pictures at home, demonstrating the longer-term influence of the Grand Tour in shaping aristocratic collections. There is no firm evidence that John acquired other works of art, additional to the Canaletto paintings, on his Grand Tour. In fact, the availability of such an active art trade in England reduced the necessity of shipping artworks directly from abroad.[118] Italian paintings were especially prized, including religious pictures at odds with Protestant Whig sensibilities. In London, the Duke engaged an artist-conservator, Isaac Colivoe (c.1702-1769), who accompanied him to sale rooms to advise on acquisitions.[119] In addition to frequenting sale rooms, the Duke also commissioned artists to paint decorative works for his new house, such as two overmantles by Thomas Gainsborough (1727-1788) purchased in 1755 (figs. 5 and 6).[120]

Today, we regard the furniture and decorative arts as an integral part of the collection at Woburn Abbey, although John would have seen them as essential furnishings and equipment. He added vast quantities of new English furniture by the leading craftsmen of the day to decorate the rooms, which now form an important expression of his taste. For example, a suite of impressive table silver was supplied by a number of Huguenot craftsmen, including Paul de Lamerie (1688-1751).

In 1767, the 4th Duke's son Francis (fig. 7; see cat. no. 27) suffered a tragic accident and predeceased his father. His collection of artworks was absorbed into the family collection, or sold. Whilst on his Grand Tour five years earlier, he had been cautious of the agents and dealers lying in wait to exploit the naivety of a young man culturing an interest in art. He was particularly suspicious of Thomas Jenkins (1722-1798), painter-turned-dealer, whom he felt had 'great hopes of plundering me', but with whom he did spend £457.4.0.[121] Francis tried to cultivate the expected interest in art, though the tone of his correspondence is revealing. To his friend Thomas Robinson (1738-1786), he sent bored, gossipy letters and – just at Genoa – remarked that he had seen enough paintings 'to amuse me (I think) for a whole year'.[122] Returned home to his responsibilities, his letters to his impressionable young cousin were more didactic and erudite. As well as the surviving correspondence, he annotated guidebooks and notebooks, updating the margins with things he had seen, missed or which made no impression. The notebook for Rome is arranged by type rather than following a sequence of viewing, reflecting the view that Rome was a city of 'objects'.[123] As well as acquiring works of art, prints, and sculpture on his travels, he also acquired a series of marble discs, which were later inset into pier tables by Benjamin Vulliamy (1747-1811).

Francis was most impressed with sculpture, particularly 'the *Apollo Belvedere*, the *Laococoon* & *Antinous* (which are all I have seen at Rome) have at once opened my eyes to the beauties of this branch. The first is the finest object of any sort of kind ever beheld'.[124] He acquired a copy of the *Apollo Belvedere* from Pietro Pacilli (1720-1773) on behalf of his father for £250.0.0, and it stood in the entrance hall of Bedford House, Bloomsbury, before the house was demolished around 1800.[125] From Florence, he wrote to his father to complain that none of the women would talk to him in French, though it was clear they could understand it, and that he was amused that he had engaged the same valet who had accompanied his father decades previously.[126] Whilst there, he acquired two scagliola tops from Lamberto Cristiano Gori (1730-1801), which were subsequently incorporated into commodes upon return to England.

Francis did not have the opportunity to continue developing his collection or make alterations to the family seat. On his death, his collections – including a case with patterns of curious marble, books, maps, and prints – were sent to Bedford House for safekeeping. The homes he had recently refurbished were abandoned: Houghton House was dismantled and gutted in 1794. Adjacent to his cousin Lord Ossory's Ampthill Park, the ruins were included as a point of interest in Lancelot 'Capability' Brown's (1716-1783) proposals for relandscaping, before being formally acquired by Ossory in 1804. His ruined house therefore survives today as a melancholy reminder of this chapter in the family's history, but the remnants of his collection have long been incorporated into those of his ancestors and descendants at Woburn Abbey. In 1804, his son John Russell, 6th Duke of Bedford (1766-1839), wrote about discovering some bronzes and marbles bought by his father in Rome, 'which till very lately had not been unpacked'. It is likely that this discovery prompted the conversion of the Orangery into a Sculpture Gallery and the development of the significant sculpture collections at Woburn.[127]

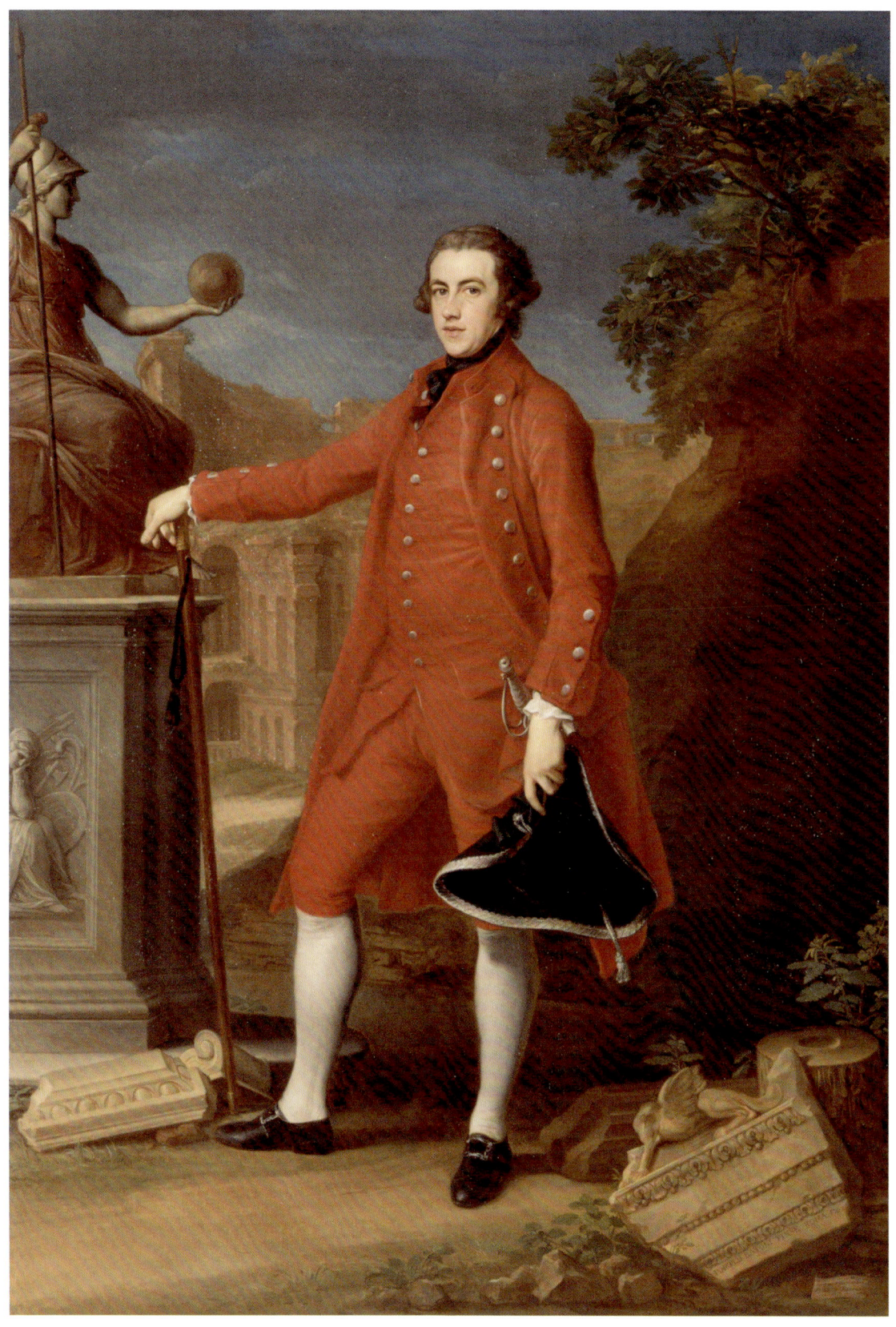

Fig. 7
Pompeo Batoni, *Portrait of Francis, Marquess Of Tavistock*
(1739–1767), 1762. Canvas, 241.3 x 166.4 cm. Woburn Abbey

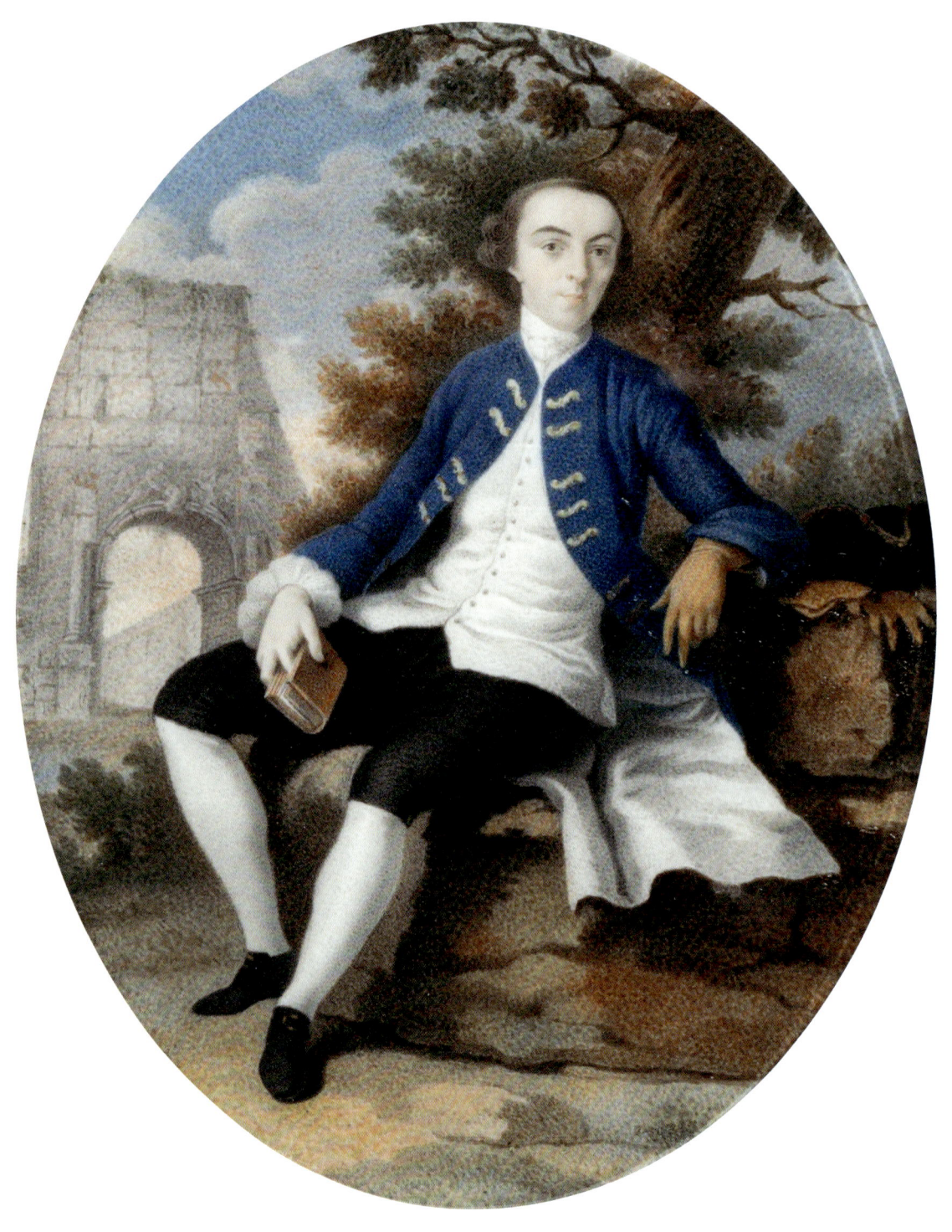

26

ORSOLA URBANI (ATTRIBUTED TO)

Portrait of a Man Traditionally Identified as Lord John Russell, later 4th Duke of Bedford (1710-1771), c.1730

Watercolour on ivory, 15.4 x 12 cm

—————

Woburn Abbey

A Grand Tourist, traditionally identified as John Russell, 4th Duke of Bedford, relaxes against a rock, with a finger holding the page of a pocketbook or guide. In the background is the ruin of the Arch of Titus in Rome, with reclining figures in the spandrels and the distinctive sloped edge. It shows the eastern elevation with the rough stonework entablature, rather than the western side which still retained its travertine marble inscription. The portrait has been attributed to Orsola Urbani, a copyist and painter of miniature portraits in Rome (active 1738-1757).

The Duke, then Lord, embarked on the Grand Tour in 1728 and was in Rome by the Autumn of 1730. Unlike his son, Francis Russell, Marquess of Tavistock (1739-1767; see cat. no. 27), there is little evidence for his personal thoughts and feelings by way of correspondence or journals. What does survive is a curious pocketbook – possibly the one depicted on this miniature – listing an ambitious itinerary representative of the most 'indefatigable', 'intrepid' or 'inveterate' traveller, with a Tour that extended into the Netherlands, Spain, Scandinavia, Poland, Russia, Germany, and the Ottoman Empire.[128] Previously overlooked and attributed to his elder brother, Wriothesley, 3rd Duke of Bedford (d.1732), it has been proven beyond reasonable doubt that the book fleetingly records John's travels and can be reconciled with the 'fragment' mentioned in his published correspondence.[129] The book in Woburn Abbey's archive is dirty and stained, as to be expected from the pocketbook of a well-travelled Grand Tourist. It is an incomplete record of financial transactions, but offers some evidence of destinations on his travels. It has not yet been possible to corroborate the itinerary against the notes on the pages. His Grand Tour may have been curtailed by the death of his brother in 1732, and a shift in priorities towards the management of the Bedford Estates.

VP

27

JOSHUA REYNOLDS

Portrait of Francis Russell, Marquess of Tavistock (1739-1767), 1765-1766
Canvas, 123 x 98 cm

———

Woburn Abbey

Francis Russell, Marquess of Tavistock, son of the 4th Duke of Bedford, is shown here in a pensive pose, surrounded by attributes of a Grand Tourist. A bronze statue of *Samson Slaying the Philistine* after Michelangelo (1475-1564; see cat. no. 28), a souvenir from his travels, acts as a paperweight for the loose rolled papers and prints on the gilt-wood table. Leaning against the table is an oval painting, *en grisaille*, which is likely to be the 'shield with a Battle Painted on it with a Brass rim' recorded in the inventory of his effects taken in 1767.[130]

Writing to his friend Thomas Robinson (1738-1786), future 2nd Baron Grantham, in March 1762, Francis reports that so far in Rome he had 'only bought some prints & a little basso relievo'.[131] This is confirmed by the account books of his personal servant, George Rawson, which record consecutive payments to porters for the sculpture, and a bill for prints.[132] In the painting, volumes and papers are casually stacked on a stool, one mezzotint slightly folded over the open-book by Francis's bent knee.

Tavistock undertook an intense Tour of Italy, commencing in the winter of 1761 and returning to London in May 1762. He had a relatively short sojourn compared to many peers, but extensive nonetheless. Correspondence places him in Turin in December 1761, Florence in January 1762, Naples in February, and Rome in March; then in Bologna, Vicenza, Verona, San Michele, Brescia, and Milan during April and May, following the itinerary set by his friend Robinson. Despite writing in thanks to him that he had 'sure seen more in six months than many have done in 2 years', he advised his cousin John Fitzpatrick, 2nd Earl of Upper Ossory (1745-1818), to experience Italy at a more leisurely pace, with at least three months in Rome and a month in Bologna.[133]

He recollected his travels with great fondness, and travelled vicariously through his cousin when he embarked on his own Tour: 'I long to hasten to Italy (in idea only, I mean)' and provided a detailed itinerary 'for I shall observe the route I went in, speaking of the different places', entreating John Fitzpatrick to return the letter as a useful personal reminder.[134] Perhaps another sign of Francis's wistful longing for Italy is evidenced in his acquisition in London of a painting by Richard Wilson (1714-1782) of *Rome from the Villa Madama*, in the same year he sat for this portrait.

Although displaying typical characteristics of a Grand Tour portrait painted in Italy, this portrait was in fact painted several years after he returned from his travels, by one of the leading British portraitists. Joshua Reynolds (1723-1792) had travelled in Italy in 1749, a journey that was enabled by Francis's future brother-in-law, Captain Augustus Keppel.[135] He did not seek to monetise his trip by painting souvenir portraits, but his work was greatly influenced by his time in Italy and the sketchbook after Old Masters he compiled there.

VP

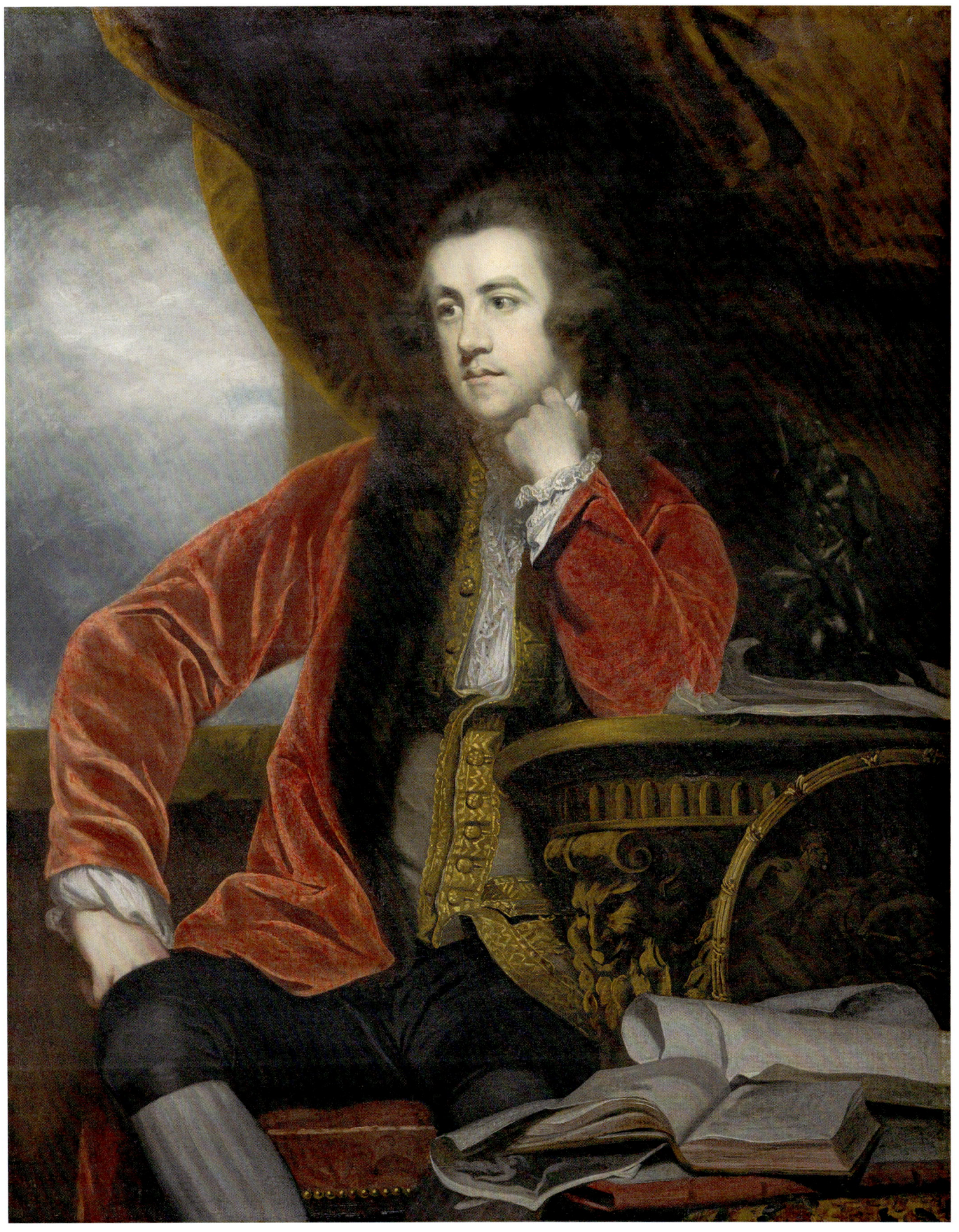

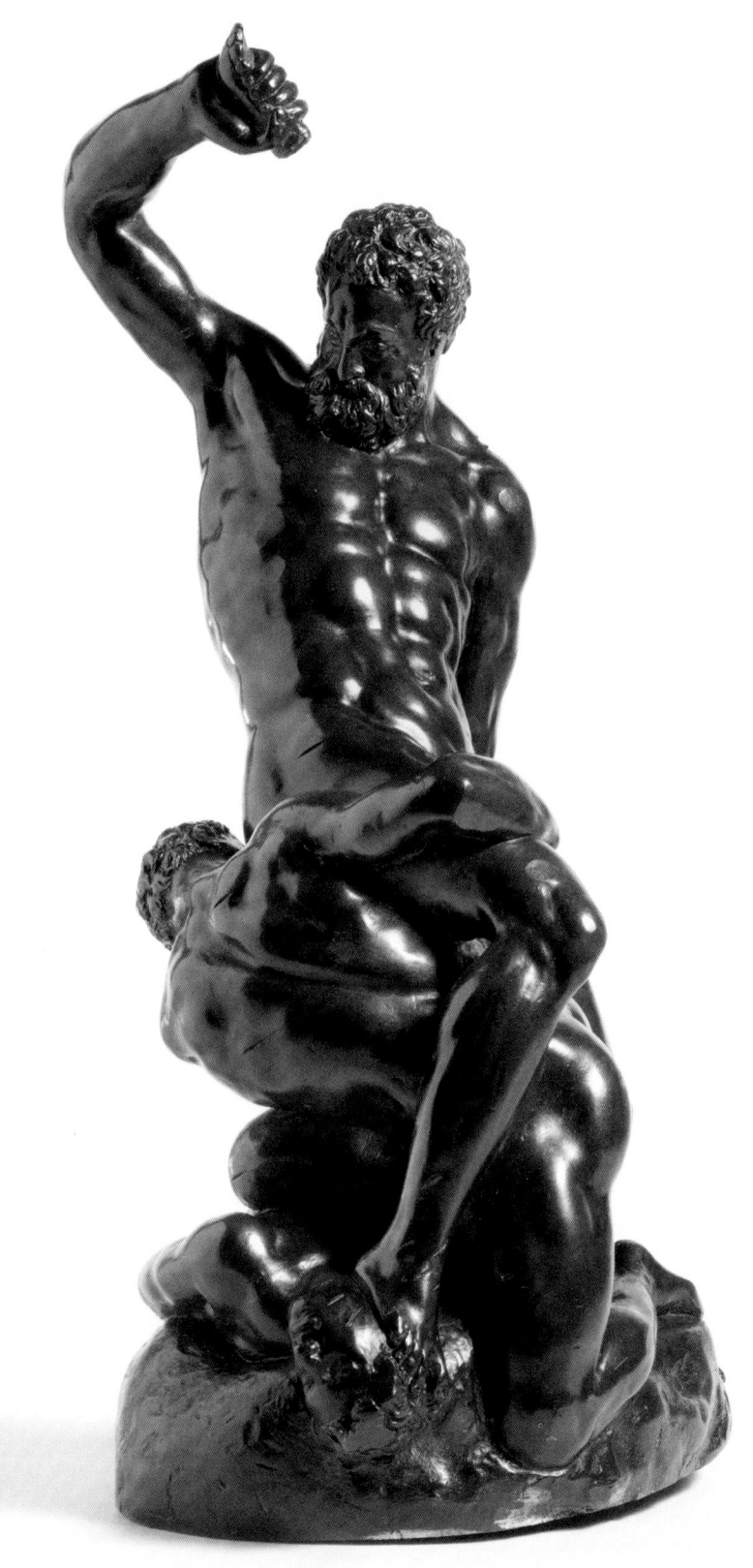

28

ANONYMOUS ARTIST AFTER A MODEL BY MICHELANGELO

Samson Slaying the Philistine, 17th century
Bronze, 38 x 18.5 x 18 cm

———————

Woburn Abbey

This bronze is one of a group of thirteen similar pieces that are probably based on a now-lost preparatory work by Michelangelo (1475-1564) for an unrealised project for the Piazza della Signoria in Florence.[136] In his book *Le vite de' più eccellenti pittori, scultori, e architettori* (The Lives of the Most Excellent Painters, Sculptors, and Architects), the Italian artists' biographer Giorgio Vasari (1511-1574) identifies the subject as *Samson Slaying the Philistine*. The biblical hero Samson raises an arm to strike the philistine, and a third figure is trampled underfoot. This third figure has erroneously been described as a 'reclining woman' in historic records, overlooking their involvement in the combat. Some related versions of the sculpture omit this figure altogether.

The bronze is depicted in a portrait of Francis Russell, Marquess of Tavistock (1739-1767) painted by Joshua Reynolds (1723-1792) in 1765-1766, a couple of years after the Marquess's journey through Italy (see cat. no. 27). It may also be recorded as 'Gladiators' in one of his inventories of Woburn Abbey. The painting shows the sculpture complete with the jawbone that Samson wields in his right hand, which has unfortunately been lost today.

Bronze replicas of ancient and Renaissance sculptures began to appear towards the end of the seventeenth century. They proliferated to satisfy the Grand Tourist market, especially following the foundation of the Zoffoli foundry in Rome. Founded by Giacomo Zoffoli (c.1731-1785), the foundry produced affordable miniature replicas of some of the most famous and recognisable Italian statues, which were often acquired as sets.

The Marquess acquired both bronze and marble sculptures in Italy. When in Rome in 1762, he commissioned the Scottish dealer Gavin Hamilton (1723-1798) as agent to purchase statues and busts 'of merit and curiosity' for a gallery he hoped to build.[137] Other bronze statues include copies of the 'excellent bronze' Marcus Aurelius – the famous equestrian monument he so admired in Rome – a small bird now attributed to Giambologna (1529-1608), and an early Zoffoli set including copies after the Furietti centaurs excavated near Tivoli.[138] Many were displayed in his study as a signifier of his classical learning.

VP

29

ANNIBALE CARRACCI (CIRCLE OF)

Noli Me Tangere, **c.1690**
Canvas, 162 x 119 cm

Woburn Abbey

This painting depicts Christ after his resurrection appearing to Mary Magdalene in the Garden of Gethsemane as described in John, 20:14. The painting was noted at the Palazzo Barberini in Rome by Francis Russell, Marquess of Tavistock (1739-1767) on his Grand Tour in 1762. He described it as 'finely drawn & composed'.[139]

The Marquess annotated the margins of his copy of Charles-Nicolas Cochin's *Voyage d'Italie* (1753) with his observations and, as Rome is represented by a single page in these volumes, he wrote a separate handwritten addendum to cover the city and its environs.[140] Of the Palazzo Barberini, he praised the ceiling of the Great Hall by Pietro da Cortona, and works by such masters as Francesco Albani, Domenico Fetti, Guido Reni, Raphael, Giuseppe Chiari, Claude Lorrain, Guercino and Nicolas Poussin, amongst others: 'there are numberless pictures, busts &c in the palace & several very good but much neglected & damaged'.[141]

On 6 March 1762, the Marquess wrote from Rome to his friend Thomas Robinson (1738-1786): 'the [Barberini] family is involved in a law suit & poor & I believe will sell anything for a good price. Hamilton is my operator and we have together pitched upon some things which if I do pay a little too much for, will not afterwards be a disgrace to my collection – one is the famous *Death of Germanicus* by Poussin, tho' I almost despair of succeeding there – the others tho' not entirely capital are far from bad. As nothing is yet determined, I beg you not to talk of it'.[142]

The Marquess failed to acquire the work by Poussin, but *Noli me Tangere* was amongst a collection which was arriving in England over two years later.[143] On 29 July 1764, the Marquess wrote excitedly to the Earl of Upper Ossory 'My Barberini pictures are arrived in the river & will be unloaded next week. You may guess at my impatience to see them especially the Carraci which is the only picture I pride myself upon as a capital one'.[144] This coincided with the Marquess's refurbishment of both his town and country residences.

The painting was described in the 1767 inventory of his London home on Great Russell Street in the Drawing Room, as 'Our Saviour in the character of a Gardiner, with the Woman by Hannibal Carrachi'. After the Marquess's death, the painting was displayed in the Red Drawing Room at Bedford House, which absorbed most of the collection before being transferred to the Saloon at Woburn Abbey.[145] Another painting acquired from the Barberini family was Guercino's *Samson Bringing Honey to His Parents*, which was also displayed in the Saloon at Woburn before it was sold in 1951.[146]

VP

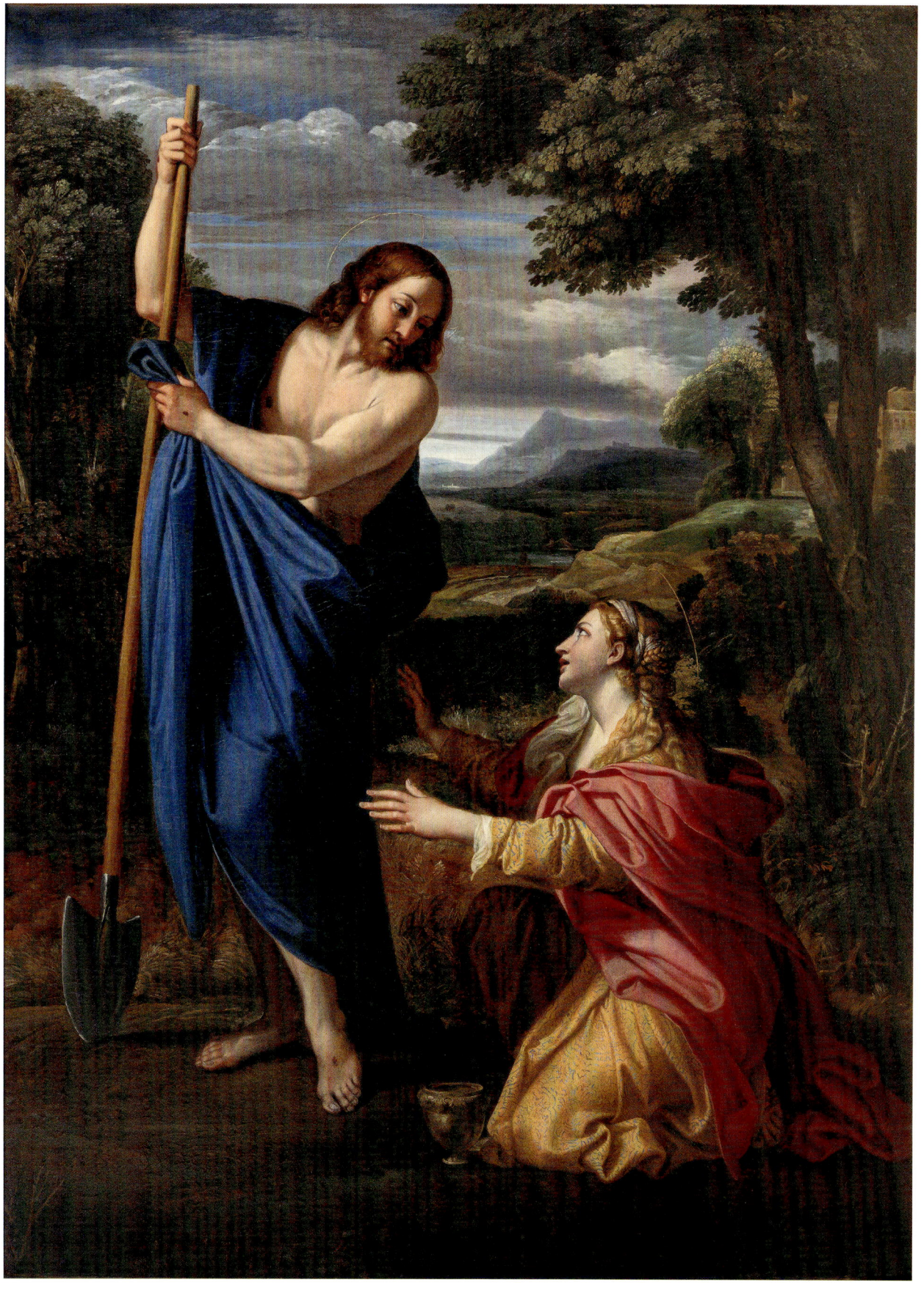

COLLECTING ITALIAN VEDUTE:
THE CANALETTO SERIES AT WOBURN ABBEY

Victoria Poulton

Venice long held a strong place in the visual imagination of the eighteenth-century Grand Tourist, surpassing almost every other destination on the itinerary except Rome.[147] Prints, maps and descriptions had been in wide circulation since the sixteenth century ensuring familiarity, yet as tourist William Freeman observed in 1729: 'the description of the situation of Venice every one knows but still it surprises when you first enter the town'.[148] Unlike Rome, the city had neither ancient ruins nor a great number of antiquities. It was the architecture, unique archipelago, canals, entertainments, festivals and blend of cultures that made Venice intriguing and memorable.

The tradition of *vedute* (view or cityscape) painting was not exclusively Venetian, but it is strongly associated with the city. In Venice, the market largely operated with local artists supplying foreign travellers who were keen to take home a reminder of this unusual city. Travellers in the early eighteenth century became keen patrons of *vedute* painters like Giovanni Antonio Canal, better known as Canaletto (1697-1768). Lord John Russell, later 4th Duke of Bedford (1710-1771), commissioned the largest series executed by the artist, with twenty-four paintings in the collection at Woburn Abbey. The set comprises views of the Grand Canal alongside well-known squares and other landmarks. Whilst some viewpoints reproduce other extant versions by Canaletto, with minor variations, other scenes are unique in his oeuvre. Each scene is peppered with mundane activity – people chatting, washing billowing on the line – against the backdrop of Venice's unique topography of canals and squares.

Representing the canal views, *The Grand Canal in Venice* focuses on the Custom's House (Dogana di Mare). Behind it rises the dome of the Church of Santa Maria della Salute; a large barge is moored next to it, and around it, porters bustle along the pavement (fig. 1). Weeds have taken root in the architrave of the building, set against the imposing grandeur of Bernardo Falcone's (c.1620-c.1696) sculpted Atlantes figures, bearing the weight of a globe and a weathervane in the form of fortune bearing a sail, alluding to the city's success in maritime trade (fig. 2).

Illustrative of the Venetian squares in the series is *The Piazza S. Marco in Venice*. It is painted from a low viewpoint. On the left, one can see the base of the clock tower, the Campanile, and, across the square, an accurate rendering of Jacopo Sansovino's (1486-1570) façade of the church of San Geminiano, with its paired columns, rose window, and off-centre sculpted lion (fig. 3). The tall flagpoles punctuate the composition but are inaccurately scaled to fit within the confines of the picture plane; they are truncated, and the clouds between them have been repainted as the artist changed his mind. Populated with the quotidian, the tooth dangling from a post advertises the services of a dentist (fig. 4).[149]

The paintings were probably acquired with the assistance of Joseph Smith (c.1674-1770), merchant banker turned dealer, and part of the network which facilitated cash withdrawals at various stations on the Grand Tour. Smith was a junior partner in Williams & Smith bankers, who had many British clients in Italy, and also provided a complementary service as agent. The firm had previously been bankers to Thomas Coke (1697-1759), future Earl of Leicester, during his Grand Tour (1712-1718), and Smith negotiated the purchase of several manuscripts for him.[150] By 1723, Smith had met Canaletto, and together they formed a successful partnership in the market for Venetian *vedute*, though there is no surviving evidence of the finances of the agreement.[151] The pocketbook of Lord John Russell records a receipt of 300 sequins (£150) withdrawn from 'Mr Smith' in March 1731, which is probably evidence of the two men meeting.[152]

By the time Russell and Smith were acquainted, Smith had commissioned a set of twelve Grand Canal views for display at his own home in Venice, 'The House of Joseph Smith, Englishman'. There can be little doubt that this was intended as a showroom so visitors could be persuaded to order similar views, and that John saw them there.[153] *The Grand Canal in Venice* from the Woburn Abbey Collection is similar to the same scene in Smith's collection, with a different cast of activity, and taking a slightly wider viewpoint to capture the moored boat to the left (fig. 5). Potted plants and awnings appear in the Woburn picture, adding greater variety and perhaps suggesting a different time of year. The bend of the canal has changed, repositioning the bell tower of the Santa Maria della Carita tighter to the right.

Canaletto's stylised topographical views lent themselves well to large series of this kind, and were almost exclusively conceived as pairs, groups or sets, taken back to Britain and hung in Country Seats or Town Houses as decorative artworks.[154] Canaletto built on the established tradition of Caspar van Wittel (1653-1736) in Rome (see cat. no. 5), and of Luca Carlevarijs (1663-1730) in Venice, likely aided by the business acumen of Smith and by his own skilled blend of topographical accuracy and aesthetic contrivance. The

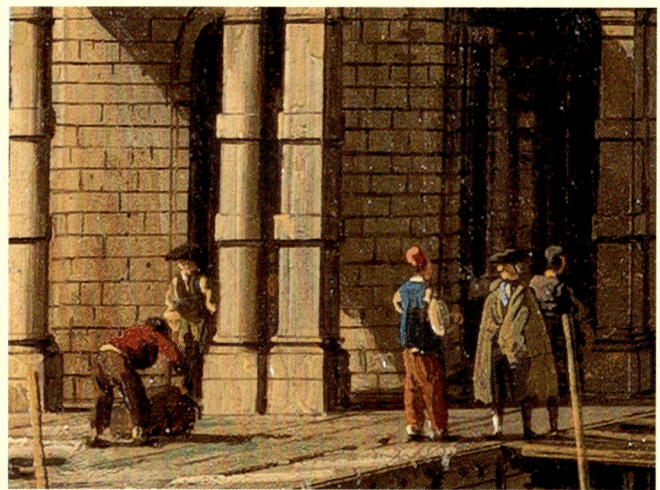

Fig. 1
Detail of Canaletto, *The Grand Canal in Venice*
(cat. no. 30)

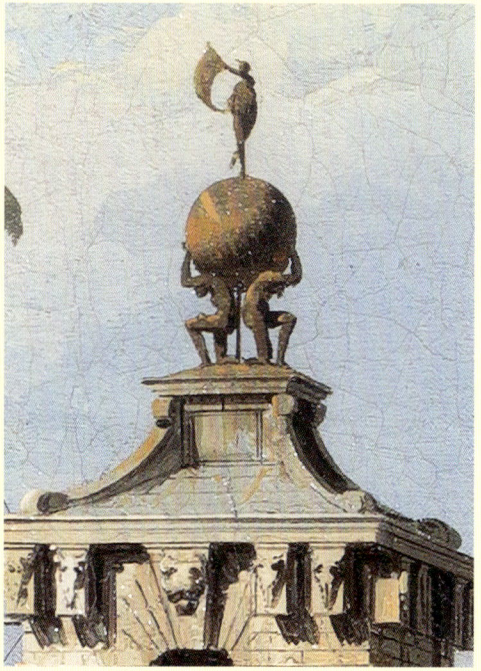

Fig. 2
Detail of Canaletto, *The Grand Canal in Venice*
(cat. no. 30)

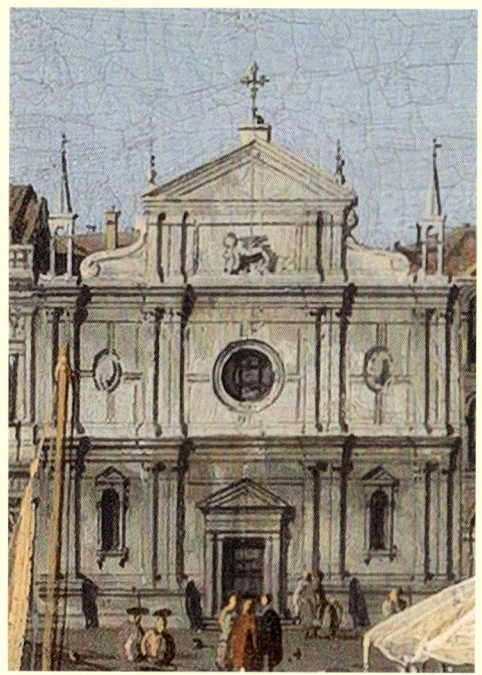

Fig. 3
Detail of Canaletto, *The Piazza S. Marco in Venice,*
Looking West (cat. no. 31)

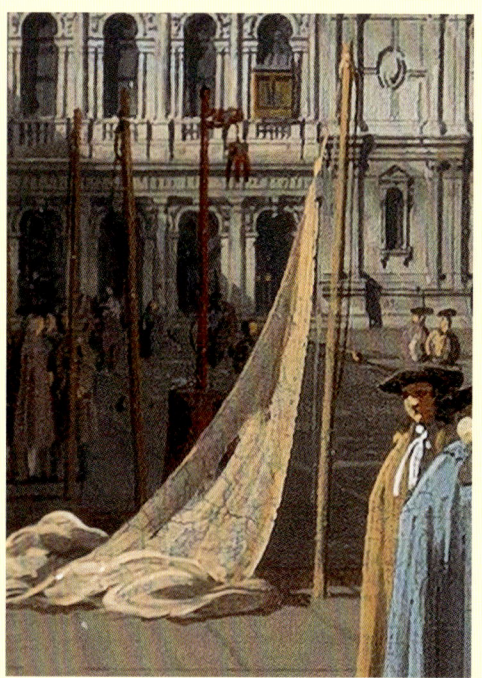

Fig. 4
Detail of Canaletto, *The Piazza S. Marco in Venice,*
Looking West (cat. no. 31)

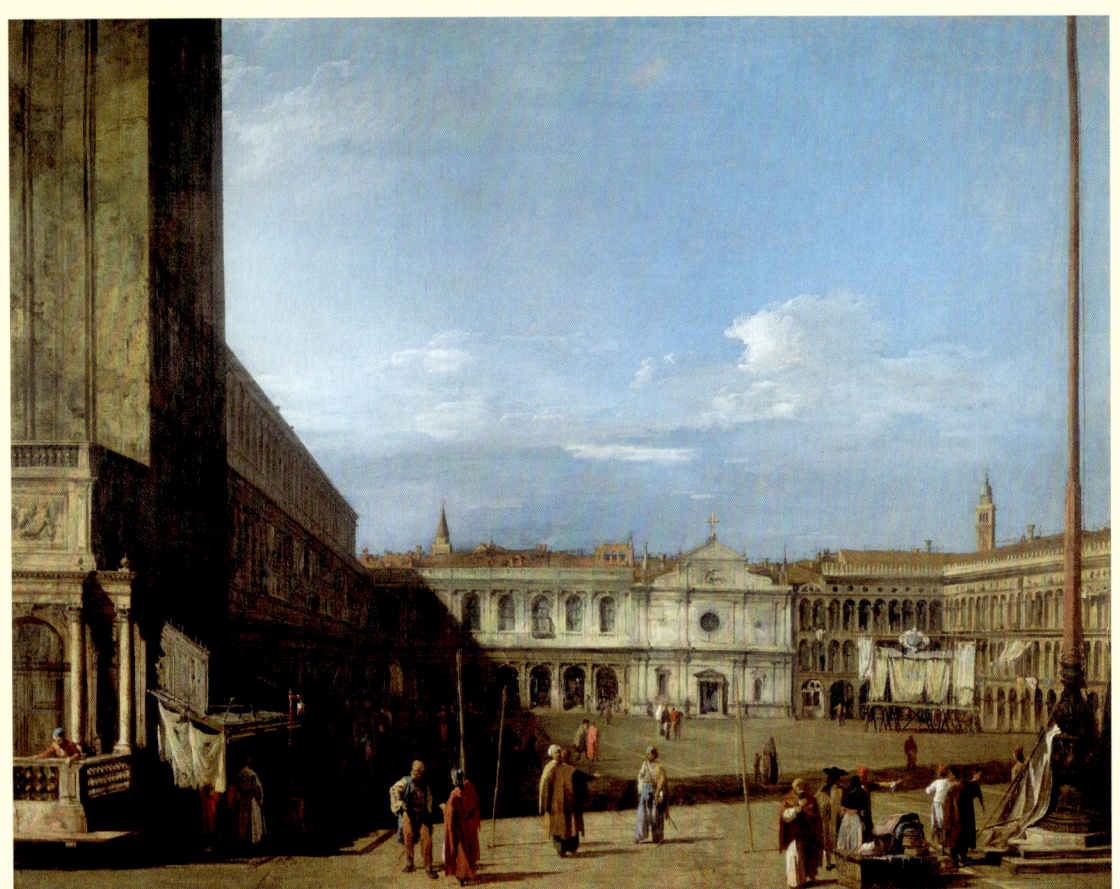

Fig. 5
Giovanni Antonio Canal, called Canaletto, *Piazza San Marco looking West towards San Geminiano*, c.1723-1724. Canvas, 134.6 x 173 cm. Royal Collection Trust, London

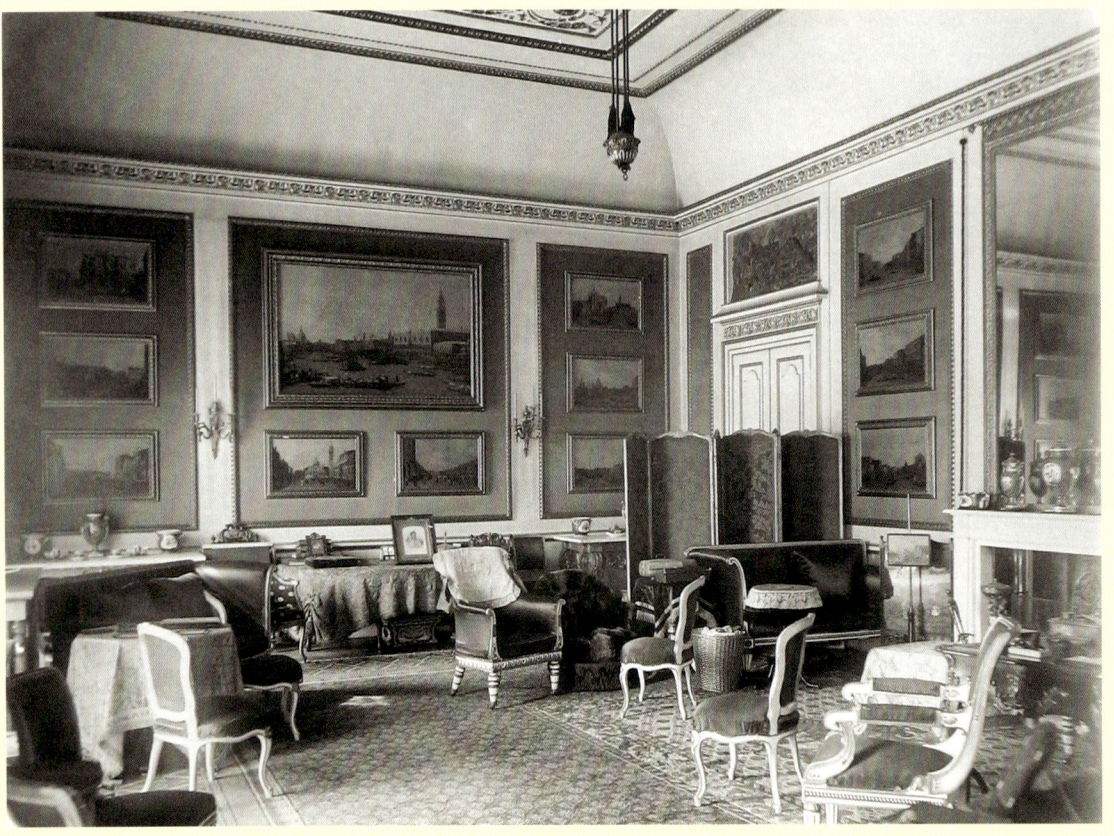

Fig. 6
The Dining Room at Woburn Abbey in 1887

paintings' small scale made them easy to package and ship, and upon arrival in London, Joseph's brother John Smith could act as intermediary – often with a patron who had placed an order several years prior.

The Woburn Abbey series is the largest for one patron, but it is not exceptional. It has been argued that nothing better represents Canaletto's work from this period than two large groups of paintings executed for British aristocratic patrons: the Duke of Bedford and the Duke of Marlborough. These two sets, comprising 44 works in total, represent a wide-ranging tour of the city, with no repetition across the group.[155] Other significant patrons include Thomas Osborne, 4th Duke of Leeds (1713-1789) who ordered 11; William, 3rd Earl Fitzwilliam (1719/20-1756) had 8; Henry Howard, 4th Earl of Carlisle (1694-1758) acquired not only 5 Canalettos, but also 15 views from Bernardo Bellotto (1722-1780) and 18 from Michele Marieschi (1710-1743), amongst others.[156] Additionally, Russell's sister, Elizabeth Capell, Countess of Essex (1704-1784), acquired a group of Canaletto paintings from Smith. In 1734, Smith wrote to her to advise that Canaletto would set other work aside to focus on completing her commission.[157] The Countess and her husband were resident in Italy, and she is recorded in Venice in 1731 alongside her brother. She returned in 1734, when her husband negotiated with Smith for soprano castrato Farinelli (1705-1782) to sing at the Haymarket Opera House in London.[158]

For the slightly less wealthy traveller, unable to acquire a group of oil paintings, Smith's own series of paintings was engraved and published. The plates were ready for publication in 1730, but were delayed by the addition of two large festival paintings to Smith's gallery. The first edition was published in 1735.

Analysis of the pace of Canaletto's output proves difficult, as the scant documentary evidence represents the bias of the agent, who was keen to prove their value and presumably earn a commission. In July 1730, Smith was writing to patron Samuel Hill (c.1691-1758) that his two Canaletto paintings would be finished within a year – in the event, the paintings arrived in England within five months.[159] The delivery of the Woburn Canalettos took place over an extended period of time: a preparatory drawing for the *Piazzetta Looking North-West* is dated July 1732 in Canaletto's sketchbook; *Regatta on the Grand Canal* bears the arms of Doge Pisani (in office 1735-1741) indicating that it was painted no earlier than 1735.[160] It was not uncommon for Grand Tourists to wait for their works of art to arrive home – the following generation saw similar complaints

about Pompeo Batoni (1708-1787), who also balanced a long client list, and sometimes took years to fulfil commissions (see cat. no. 3).[161]

It is therefore difficult to ascertain whether Lord John Russell placed the order for the paintings at once, or whether it was part of an extended arrangement.[162] Young John was already a 'man of property' and money independent from the Bedford Estate. Upon the death of his mother, the wealthy heiress Elizabeth Howland (1682-1724), in 1724, he was personally left lands in several counties. Separately, a modest seventeenth-century manor house in Cheam, Surrey, was given to him in 1730.[163] With the fragile health of his brother Wriothesley an ongoing family concern, he can have been relatively assured that one day he himself would become Duke of Bedford. When he did marry in 1731, he bought the family estate at Stratton from his brother and set about an ambitious programme of redevelopment before the 3rd Duke's death. It is likely that the Canalettos were originally intended to be displayed there.

Few of John's papers survive prior to his inheritance. Five letters sent from Italy are known, but make no reference to the acquisition of works of art.[164] References to the Canaletto paintings first appear in the form of three receipted payments in the Bedford Estates Archive, totalling £188.2s.3d and spanning the years 1732-1736, when the paintings arrived in England.[165] This relatively modest sum is unlikely to cover the full cost of a commission of such a large group of paintings, so it is often assumed that there must be other payments for which the vouchers do not survive. Two of the known vouchers reconcile with a cash account, which also reveals additional payments to 'John Smith':

11 January 1733: John Smith £11.11.0.
16 September 1733: Mr John Smith, £27.1.8
20 November 1733: Mr John Smith, £27.16.5
28 September 1734: Mr John Smith, £27.7.1

The second payment perhaps relates to the receipt dated 27 February 1733 for £27.1.8, which is not recorded elsewhere in the account.[166] The fact that the sums are comparable, and fall within accepted parameters for the commission, framing, and shipping of two paintings, make these compelling clues, though unfortunately it has not yet proven possible to find any corroborating vouchers that may provide additional details.

What is irrefutable is that the Canalettos at Woburn represent a legacy of the 4th Duke's Grand Tour. Details in many of the paintings can also be linked to many of the compositions within Canaletto's surviving sketchbook, making the Russell commission a valuable example in understanding the artist's methods.[167]

As is typical of inventories of the period, it is impossible to locate the precise original positions of the paintings, described as 'Views of Venice' when they arrived to Bedford House in London.[168] They were in 1771 divided between two rooms in Bedford House: the Little Eating Room was exclusively for Canalettos, save a painting of spaniels and a parrot over the fireplace – with 'Two very large views of Venice (by Canaletto), eight smaller ditto, and eight ditto less'.[169] The rest were in the adjacent Large Dining Room, alongside an assortment of other pictures.

When Bedford House was demolished around 1800 by the 5th Duke of Bedford (1765-1802), the paintings were relocated to Woburn Abbey, to a room designed by Henry Holland (1745-1806) specifically to house them as part of a larger programme of remodelling the south and east fronts of the house. The paintings were hung together in registers of three around the room, with the two large paintings anchoring the centre of each of the shorter elevations (fig. 6). This necessitated the blocking up of a large tripartite window. This room was also used as an Eating Room, before it was turned into a Drawing Room for most of the nineteenth-century.

Here, the paintings remained for over 150 years, with minor rearrangement on several occasions, until 1955 when the 13th Duke of Bedford opened up the majority of the principal rooms of Woburn Abbey to paying visitors. Retaining the use of the Dining Room, he reopened the blocked window. This intervention disrupted the principal elevation of the room, which contained no fewer than nine Canaletto paintings centred on one of the two largest views, displacing three paintings to elsewhere in the house. Despite this dilution of the impact of all 24 views of Venice within a single interior, the Dining Room at Woburn Abbey remains a remarkable expression of the experience of the Grand Tour and the British fascination with Venice in particular.

30

GIOVANNI ANTONIO CANAL, CALLED CANALETTO

The Grand Canal in Venice, Looking West, with the Dogana di Mare and the Santa Maria della Salute, **c.1732-1736**
Canvas, 47 x 79 cm

Woburn Abbey

31

GIOVANNI ANTONIO CANAL, CALLED CANALETTO

The Piazza S. Marco in Venice, Looking West, **c.1732-1736**
Canvas, 47 x 80 cm

Woburn Abbey

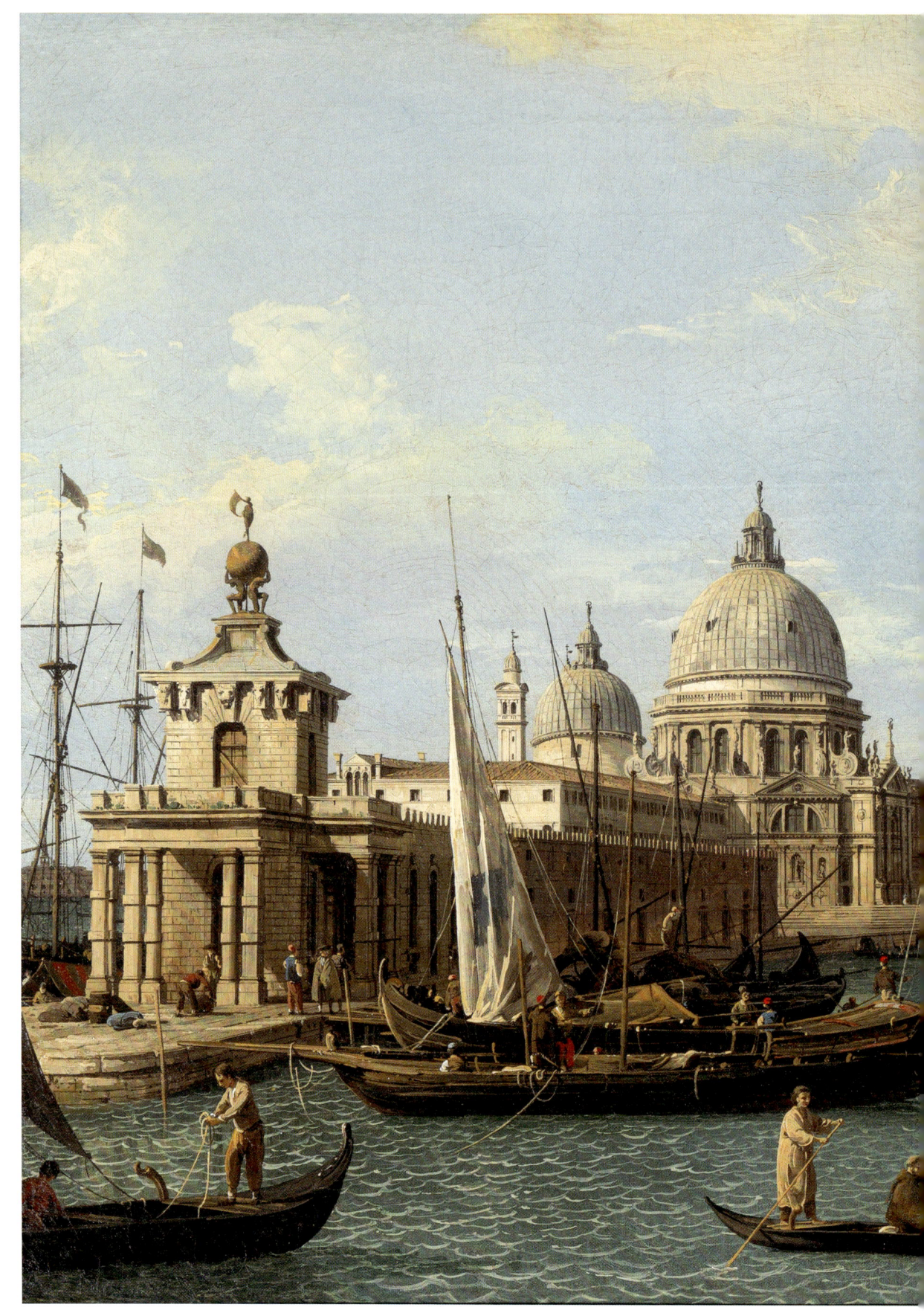

Cat. no. 30

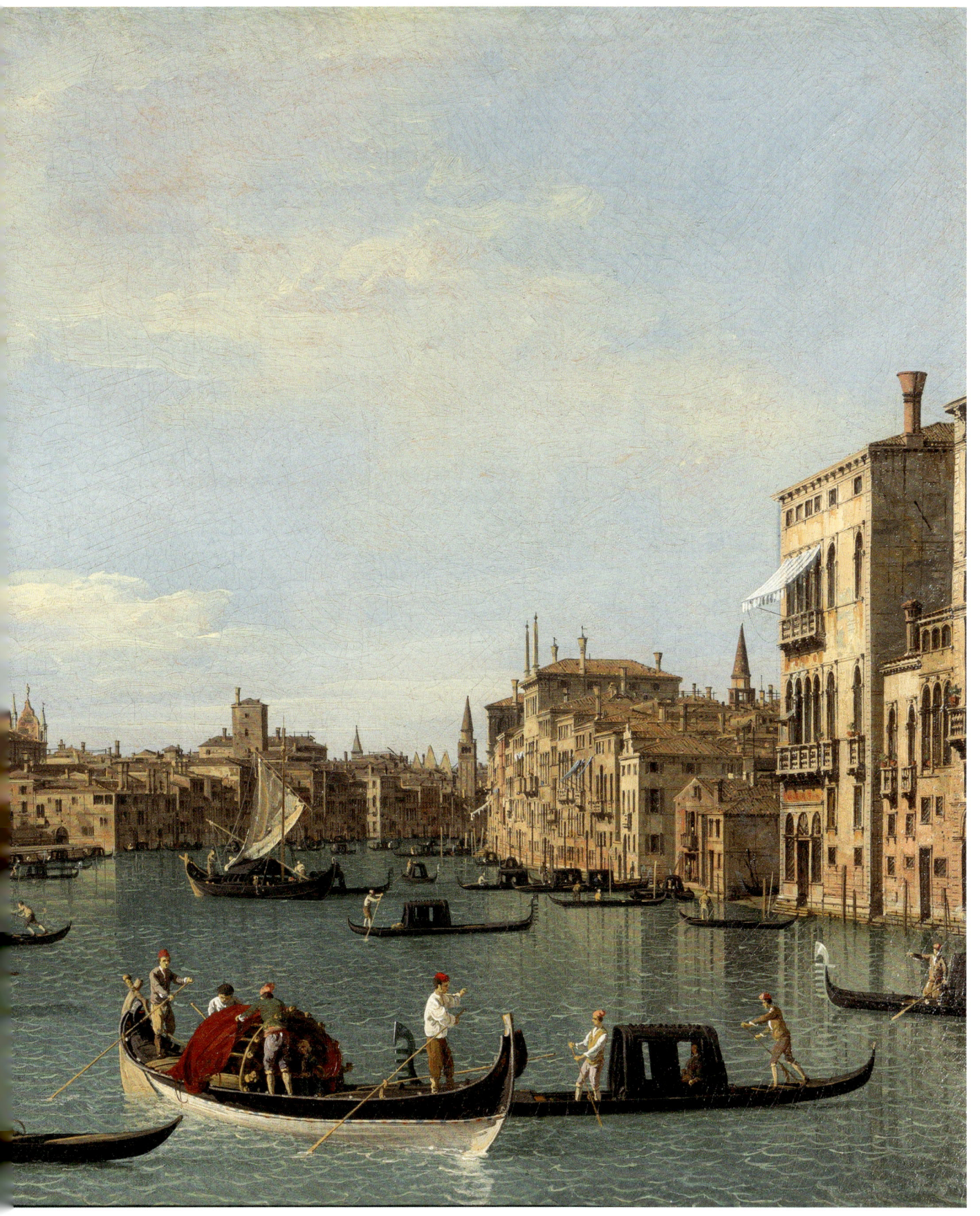

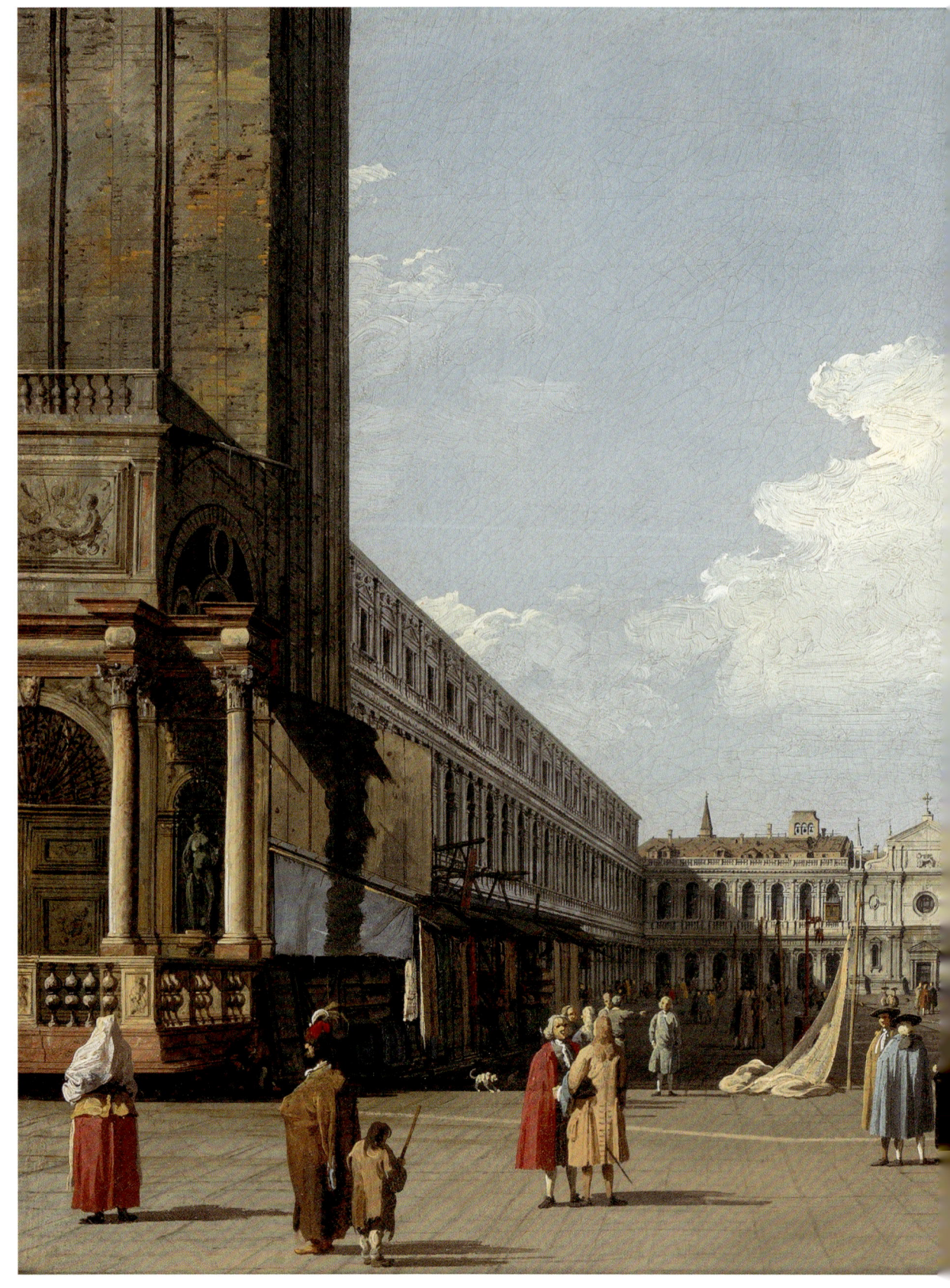

Cat. no. 31

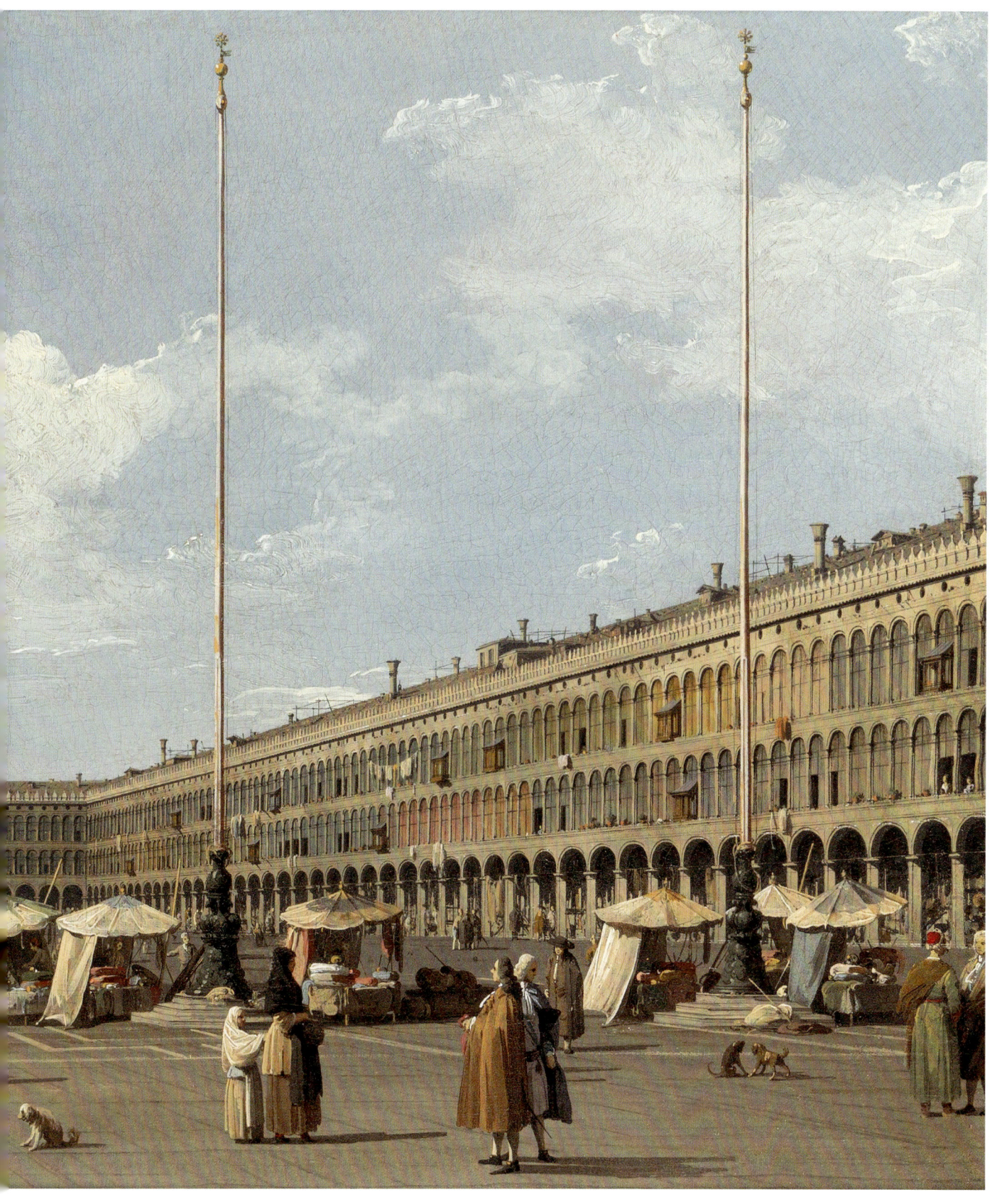

NOTES

1 This contribution is based on Budding 2018.
2 Lynch Piozzi 1789; Miller 1777.
3 Smollett 1766, p. 120.
4 Sharp 1766, p. 44.
5 Nugent 1778.
6 Thomas Coryat (1577-1617) travelled on foot to Italy and other countries and wrote about it in *'Coryat's Crudities'* (1611).
7 Miller 1777, vol. I, p. 161.
8 Miller 1777, vol. II, p. 31.
9 Garrick 1764, p. 410.
10 Miller 1777, vol. I, p. 161.
11 Sharp 1766, p. 43.
12 Beckford 1735.
13 Dolan 2002, p. 137.
14 Idem, p. 138.
15 *The Morning Post*, 1 March 1815.
16 *The Morning Post*, 4 January 1815.
17 *The Morning Post*, 28 July 1815.

18 Ingamells 1997, p. 225; Moore 1985, p. 37.
19 For the connection to the frescoes at Palazzo Pamphili, see: Moore 1985, p. 34.
20 Hiskey 2016, p. 68.
21 Moore 1985, p. 38.
22 Idem, p. 39.
23 Idem, p. 38.
24 The South Sea Bubble refers to a financial crash involving the British South Sea Company, trading with South America.
25 Palladian architecture is a European architectural style that draws heavily from the designs of the sixteenth-century Italian architect Andrea Palladio (1508-1580), who in turn was inspired by classical Greek and Roman architecture. Key features include symmetry, proportion, and the use of classical elements like columns, porticos, and pediments. This style can be seen in many country houses built in the United Kingdom in the eighteenth century.
26 Ross 2021, p. 127.
27 Idem.
28 For exact references to all of these see: Hiskey 2016, pp. 535, 556.
29 Stirling 1912, p. 38.
30 Angelicoussis/Schmidt 2025, pp. 330-331.
31 Ingamells 1977, p. 226.
32 Stirling 1912, p. 210.

33 Around 1000 pounds of today.
34 For Rosalba Carriera as a miniature painter, see Venice 2023.
35 For details on the payments received by Carriera in comparison to her fellow Venetian painters, see: Dresden 2023, pp. 52, 53 note 48.
36 Letter from Rosalba Carriera to Nicolas Vleughels, 1721, see: Sani 1985, vol. I, nos. 327, 390.

37 Carriera documented her stay in Paris between August 1720 and September 1721 in a journal, see Jeffares 2006.
38 For details on the artist's life, see Dresden 2023; N. Jeffares, *Dictionary of Pastellists before 1800*, online edition, updated 27 January 2025, http://www.pastellists.com/.

39 The painting was published in Sani 1988/2007, cat. no. 328.
40 Quoted by D. Shaw-Taylor in Dresden 2023, p. 68.
41 The pastel from Holkham Hall discussed here does not have such a talisman. For information on these talismans, see Dresden 2023.
42 See R.R. Sedgwick, 'COKE, Hon. Edward (1719-53)', online edition, https://www.historyofparliamentonline.org/volume/1715-1754/member/coke-hon-edward-1719-53, originally published in Sedgwick 1970.
43 Idem.

44 Bowron/Kerber 2007, pp. 37-38.
45 E. Peters Bowron in Rome 2005, p. 188, cat. no. 69.

46 The last cipher is not readable. G.F. Waagen, cited in Röthlisberger 1961, gives the date 1652.
47 Holkham Archives, C/BMy 1'; see also Kenworthy-Brown 1983, p. 18.
48 Röthlisberger 1961, vol. 1, LV 70, pp. 212-213; vol. 2, fig. 141.
49 Idem, vol. 1, p. 214; vol. 2, fig. 390.

50 London 2008, p. 9.
51 Brettingham 1773.
52 London 2008, p. 39, cat. no. 7b.

53 Hiskey 2016, p. 68.
54 Payment is recorded in the Holkham Archives under F/TC 4, on 1 July 1716 and under F/TC 5, on 17 August 1716.
55 Ingamells 1997, p. 225; Hiskey 2016, p. 68, 538 note 55.

56 Angelioussis 2001, cat. no. 47.
57 Schmidt/Angelicoussis 2025, p. 219.
58 The surviving account book is held in Holkham Archives, HA C/BMy 1, p. 19.
59 Idem, p. 92.
60 Brettingham 1773, p. 15.

61 This essay is based on Gialluca 2014; Hiskey/Reynolds 2014; Moore 2014; Reynolds 2014; Reynolds 2015; Hiskey 2016.
62 Holkham Archives, F/G 2(2), fols. 444-445, 24 November 1706; Hiskey 2016, p. 59.
63 Holkham Archives, F/G 2(2), fols. 422-423, 4 June 1711; Reynolds 2015, p. 2 note 8.

64 For the first quote, see: Holkham Archives, F/G 2(2), fols. 463-464; Hiskey 2016, p. 68. For the second quote, see: Holkham Archives, F/G 2(2), fol. 463; Hiskey 2016, p. 69.
65 Holkham Archives, F/G 2(2), fols. 463-464; Reynolds 2015, p. 9 note 66.
66 Garzelli 1985, vol. II, fig. 110; De la Mare 1985, vol. I, pp. 459, 488, 501; G. Mariani Canova in *The Painted Page* 1994, cat. no. 47; Reynolds 2015, pp. 236-240. For the other work by the anonymous illuminator, see: Naples, Bibllioteca Nazionale, inv. MS. IV.E.12.
67 Alexander 2016, p. 1.
68 L. Armstrong in *The Painted Page* 1994, cat. no. 84.
69 Aymonino 2025.

70 The account book is held in the Holkham Archives, HA F/TC 4.
71 In comparison, periwigs bought at the same time cost a mere 50 to 90 livres.
72 At the time, chocolate was drunk rather than eaten.
73 See HA A/3-31 for details of his charitable giving.
74 Moore 1985, p. 33.
75 Acquiring a sense of taste and to become a *virtuoso* was seen by many as the epitome of a Grand Tour. See Haskell 1981.
76 HA F/TC 4, p. 14.
77 Idem, p. 97.
78 HA F/G2 (2), fol. 463.
79 Now known as Teatro Malibran.
80 HA F/TC 4, p. 55, probably the Teatro San Angelo.
81 Idem, p. 22.
82 Idem, p. 141.
83 Idem, p. 73.
84 The Venetian architect Andrea Palladio (1508-1580) incorporated elements of Roman and Greek architecture (symmetry, perspective and proportion) to create a style whose influence can be seen in many country houses built in the United Kingdom in the eighteenth century.
85 HA F/TC 4, p. 146.
86 Idem, p. 177.
87 Idem, p. 73.
88 Hiskey 2016, p. 530.
89 Kent was acting as agent for Thomas and payments were recorded in a second account book, see: HA F/TC 5.
90 HA F/TC 4, p. 167.
91 Idem, p. 154.

92 Brownlow remained childless, so after his death the painting came into the possession of his sister, Lady Elizabeth Chaplin (1729-1813). It was acquired by the Trustees of Burghley in 2003 and has since been back at Burghley House.

93 See, among others, London 2024.

94 London 2024, cat. no. 5.

95 Cf. M. Carlova, 'Angelika Kauffman', in Amsterdam 2018-2019, pp. 140-149.

96 See Bleyerveld 2022, pp. 5-6. See also Kauffman's self-portrait of 1784, likewise with a portfolio and stylus, in London 2024, cat. no. 2.

97 London 1997, cat. no. 14.

98 Goodreau 1977. For the portrait discussed here, see idem, cat. no. 10.

99 London 2024.

100 Scarth 2009, p. 231.

101 Cf. 's-Hertogenbosch-Heino-Haarlem 1984, pp. 215-243.

102 The side panels of the triptych also ended up in English collections, in the Barber Art Institute in Birmingham and in the Chelsea and Westminster Hospital in London, respectively.

103 Pittsburgh-Edinburgh 1995-1996, cat. no. 5.

104 Cf., among others, Phoenix-Kansas City-The Hague 1999, cat. no. 11.

105 Baldassari 1995/2015, cat. no. 2.

106 González-Palacios 1994, p. 349.

107 This information was kindly supplied by Dr Jonathan Yarker, Trinity College, Cambridge.

108 See Dr Charles Avery's records at the Victoria and Albert Museum, London.

109 The whereabouts of the corresponding cup is unknown.

110 New Hollstein Dutch 1996, cat. no. 561.

111 Burghley House Archive, Exeter Mss 51.10.

112 The Crouching Venus, of which numerous Roman copies exist, was based on the original Hellenistic sculpture of 200 BCE described by Gaius Plinius Secundus (called Pliny; 23/24-79 CE) in his Naturalis Historia (77 CE) as being by the hand of the Greek sculptor Doidalsas and displayed in the temple of Jupiter Stator. One of the Roman copies is in the British Royal Collection (inv. RCIN 69746), and is likely to have been known to John Russel, the 4th Duke of Bedford. The bust of Caracalla is depicted in the now lost portrait of Laurent Delvaux by Issac Whood (1689-1752). Whood was patronised frequently by John and became his 'court' artist. He died

in Bloomsbury Square, the location of Bedford House, in 1752. See Avery 1988, pp. 253-264.

113 The seventeenth-century south range was eventually replaced in the late 1760s by the architect Sir William Chambers (1723-1796), with a new Library at its centre.

114 Woburn Abbey Collection, R5/1092.

115 Woburn Abbey Collection, HMC 58; HMC46. For a discussion on the Grand Tour destinations, see Black 1999.

116 Just as the State Apartment was being readied for habitation in 1754, there was a flurry of this kind of activity, with over £686 spent in the sale rooms that year.

117 Woburn Abbey Collection, HMC 58, vol. 2.

118 Black 2003, p. 188-189.

119 Woburn Abbey Collection, HMC 58, vol. 15. For more information on Colivoe, see: J. Simon, British picture restorers, 1600-1950 (National Portrait Gallery, online resource).

120 Thomas Gainsborough, The Milkmaid, 1755 and A Wooded Landscape, 1755, Woburn Abbey.

121 Bignamini/Hornsby 2010, vol. I, p. 288; Woburn Abbey Collection HMC8-45-22; NMR 15/5A, 'Marquess of Tavistock's Accounts', vol. I.

122 Woburn Abbey Collection, HMC 8-46-206.

123 Sweet, p. 111.

124 Woburn Abbey Collection, HMC 8-45-22.

125 Woburn Abbey Collection, '4th Duke Cash Account Books', p. 11.

126 Woburn Abbey Collection, HMC 8-46-6, 8 January 1762.

127 British Museum Archive, letter from John Russell, Duke of Bedford, to Townley, 14 May 1804.

128 Woburn Abbey Collection, HMC46. For a discussion on the Grand Tour destinations, see Black 1999. In this publication, this vocabulary is used to describe the travels of Sir Francis Dashwood, Henry, 3rd Earl Radnor, Sir Richard Worsley, Theophilus, 9th Earl of Huntingdon, amongst others, who visited the destinations on John Russel's list. The transactions listed in the book are incomplete and there are some discrepancies between the order of the destinations in the itinerary and the order of cash withdrawals.

129 Described as 'Duke of Bedford's Memorandum Book 1728-1732' in the Historical Manuscripts Commission Report. The pocketbook contains payments in respect of Mr Hetherington and Mr Bernège, and a withdrawal of cash on 29 November 1730. Ingamells 1997, p. 832 places John Russel in Rome on 30

November and records these travelling partners. The reference to the fragment in the published correspondence describes 'various places in Holland and the Low Countries' but makes no reference of Italy. The reference to this diary is repeated in Ingram 1988, but it is not clear whether he had seen it or was relying on the previous publication.

130 Woburn Abbey Collection, 4D-MT-I, 'Inventory of Great Russell Street', p. 30.

131 Woburn Abbey Collection, HMC8-45-50, 6 March 1762, Rome.

132 Woburn Abbey Collection, 'George Rawson Disbursements', November 1761-January 1765.

133 Woburn Abbey Collection, HMC8 45-66, 10 April 1762, Bologna; 4D-MT-C; Redford 1996, p. 14 argues that to qualify as a Grand Tour, the stay should be two or three years.

134 Woburn Abbey Collection, 4D-MT-C.

135 Francis married Lady Elizabeth Keppel (1739-1768) in 1764.

136 For another example, see: Samson and the Philistines, c.1550, Metropolitan Museum, New York, inv. 64.101.1444, https://www.metmuseum.org/art/collection/search/203933.

137 Quoted in Angellicoussis 1992, p. 14. Angelicoussis identifies two marbles acquired by the Marquess. Furthermore, two sculptures in the Woburn Abbey Collection came from the Marquess's nephew Lord John FitzPatrick, 2nd Earl of Upper Ossory (1745-1818). This includes a Bacchus that was formerly part of the Albani Collection and was acquired by Hamilton for Lord Ossory around 1769. See: Bignamini/Hornsby 2010, p. 334.

138 Woburn Abbey Collection, 4D-MT-D1, 'Notes taken at Rome', 1762. The Furietti Centaurs are bronze sculptures of the mythical figures that were half man, half horse. They were said to be found in Hadrian's Villa excavations in 1736. As a pair of sculptures, representing an old and young centaur, they made popular pairs to flank decorative ensembles. Now they are in the Capitoline Museums in Rome.

139 Woburn Abbey Collection, 4D-MT-D1, Francis Russell, Marquess of Tavistock, 'Notes taken at Rome', 1762.

140 Woburn Abbey Collection Library, 6949-51, Charles-Nicolas Cochin, Voyage d'Italie, 1753. The volumes are mentioned in the Marquess's inventory of Houghton House of 1767, see Woburn Abbey Collection, 4D-MT-I-1-19.

141 Woburn Abbey Collection, 4D-MT-D1, Francis Russell, Marquess of Tavistock, 'Notes taken at Rome', 1762.

142 Woburn Abbey Collection, HMC8-45-50, 6 March 1762, Rome.

143 Nicolas Poussin, *The Death of Germanicus*, 1627, Minneapolis Institute of Art, inv. 58.28. The painting remained in the Barberini family until 1958.

144 Woburn Abbey Collection, 4D-MT-C3, 29 July 1764, Woburn.

145 Woburn Abbey Collection, 4D-MT-I, 'Inventory of Great Russell Street'; HMC140, 'Woburn Abbey A Catalogue of Paintings'; 4D-H1-4, 'Inventory of Woburn Abbey', 1771.

146 Sale Duke of Bedford, London (Christie's), 19 January 1951, no. 26. Now in the Chrysler Museum of Art, Virginia, inv. 71.521.

147 Sweet 2012, pp. 203-204.

148 Quoted in Black 2003, p. 39.

149 Beddington 2021, p. 59.

150 Vivian 1989, p. 12.

151 New York 1989, p.g. Smith replaced Owen McSwinney as Canaletto's business partner. McSwinney had been instrumental in negotiating commissions in the 1720s, including small works on copper panels for the Duke of Richmond.

152 Woburn Abbey Collection, HMC 46. The pocketbook also records 'received at Venice' from 'Mr Rousscau' of 100 [?] sequins and 20 pistoles. This is probably the merchant banker Phillippe Rousseau, in Venice c.1700-1737.

153 London-Washington 1994, p. 224.

154 Clayton 2005, p. 16.

155 Links 1982 p. 76. The Duke of Marlborough became Bedford's brother-in-law in 1732. The Marlborough set, formerly known as the Harvey set, was sold by the family in situ at Langley Park in 1788.

156 Beddington 2021, p. 45; Razzall/Whitaker 2017, p. 131.
The Carlisle commission may have been brokered by a different agent than Smith, owing to the disparity among the paintings historically attributed to Canaletto, see Links 1982, p. 83.

157 Links 1977, p. 44.

158 McGeary 2024, p. 118; Links 1977, p. 45.

159 Quoted in: Razzall/Whitaker 2017, p. 130.

160 Links 1982, p. 87.

161 Beddington 2021, p. 15.

162 See Beddington 2021 for a proposed order of the paintings.

163 Draper 1988, p. 387.

164 A very brief description of the letters is provided in the research notes of former Archivist of the Bedford Estates, Marie Draper. They are today untraced.

165 Woburn Abbey Collection, 4D-A7-3-50 comprise payments of £27.1.8 (27 February 1733); £55.6.5 (7 January 1735) and £105.14.2 (27 April 1736).

166 Woburn Abbey Collection, 4D-A7-3-50, no 1.

167 Beddington 2021, p. 13.

168 New York 1989, p. 31.

169 Woburn Abbey Collection, 4D-H1-4, 'Inventory of Woburn Abbey', 1771.

BIBLIOGRAPHY

Amsterdam 2018-2019
S. Androsov, E.M. Moormann, T. Coppens, *Classic Beauties. Artists, Italy, and the Aesthetic Ideals of the 18th Century*, Amsterdam (Hermitage), 2018-2019

Angelicoussis 1992
E. Angelicoussis, *The Woburn Abbey Collection of Classical Antiquities*, Mainz 1992

Angelicoussis 2001
E. Angelicoussis, *The Holkham Collection of Classical Sculptures*, Mainz 2001

Angelicoussis/Schmidt 2025
E. Angelicoussis, L. Schmidt, *Holkham*, Munich 2025

Avery 1988
C. Avery, 'Laurent Delvaux's Sculpture at Woburn Abbey', in C. Avery (ed.), *Studies in European Sculpture II*, London 1988, pp. 312-321

Aymonino 2025
A. Aymonino, 'La Gran Bretagna e lo sviluppo del Grand Tour nel primo Settecento', lecture organised by Brevissme, Florence, 20 March 2025

Baldassari 1995/2015
F. Baldassari, *Carlo Dolci*, Turin 1995, second edition Florence 2015

Beckford 1735
William Beckford, *Dreams, Waking Thoughts, and Incidents; In a Series of Letters, From Various Parts of Europe*, 1735

Beddington 2021
C. Beddington, *Canaletto, Painting Venice: the Woburn series*, London, 2021

Bignamini/Hornsby 2010
I. Bignamini, C. Hornsby, *Digging and Dealing in Eighteenth-Century Rome*, New Haven 2010

Black 1999
J. Black, *Eighteenth-Century Europe*, London 1999

Black 2003
J. Black, *Italy and the Grand Tour*, New Haven 2003

Bleyerveld 2022
Y. Bleyerveld, *Landschappen op royaal formaat - Noord-Nederlandse Kunstenaars tekenen in de Buitenlucht, ca. 1580-1700*, Leiden 2022

Bowron/Kerber 2007
E.P. Bowron, P.B. Kerber, *Pompeo Batoni: "The Best Painter in Italy"*, New Haven 2007

Brettingham 1773
Matthew Brettingham, *The Plans, Elevations and Sections of Holkham in Norfolk…to which are added, the ceilings and chimney pieces; and also a descriptive account of the statues, pictures and drawings not in the former edition*, London 1773

Budding 2018

J. Budding, *De Grand Tour in de 18e Eeuw. Op Reis door Frankrijk en Italië*, Amsterdam 2018

Clayton 2005

M. Clayton, *Canaletto in Venice*, London 2005

Coryat 1611

Thomas Coryat, *Coryat's Crudities*, London 1611

Dolan 2002

B. Dolan, *Ladies of the Grand Tour: British Women in Pursuit of Enlightenment and Adventure in Eighteenth-Century Europe*, London 2002

Draper 1988

M.P.G. Draper, 'The Houses of the Russell Family', *Apollo* 127 (1988), no. 316, pp. 387-392

Dresden 2023

R. Enke, S. Koja, *Rosalba Carriera. Perfection in Pastel*, Dresden (Staatliche Kunstsammlungen), 2023

Garrick 1763

David Garrick, *The Journal of David Garrick Describing his Visit to France and Italy in 1763*, London 1763

González-Palacios 1994

A. González-Palacios, 'Cornici di Pio VI', in M. Boskovits (ed.), *Studi di Storia dell'arte in onore di Mina Gregori*, Milan 1994

Goodreau 1977

D. Goodreau, *Nathaniel Dance (1735-1811)*, London 1977

Haskell 1981

F. Haskell, *Taste and the Antique: the Lure of Classical Sculpture*, New Haven 1981

's-Hertogenbosch-Heino-Haarlem 1984

R. de Leeuw (ed.), *Herinneringen aan Italië - Kunst en Toerisme in de 18de eeuw*, 's-Hertogenbosch (Noord-Brabants Museum), Heino (Kasteel het Nijenhuis), Haarlem (Frans Hals Museum), 1984

Hiskey 2016

C. Hiskey, *Holkham: The Social, Architectural and Landscape History of a Great English Country House*, Norwich 2016

Ingamells 1997

J. Ingamells, *A Dictionary of British & Irish Travellers in Italy 1701-1800*, London 1997

Ingram 1988

T.L. Ingram, 'John, the Fourth Duke of Bedford, 1710-71', *Apollo* 127 (1988), no. 316, pp. 382-386

Jeffares 2006

N. Jeffares, *Dictionary of Pastellists Before 1800*, Milton Keynes 2006

Kenworthy-Browne 1983

J. Kenworthy-Browne, 'Matthew Brettingham's Rome account book 1747-1754', *The Volume of the Walpole Society* 49 (1983), pp. 37-132

Links 1977

J.G. Links, *Canaletto and his Patrons*, London 1977

Links 1982

J.G. Links, *Canaletto*, London 1982

London 1997

A. Wilton *et al.* (eds.), *The Lure of Italy in the Eighteenth Century*, London (The Tate Gallery), 1997

London 2008

L. Laureati, 'Vanvitelli-Gaspar Van Wittel', in L. Laureati (ed.), *Vanvitelli: Gaspar Van Wittel*, London (Robilant + Voena), 2008

London 2024

B. Baumgärtel *et al.* (eds.), *Angelica Kauffman*, London (Royal Academy of Arts), 2024

London-Washington 1994

J. Martineau, A. Robinson (eds), *The Glory of Venice: Art in the Eighteenth Century*, London (Royal Academy of Arts), Washington (National Gallery of Art), 1994

Lynch Piozzi 1789

Hester Lynch Piozzi, *Observations and Reflections Made in the Course of a Journey through France, Italy and Germany*, London 1789

McGeary 2024

T. McGeary, *The Cultural Politics of Opera, 1720-1742: The Era of Walpole, Pope, and Händel*, Martlesham 2024

Miller 1777

A. Miller, *Letters from Italy Describing the Manners, Customs, Antiquities, Paintings, &c. of that Country, in the Years MDCCLXX and MDCCLXXXI: to a Friend Residing in France*, London 1777

Moore 1985

A. Moore, *Norfolk and the Grand Tour*, Norwich (Norwich Castle Museum), 1985

New Hollstein Dutch 1996

F.W.H. Hollstein *et al.*, *The New Hollstein Dutch & Flemish Etchings, Engravings & Woodcuts 1450-1700*, Rotterdam 1996

New York 1989

K. Baetjer, J.G. Links (eds.), *Canaletto*, New York (Metropolitan Museum of Art), 1989

Nugent 1778

Thomas Nugent, *The Grand Tour, or, A Journey Through the Netherlands, Germany, Italy and France*, London 1778

Phoenix-Kansas City-The Hague 1999

M.K. Komenicky *et al.*, *Copper as Canvas - Two Centuries Masterpiece Paintings on Copper 1575-1775*, Phoenix (Phoenix Art Museum), Kansas City (Nelson Atkins Museum of Art), The Hague (Mauritshuis), 1999

Pittsburgh-Edinburgh 1995-1996

H. Brigstocke *et al.*, *Italian Paintings from Burghley House*, Pittsburgh (Frick Art Museum), Edinburgh (National Gallery of Scotland), 1995-1996

Razzall/Whitaker 2017

R. Razzall, L. Whitaker, *Canaletto and the Art of Venice*, London 2017

Redford 1996

B. Redford, *Venice and the Grand Tour*, New Haven 1996

Reynolds 2015

S. Reynolds, *A Catalogue of the Manuscripts in the Library at Holkham Hall*, Turnhout 2015

Rome 2005

A. Lo Bianco, A. Negro (eds.), *Il Settecento a Roma*, Rome (Palazzo Venezia), 2005

Röthlisberger 1961

M. Röthlisberger, *Claude Lorrain. The paintings*, New Haven 1961

Sani 1985

B. Sani, *Rosalba Carriera. Lettere, diari, frammenti*, Florence 1985

Sani 1988/2007

B. Sani, *Rosalba Carriera, 1673-1757*, Florence 1988, second edition Turin 2007

Scarth 2009

A. Scarth, *Vesuvius. A Biography*, Princeton 2009

Scott Thomson 1949

G. Scott Thomson, *Family Background*, London 1949

Sedgwick, 1970

R. Sedgwick, *The History of Parliament. The House of Commons, 1715-1754*, London 1970

Sharp 1766

Samuel Sharp, *Letters from Italy, Describing the Customs and Manners of that Country in the Years 1765 and 1766*, London 1766

Smollett 1766

Tobias Smollett, *Travels through France and Italy*, London 1766

Stirling 1912

A.M.W. Stirling, *Coke of Norfolk and His Friends*, 2nd edition, London 1912

Sweet 2012

R. Sweet, *Cities and the Grand Tour. The British in Italy, c.1690-1820*, Cambridge 2012

Trusted 1996

M. Trusted, *Spanish Sculpture. Catalogue of the Post-Medieval Spanish Sculpture in Wood, Terracotta, Alabaster, Marble, Stone, Lead and Jet in the Victoria and Albert Museum*, London 1996

Venice 2023

A. Craievich (ed.), *Rosalba Carriera. Miniature su avorio / a cura di Alberto Craievich*, Venice (Ca' Rezzonico), 2023

Vivian 1989

F. Vivian, *The Consul Smith Collection, Masterpieces of Italian Drawing from the Royal Library, Windsor Castle: Raphael to Canaletto*, Munich 1989

This catalogue was published
to accompany the exhibition
The Grand Tour – Destination Italy
Mauritshuis, The Hague
18 September 2025 – 4 January 2026

AUTHORS
Janneke Budding
Jon Culverhouse (JC)
Matthew Hirst
Laura Nuvoloni
Maria de Peverelli (MdP)
Victoria Poulton (VP)
Lucy Purvis (LP)
Ariane van Suchtelen (AvS)

EDITING
Ariane van Suchtelen

COPY EDITING
Dorine Duyster, with the assistance of
Daphne Martens and Robin de Vries

TRANSLATION
Diane Webb

PROCUREMENT OF PHOTOS
Robin de Vries

DESIGN
Gert Jan Slagter

PRODUCTION
Stichting Koninklijk Kabinet van Schilderijen
Mauritshuis, The Hague

PUBLISHER
Waanders Publishers Zwolle

COLOUR MANAGEMENT
Benno Slijkhuis, Wilco Art Books

PRINTING
Wilco Art Books, Amersfoort

©2025 Waanders Uitgevers b.v., Zwolle /
Stichting Koninklijk Kabinet van Schilderijen
Mauritshuis, The Hague

ISBN 9789462626461
NUR 644

This catalogue has also been published
in a Dutch edition
ISBN 9789462626454

www.mauritshuis.nl
www.waanders.nl

PHOTO CREDITS

The photographic material was provided by
the owners mentioned in the captions, as well
as by the following:

London, Royal Collection Trust: p. 116, fig. 5
(© Royal Collection Enterprises Limited 2025
| Royal Collection Trust), British Museum:
p. 18, figs. 1, 3, 4 (© The Trustees of the British
Museum); New Haven, Paul Mellon Collection,
p. 18, fig. 2 (© Yale Center for British Art,
Paul Mellon Collection); Norfolk, Holkham
Hall: p. 26, fig. 1, p. 29, figs. 5, 6, p. 30, figs. 9,
11 (© photography Pete Huggings and with
the kind permission of the Earl of Leicester
and the Trustees of the Holkham Estate),
cat. nos. 1-9, p. 26, figs. 2, 3, 4, p. 29, fig.
8, p. 30, fig. 10, p. 49, fig. 1, p. 56, figs. 2, 3
(© with the kind permission of the Earl of
Leicester and the Trustees of the Holkham
Estate), p. 14, fig. 11, p. 38, cat. nr. 4, p. 45,
cat. nr. 6 (by kind permission of the Earl of
Leicester and the Trustees of the Holkham
Estate / Bridgeman Images), pp. 22-23
(© photography by Ivo Hoekstra); Stamford,
Burghley House: pp. 58-58 (© photography by
Ivo Hoekstra)

Front cover
    Canaletto, *The Entrance to the Grand Canal
    in Venice* (30)
Back cover
    Angelica Kauffman, *Portrait of Brownlow
    Cecil, 9th Earl of Exeter (1725-1793)* (10)
Page 2
    Anonymous, *The Head of the Goddess
    Roma mounted on a post-antique Bust* (7)
Page 8
    Canaletto, *The Entrance to the Grand Canal
    in Venice* (30)

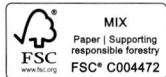